Regional Investment Pioneers in South Asia

SOUTH ASIA DEVELOPMENT FORUM

Regional Investment Pioneers in South Asia

The Payoff of Knowing Your Neighbors

SANJAY KATHURIA, RAVINDRA A. YATAWARA, AND XIAO'OU ZHU

South Asia Development Forum

Home to a fifth of humankind, and to almost half of the people living in poverty, South Asia is also a region of marked contrasts: from conflict-affected areas to vibrant democracies, from demographic bulges to aging societies, from energy crises to global companies. This series explores the challenges faced by a region whose fate is critical to the success of global development in the early 21st century, and that can also make a difference for global peace. The volumes in it organize in an accessible way findings from recent research and lessons of experience, across a range of development topics. The series is intended to present new ideas and to stimulate debate among practitioners, researchers, and all those interested in public policies. In doing so, it exposes the options faced by decision-makers in the region and highlights the enormous potential of this fast-changing part of the world.

Contents

Tables

Acknowledgments

This report was conceived under the World Bank Group's program on building a more positive narrative for regional integration in South Asia, as part of a broader engagement on intraregional cooperation and connectivity. Given that investment and trade are deeply interlinked, it was designed to complement and follow up on the earlier report on trade, *A Glass Half Full: The Promise of Regional Trade in South Asia*. The authors of this report are Sanjay Kathuria, Ravindra A. Yatawara, and Xiao'ou Zhu.

The report's underpinnings are provided by the survey data and the case studies of different regional investment pioneers. The authors would like to acknowledge the very valuable efforts of the teams from different partner organizations in South Asia, for providing feedback on the survey instrument and conducting the survey: Sadat Anowar, Nabila Hasan, Muhammad Moshiur Rahman, and Selim Raihan (South Asian Network on Economic Modeling, Bangladesh); Sanjeev Mehta and Sonal Mehta (Royal Thimphu College, Bhutan); Neha Anand, Prerna Dani, and Manab Majumdar (Federation of Indian Chambers of Commerce and Industry, India); Sameer Ahmad, Subrata Bandopadhyay, and Afaq Hussain (Bureau of Research on Industry and Economic Fundamentals, India); Nav Raj Dahal, Prisha Khanal, Kishor Mahajan, Posh Raj Pandey, Dhrubesh Regmi, and Nirmal Sharma (South Asia Watch on Trade, Economics and Environment, Nepal); Kithmina Hewage, Rangani Ranasinghe, and Vishvanathan Subramaniam (Institute of Policy Studies, Sri Lanka, for the Maldives survey); Shujaat Ahmed, Vaqar Ahmed, and Asif Javed (Sustainable Development Policy Institute [SDPI], Pakistan; SDPI also conducted the Afghanistan survey); and Hitheshi Almeida, Dilini Jayasuriya, and Rangani Ranasinghe (Breakthrough Business Intelligence, Sri Lanka). Partners for the case studies included Shiromani Dhungana for Nepal and Sanjeev Mehta for Bhutan. Other case studies were done by the authors.

The team is grateful to Maggie X. Chen (George Washington University) for key inputs on the econometric exercises as well as other ideas. The team would also like to acknowledge Ann Harrison (University of California, Berkeley), Pravin Krishna

(Johns Hopkins University), Priya Mathur (World Bank), and Aaditya Mattoo (World Bank) for valuable ideas and comments. Grace James supported the team during the entire cycle of the production, and World Bank staff in different capitals of South Asia facilitated meetings with investment pioneers. Pawan Bali, Nikita Singla, and Julie Ann Vorman (all World Bank) are supporting the dissemination process.

The authors thank the following peer reviewers for valuable comments: Vaqar Ahmed (Sustainable Development Policy Institute), Michael Engman (World Bank), and Michael Joseph Ferrantino (World Bank).

Sherrie Brown and Sandra Gain edited the report. The cover was designed by Sergio Andrés Moreno Tellez. Graphics were designed by Aletz Espinosa. Production and editorial logistics were led by Mark McClure.

The report was prepared under the supervision of Manuela Francisco, and, earlier, Esperanza Lasagabaster, and under the stewardship of Hans Timmer, Cecile Fruman, Zoubida Kherous Allaoua, and (earlier) Salman Zaheer, Philippe Dongier, and Robert Saum.

The team expresses its sincere thanks to the Foreign, Commonwealth and Development Office of the United Kingdom (previously the Department for International Development) for its steadfast support for the preparation of this report and the broader regional economic cooperation agenda.

About the Authors

Sanjay Kathuria is a fellow at the Wilson Center, a senior visiting fellow at the Centre for Policy Research in India, and a nonresident senior fellow at the Institute of South Asian Studies in Singapore. He is also an adjunct professor at Georgetown University and visiting faculty at Ashoka University. Previously, he was a lead economist at the World Bank. He is one of the leading thinkers and commentators on economic integration in South Asia and the economic development of the region. In 27 years at the World Bank, from 1992 to 2019, he worked in Eastern Europe, Latin America and the Caribbean, and South Asia, including field assignments in New Delhi and Dhaka. Before joining the World Bank, he was a fellow at the Indian Council for Research on International Economic Relations in New Delhi, from 1982 to 1992. He holds a master's degree in economics from the Delhi School of Economics and MPhil and PhD degrees in economics from Oxford University.

Ravindra A. Yatawara is a senior economic consultant in South Asian regional integration in the World Bank's Macroeconomics, Trade, and Investment Global Practice. He was the manager of the World Trade Indicators 2010 project and has been working on the impact of the global recession on developing countries and their policy responses to it. His research interests are in political economy of trade reform, competitiveness, trade and poverty, gender, and the interaction between trade and macroeconomic policies and regional integration. He has held faculty positions at Columbia University and the University of Delaware, and has also worked for the government of Sri Lanka. He holds a BA from Reed College and a PhD in economics from Columbia University.

Xiao'ou Zhu is a consultant in South Asian regional integration in the World Bank's Macroeconomics, Trade, and Investment Global Practice. Her research interests include international trade policies, global value chains, regional integration, emerging technologies, state-owned enterprise reform, and industrial policies in international trade and investment. Before joining the World Bank, she worked in impact investment to combine global stakeholder efforts to launch business-driven development programs in which investors' interest and development priorities intersect. She holds a BA from the School of Asia and Africa Studies of Beijing Foreign Studies University and an MA from the Middlebury Institute of International Studies.

Abbreviations

BITs   bilateral investment treaties
CDIS   Coordinated Direct Investment Survey
CEO   chief executive officer
DTAA   Double Taxation Avoidance Agreement
EU   European Union
FDI   foreign direct investment
FEMA   Foreign Exchange Management Act
FERA   Foreign Exchange Regulation Act
FTA   free trade agreement
GATT   General Agreement on Tariffs and Trade
GDP   gross domestic product
GVC   global value chain
IAB   Investing Across Borders
IFDI   inward foreign direct investment
IMF   International Monetary Fund
LRS   Liberalized Remittances Scheme
MNE   multinational enterprise
NER   North Eastern Region of India
OECD   Organisation for Economic Co-operation and Development
OFDI   outward foreign direct investment
R&D   research and development
RBI   Reserve Bank of India
REVC   Regional Engagement and Value Chain Survey

SAFTA   South Asian Free Trade Agreement
SEZ   special economic zone
UNCTAD   United Nations Conference on Trade and Development
US   United States
WTO   World Trade Organization

$ = US dollars unless otherwise stated.

Overview

Key Messages

- **Economic links between the countries of South Asia are well short of their promise.** For example, intraregional goods trade in the region is less than one-third of its potential. This shortfall hurts the welfare of consumers, workers, and firms.

- **COVID-19 (coronavirus) and its aftermath, which is accentuating other factors, is likely to have made the case for regional economic integration in South Asia even more compelling.** These factors include a widespread push to diversify global value chains; pressure to relocate such value chains at home or nearer home; rising trade costs; a drop in global air transport capacity, at least in the near term; the importance of services growth in global recovery and the large services sectors in the region; growing South Asian consumer markets; and the potential for regional trade to provide the buoyancy absent or muted in world trade.

- **Trade and investment are intimately connected, and, if anything, intraregional investment is even lower than intraregional trade.** The region reveals inadequate levels of intraregional investment, global inward foreign direct investment (IFDI), and outward foreign direct investment (OFDI), all potentially important to stimulating trade. As of 2018, IFDI stocks ($524 billion) and OFDI stocks ($82 billion) are relatively low compared with those of other developing regions. Intraregional investment of $3 billion (as of 2017) accounts for only 0.6 percent of IFDI from the world and 2.7 percent of OFDI to the world. Intraregional exports stand at a higher 7.9 percent of exports.

- **This report explores two understudied factors that may be key to unlocking the potential of regional trade and regional value chains in South Asia:**

knowledge connectivity and intraregional investment. Knowledge connectivity refers to how well firms know the economic and investment environment in another country; poor knowledge connectivity reflects high information frictions and costs of economic engagement with that country.

- **South Asia exhibits limited and polarized knowledge connectivity and low bilateral trust.** In a survey of 1,274 firms across the eight countries of South Asia, the average score on knowledge connectivity among country pairs was only 1.9, falling between "not at all" and "not very well" informed (scores ranged from 1 to 4). Information and network frictions, along with bilateral mistrust, reflect the high costs of search, matching, and contracting across borders and the market failures in providing channels to alleviate these frictions.

- **Knowledge connectivity is important in investment decisions, and such connectivity can have different roots.** Social and ethnic networks increase cross-border investment. For services FDI, such networks are even more important than productivity improvements. In general, investments grow gradually as firms learn from exporting and from affiliated firms in a conglomerate. FDI offers the best opportunity for developing regional value chains in a low-trust environment.

- **Distortions in the region's investment policies persist, particularly in OFDI regimes.** Except for India and to a lesser extent Sri Lanka, most OFDI policies in South Asia are restrictive, discretionary, or nontransparent. IFDI regimes are liberalizing but remain challenging by global standards, owing to the time it takes to resolve disputes, restrictions on land ownership, and some sector-specific restrictions. Region-specific IFDI and OFDI policies—some countries have additional layers of approval for specific bilateral partner countries—are in place and on balance deter intraregional investment.

- **Despite the handicaps, regional investment pioneers in South Asia have succeeded in establishing profitable ventures in different sectors.** Outward investment pioneers tend to be large, highly productive firms with surplus internal funds. Trade-supporting investments and services operations investments dominate, by number. Investors are driven by diverse motivations and use market entry strategies with varying initial costs.

- **Many of these entry strategies and motivations for outward engagement are reflected in the case studies of regional investment pioneers in the report.** Examples in the apparel value chain include Sri Lankan firms' investments in India's garment sector; a Pakistani firm initially investing in marketing, followed by a production investment in Bangladesh; and an Indian firm franchising its garments and fabrics brand in four South Asian countries. There are also several examples in the automotive value chain. In the services sector, the case studies include a joint venture between an Indian and Nepalese firm in Sri Lanka's hotel industry.

- **Government policies will benefit from a more integrative approach to firms' connectivity and international engagement, keeping in mind that firms' international strategies involve not only trade and IFDI, but also OFDI.** Similarly, connectivity involves knowledge and digital connectivity in addition to physical transport connectivity and trade facilitation. This integrative approach will not only be cost-effective, but will also have a greater impact.

- **The report offers four key considerations for policy:**

  ° **First, it makes a case for relaxation of OFDI regimes, both from a competitiveness standpoint and a need to be agile in crisis situations such as the COVID-19 pandemic.** This approach is important even for small economies and those with balance of payments concerns. Active support for OFDI could be restricted to information support and network formation abroad, but without the creation of new institutions.

  ° **Second, the analysis spells out details of smart IFDI promotion strategies and investment facilitation.** Given the role of sunk costs in investing, smaller countries may find it practical to target affiliates of global firms in larger South Asian countries that have already incurred the high entry costs of investing in the region. Governments could seek out and court these firms for IFDI. Similarly, targeting high-quality and high-visibility foreign investors is important because such firms engage for the long term and can attract follower investors.

  ° **Third, the report identifies distinct cross-border information-enhancing and network development activities, distinct from traditional connectivity, that can support intraregional investment as well as trade.** Examples include support for regional and international business associations, industry meetings, match-making events, investment missions abroad, and cross-border women's networks. Industry associations can seek out industry veterans for guidance and mentoring in addition to tapping into their networks. Industry-specific web portals with in-depth information can also be useful. Following COVID-19, regional air travel may become more important relative to global travel, at least in the near term, which will help regional networking and relationship building.

  ° **Fourth, the report suggests that digital connectivity and continued interventions to reduce trade costs are warranted to increase investment as well as trade flows.** These approaches have become even more important because health security and other trade costs have increased during the pandemic. There is particular scope to build on the digitization initiatives in trade and investment facilitation that many countries have undertaken during the pandemic, such as accepting electronic copies of trade documentation.

Electronic national single windows in the region need to be interoperable between trading partners, and extending digital acceptance of sanitary and phytosanitary documents will have positive region-specific effects.

- **Amid the pandemic, these policy recommendations are particularly relevant.** Many of these interventions do not entail large fiscal outlays, but could have a significant positive impact on FDI inflows and provide new strategies for national firms to enhance resilience. Investments in digital connectivity are a priority.

- **Trade and FDI will continue to be critical for growth and development in the post-COVID-19 world.** In South Asia, low levels of intraregional trade and investment indicate the presence of significant unexploited development potential. Moreover, regional value chains and regional trade may become relatively more important in the post-COVID-19 environment, boosting the importance of reforms and investments that would unlock regional trade and investment. Whichever direction the post-COVID-19 world takes, the messages in this report on trade and investment remain valid, and the associated policy reforms merit consideration.

Context and Motivation

South Asia has been among the fastest-growing regions in the world over the past decade. Yet intraregional trade is low and well below expected levels, suggesting that regional spillovers from individual country growth are muted. Given that trade is a conduit for growth, job creation, and poverty reduction, understanding and addressing the factors exacerbating the suboptimal levels of engagement is important.

The rising demand for goods and services from the expanding middle classes in South Asia has created significant opportunities for trade and investment expansion and diversification. Similarly, the region offers many opportunities to generate production efficiencies along value chains in partnership with regional players. Countries in the region now have greater differences in their endowments than a few decades back and have gained comparative advantages in a varied set of goods and services. Each country has a set of globally competitive firms. These firms have emerged relatively recently, albeit at different times in different countries.

Much has been written about the low levels of intraregional trade in South Asia and high intraregional trade costs. More than 40 years of development that has been largely disengaged from the region has meant low intraregional trade with cumbersome nontariff measures and neglect of intraregional connectivity in physical transportation and trade infrastructure. The size asymmetry of countries, high natural trade costs, and a trust deficit play against the coalescing power of proximity and shared roots. Addressing trade frictions with investments in transportation infrastructure, better trade facilitation, and extension of tariff preferences unilaterally and through free trade agreements have, however, produced less-than-anticipated trade responses.

This report explores two understudied factors that may be key to unlocking the potential of regional trade: intraregional investment and knowledge connectivity. The importance of foreign direct investment (FDI) flows has been evidenced in the rise of multinational enterprises from advanced economies that coordinate global value chains through a web of equity and nonequity relationships across the globe. More recently, there has been a rise of multinational firms from emerging economies. Their experience points to important benefits of outward investment from a firm and value chain perspective.

Recognition of the importance of information and network frictions for trade is growing, and they may be even more important than typical trade frictions for developing economies. Frictions in knowledge connectivity reflect the high costs of search and matching across borders and high costs or market failures in the provision of channels to alleviate these frictions. How these frictions work, how to quantify the power of information, and what remedial actions may be needed to address these frictions are only now beginning to be understood.

This report is framed within the same context as its predecessor, *A Glass Half Full: The Promise of Regional Trade in South Asia* (Kathuria 2018), namely, the suboptimal level of economic engagement within South Asia. It focuses on intraregional investment from an outward investment lens using a unifying framework of international engagement strategies (trade, investment, and other nonequity modes such as licensing). The current report is relevant to South Asia's development for several reasons, from both a regional and a global perspective. One, it brings the role of knowledge connectivity and information barriers, a much-neglected issue, into the decision to export or invest. This has powerful policy implications. Two, it draws attention to the distortionary outward investment arrangements in South Asia that restrain countries' dynamic firms and restrict regional value chains. Three, given trade-investment links, improving regional FDI will also improve regional trade. Improvements in trade also come through FDI's role in developing regional value chains in low-trust environments and its scope for trust building in the longer term. Finally, regional engagement can provide a springboard for a more global push in both trade and investment.

To investigate the relationship between investment and information barriers, this report embarked on an extensive data-collection exercise that provided detailed information on 1,274 firms and entrepreneurs across all eight countries in the region. This firm-level survey enabled rich diagnostic and econometric exercises, which are combined with aggregate national data analysis and distillation of case studies of regional pioneers. A framework of heterogeneous firms for which productivity drives self-selection of firms into export and investment is used to provide an analytical lens for case studies and to discipline the empirical analysis. The survey instrument was informed and enhanced by intensive case studies of pioneer South Asian firms. Thus, the analysis attempts to provide a holistic view of the main factors that determine global engagement by South Asian firms. The survey facilitated the compilation of original bilateral indicators of knowledge connectivity, networks, and trust, as well as entrepreneur characteristics, which are vital to the study.

Although the survey was conducted before the COVID-19 (coronavirus) pandemic broke out, the analysis remains valid and relevant. Apart from the public health challenges, the pandemic has only accelerated the developments already being witnessed in the global economy, including a rise in trade protection measures, the potential restructuring of value chains toward greater regionalization and reshoring or nearshoring, and diversification pressure induced by, among other factors, the need to make supply chains more resilient and the trade tensions between the United States and China. Further, just as in the post–global recession period, foreign investment will be an important building block in the recovery from the pandemic and recasting the "next normal." This report points to innovative approaches to building resilience and gaining from the opportunities that emanate from the evolving paradigm.

Amid the challenges of reengagement within the region, pioneering regional entrepreneurs have chartered innovative paths to regional engagement. What key drivers lead these firms to invest? What are the main constraints? Which firms are successful and which firms are not? What are the implications for policy and for the private sector? These are the central questions addressed in this report, and this overview is structured around these questions. Before exploring these issues, the overview provides an analysis of the South Asian investment landscape relative to other developing regions using aggregate bilateral data on the stocks of inward FDI (IFDI) and outward FDI (OFDI).

Investment Landscape: Low Levels of Inward FDI

South Asia shows weak performance relative to other low- and middle-income economies in other regions in attracting global FDI. The region is home to only 1.3 percent of the global stock of IFDI of US$39.5 trillion as of 2017,[1] despite producing more than 4 percent of global gross domestic product (GDP). Globally, most foreign investment flows are between high-income economies. Middle-income and low-income economies receive only 19 percent of all IFDI stock, of which 46 percent is situated in East Asian developing economies. The main sources of IFDI for East Asia and Europe and Central Asia are regional high-income economies, at 64 percent and 71 percent, respectively. South Asia has the highest amount of IFDI from extraregional developing economies, reflecting investments from Mauritius (an investment hub).[2]

In 2018, India accounted for 87 percent of South Asia's IFDI stock; in South Asia the relative importance of FDI to domestic output is relatively low; and most FDI is in the services sector. In absolute values, South Asia's IFDI stock is estimated at US$524 billion. The IFDI stock of Afghanistan, Bhutan, Maldives, and Nepal is valued at less than US$2 billion each. India and Sri Lanka have the highest value of IFDI stock as a share of GDP, at 16.9 percent and 14.4 percent, respectively, followed by Pakistan (10.8 percent) and Maldives (9 percent). Bangladesh, Bhutan, and Nepal have IFDI stocks of 6 percent or less, while foreign investment, at 3.1 percent of GDP, has been less important in Afghanistan (see box 1.1). In comparison, the respective figures for China and Vietnam are 20.3 percent and 26.8 percent, and 24.6 percent for Peru.

Investment Landscape: Low Levels of Outward FDI

The share of outward investment stock attributable to multinationals from low- and middle-income economies is about 6.0 percent using the IMF's Coordinated Direct Investment Survey, and 10.8 percent using UNCTAD data (data as of the end of 2017, and in this case both figures are stocks, based on the World Bank's income classifications). These figures may be smaller than usually seen in the media, which can be explained by two factors. One, most figures popularly quoted usually refer to flows, whereas stocks incorporate historical FDI, including earlier periods when firms from high-income economies accounted for almost all of OFDI. Two, both the 6.0 percent and 10.8 percent figures use the World Bank's classification of low- and middle-income economies (non-high-income economies) to define emerging market or developing economies. However, the figures that are frequently quoted are based on UNCTAD's investment data and classification, which include high-income economies from East Asia and the Middle East in its definition of "developing economies."

Using Coordinated Direct Investment Survey data for the end of 2017, South Asia has a low share of world OFDI stock (0.3 percent) compared with other developing regions. Among developing economies, East Asia has the largest share of global OFDI (2.4 percent), followed by Latin America and the Caribbean (1.1 percent). South Asia OFDI exceeds only that of the developing economies of the Middle East and North Africa (0.1 percent).

Most outward investment flows from developing economies go to high-income economies, and almost half originates from East Asia, with just 5 percent from South Asia (data as of the end of 2017). Of the total outward investment stock of US$2.2 trillion from developing economies, 71 percent goes to high-income economies, mostly in the same geographic region for East Asia, Europe and Central Asia, and Latin America and the Caribbean. The other developing regions, including South Asia, favor extraregional destinations. The high share of OFDI from Sub-Saharan Africa to developing economies in its region and outside the region reflects Mauritius's role as an investment hub, particularly for Sub-Saharan Africa and India.

India dominates OFDI from South Asia, but Maldives has higher OFDI as a share of GDP. India's share of South Asia's total OFDI stocks is greater than 94 percent (data as of the end of 2018). Maldives, however, reports a higher OFDI share of 5 percent of GDP. Afghanistan and India report OFDI stocks of 3.6 percent and 2.8 percent of GDP, respectively, with Sri Lanka's at 1.9 percent of GDP.

Investment Landscape: Lowest Intraregional Investment Share among Developing Economies

The South Asian intraregional stock of investment is low, at US$3 billion. South Asia ranks lowest among developing regions in intraregional investment as a share of total regional inward investment stocks (0.6 percent) or total regional outward investment stocks (2.7 percent). In comparison, Sub-Saharan Africa has the highest shares of intraregional inward and outward investment stocks (all comparisons refer to developing economies; see note in figure O.1). Other regions—such as East Asia, Latin America and the Caribbean, and Europe and Central Asia—also have high shares, reflecting the development of regional value chains in these areas (figure O.1).

Almost 75 percent of intraregional investment funds flow from India, but this amount accounts for only 2 percent of India's total outward investment and is at least six times *lower* than Indian investments in Sub-Saharan Africa. However, for the next-largest outward investors, Sri Lanka and Pakistan, the region is a more important destination, accounting for 26 percent and 19 percent, respectively, of total national outward investments. Bhutan and Nepal register the lowest amount of outward investment.

FIGURE O.1 **Low South Asian Intraregional Investment**

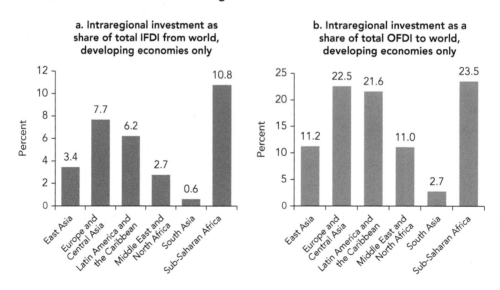

Source: International Monetary Fund Coordinated Direct Investment Survey augmented data.
Note: Developing economies are defined as non-high-income economies as classified by the World Bank income classification valid for the period July 1, 2019–June 30, 2020. Mauritius graduated to high-income country status in July 2020. Intraregional share of IFDI = IFDI from all developing economies in a region to all developing economies in that region as a percentage of IFDI from the world to all developing economies in that region. Intraregional share of OFDI = OFDI from all developing economies in a region to all developing economies in that region as a percentage of OFDI from the world to all developing economies in that region. IFDI = inward foreign direct investment; OFDI = outward foreign direct investment.

The top recipients of regional investments are Sri Lanka and Bangladesh. Pakistan and Bhutan receive the lowest amounts. Investment hubs—particularly Hong Kong SAR, China; Mauritius; Singapore; and the United Arab Emirates—play an important role in facilitating both inward and outward FDI. About 50 percent of all South Asian OFDI is destined for these four locations, and this figure rises to 77 percent when other investment hubs are included.

At the firm level, the collected data identify four types of outward investments. Trade-supporting services (for example, representative offices for sourcing and marketing purposes) and services operations dominate, amounting to 45 percent and 38 percent of the number of outward investments, respectively. Goods (agriculture and manufacturing) production and turnkey (with equity finance) investments account for just 14 percent and 3 percent of investments, respectively. The largest sectors of investor origin are manufacturing (39 percent), wholesale and retail trade (17 percent), and transportation and storage (11 percent). However, at a deeper level of industry disaggregation, the single largest origin sector is retail, with other important services sectors including warehousing, financial services, and travel agencies. Within manufacturing, the largest origin sectors are textiles and apparel, food products, and pharmaceuticals.

The share of women-led firms is small in the overall sample. However, at 2 percent, the share of women-led investor firms is even smaller than the 3.6 percent share of women-led non investor firms in the sample.

Key Drivers of Outward Investment of South Asian Firms

The experience of regional pioneers highlights the opportunities that outward investment offers emerging market firms. The case studies capture the experience of investors from four value chains: apparel, agri-food, automotive, and the hospitality (hotel) industry. The investors are from Bangladesh, India, Nepal, Pakistan, and Sri Lanka. The host economies comprise Bangladesh, India, Nepal, and Sri Lanka.

Although small, South Asia has a varied and rich investment landscape of investment types, sectors of origin, and modes of engagement, with varying initial capital costs. The region also highlights the different drivers of OFDI and identifies new value chain–based motivations for emerging market multinationals. For example, OFDI allows firms to reach higher profit margins along a value chain when the associated activities are located across the border; to cater to the higher volume and product scope requirements of buyers; to increase learning and build direct relationships with clients and suppliers; and to buy technology, brands, or other intellectual property when developing these at home may be constrained by capabilities or take too much time.

A wide array of motivations for investment and modes of engagement are recorded in survey data and firm-level case studies. The four primary motivations for investing in South Asia were market sales development, connectivity, cost considerations, and value chain management and upgrading. Firms set up retail and wholesale investments to expand market sales and capture wholesaler or retailer margins, get better control of their distribution, and build relationships and acquire knowledge about continuously changing consumer preferences. For example, Sri Lanka's Timex Garments made retail investments to sell its Avirate brand women's fashionwear, and Bangladesh's Rahimafrooz Batteries and Sri Lanka's MAS Brands made distribution investments to increase the efficiency of their distribution systems. Pakistan's denim manufacturer Soorty Enterprises made a trade-supporting investment in Bangladesh to facilitate sales of its denim textiles and increase connectivity with global buyers. India's Raymond expanded the markets for its custom suiting services using franchising agreements to reach consumers in Bangladesh, Nepal, Pakistan, and Sri Lanka.

The importance of cost factors, particularly labor costs, provides evidence contradicting assertions that South Asian nations continue to have similar endowments. South Asian firms that were driven by production cost considerations include India's tire manufacturer CEAT, which invested in tire plants in rubber-producing Sri Lanka, while Sri Lanka's Brandix invested in an apparel park in Andhra Pradesh, India, where land costs were cheaper. Another example of an Indian vertical investment is Dabur's investment in nurseries in Nepal to develop plants with high health benefits, which it uses in its division for herbal medicinal products in India.

Based in a small economy, Bhutan Ferro Silicon Alloys has managed to integrate itself into India's auto value chain, becoming a dominant supplier of ferrosilicon to the Indian steel industry, which produces auto bodies and components. The region also provided opportunities for firms to move into higher-profit-margin segments of the value chain: Sri Lankan apparel manufacturers moved into developing their own brands in India, and Indian and Sri Lankan hoteliers invested in the high-end Maldivian resort hotel industry. Having factories in more than one country has allowed Soorty Enterprises and Brandix to offer a greater range of products to their key clients, and to be able to meet requests to do so.

The region has also served as a platform for coping with difficulties at home. For example, Nepal's CG Foods invested in factories in the North Eastern Region of India at the height of Nepal's insurgency, and Sri Lankan retailers invested in Bangladesh in the face of policy uncertainty under a coalition government at home during 2015–19. In addition, regional investors tend to be less risk averse compared with global investors, such as when Nepal's CG Hospitality invested in India's Taj hotels in Sri Lanka at the height of Sri Lanka's civil war in 2008.

Key Constraint: Restrictiveness of South Asian Inward and Outward FDI Policy Arrangements

The policy arrangements for direct investment exacerbate the low volumes of investment. For outward investors, both the regulations for OFDI at home and IFDI abroad matter. Most IFDI policy arrangements have progressively liberalized but remain challenging by global standards, owing to the time it takes to resolve disputes, restrictions on land ownership, and some sector restrictions. There is significant variation across countries in different attributes of the FDI arrangements. Most arrangements have or are moving forward with special economic zones and reforming investment promotion agencies. India has moved to liberalize its investment arrangements, starting with manufacturing, extending to retail services in 2006 and to services, more broadly, in 2016. However, retail and e-commerce continue to be difficult to liberalize.

The outward investment arrangements in South Asia are largely restrictive, discretionary, and nontransparent, with India having the most progressive arrangements. India and Sri Lanka have OFDI arrangements that have an "automatic route" and a "government approval route," but in all other countries, approval from the central bank is required for all OFDI. This approval process has been liberal in Pakistan. Bhutan and Nepal have essentially banned OFDI. Bangladesh's arrangements were also very restrictive, but a few outward investments were approved following legislation in 2015. Afghanistan and Maldives and have no explicit legislation or procedures for approval that are publicly available, but they appear to allow investment abroad on a case-by-case basis.

Region-specific polices exist in both inward and outward investment arrangements. India's IFDI arrangements gradually liberalized its region-specific policies to allow Sri Lanka, Bangladesh, and Pakistan to invest in India in 2004, 2007, and 2012, respectively. However, all investments from (IFDI) and to (OFDI) Bangladesh and Pakistan are required to go through the "approval route." India extended the approval route requirement for all neighboring countries with a common land border in April 2020.

Key Constraint: Low Knowledge Connectivity and Bilateral Trust

Low and polarized knowledge connectivity characterizes South Asia. Much has been written about high intraregional trade costs due to high tariffs and paratariffs on relevant products for regional trade, nontariff measures, low-quality transportation and logistics infrastructure, and inefficient trade facilitation at land borders. However, no attempt has been made to assess the extent of information barriers. Figure O.2 presents a measure of bilateral knowledge connectivity across the 56 country pairs in the region. The measure is based on responses to questions on how well informed South Asian entrepreneurs were of opportunities in regional economies, on a scale of 1 (lowest) to 4 (highest). An average bilateral score of 1.9 (between "not at all" and "not very well" informed) indicates low overall knowledge connectivity. The results also indicate a polarization of knowledge: entrepreneurs are familiar with India and one or two nearby countries but know little about the rest of the region. For example, Nepali entrepreneurs know about opportunities in India in general and the North Eastern Region of India, but know much less about Sri Lanka, Maldives, Pakistan, and Afghanistan. India is an exception in two ways—first, most Indians have balanced knowledge about their neighbors, and second, most of the neighbors are familiar with India. Similar results were obtained with respect to the level of networks within the region.

FIGURE O.2 Bilateral Knowledge Connectivity in South Asia, by Home Country

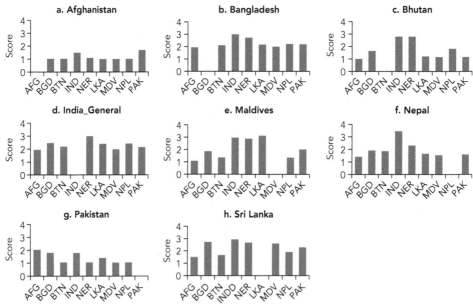

How well-informed do you feel about the opportunities abroad?
Scores range from 1 (low) to 4 (high).

Source: South Asian Regional Engagement and Value Chains Survey, World Bank.
Note: Scores are for bilateral pairs of countries with 30 or more observations. AFG = Afghanistan;
BGD = Bangladesh; BTN = Bhutan; IND = India_General (without Northeastern region); LKA = Sri Lanka;
MDV = Maldives; NER = North Eastern Region of India; NPL = Nepal; PAK = Pakistan.

Over the past two decades, many firms in South Asia have become globally competitive. However, low intraregional knowledge may result from a focus on advanced economy markets, except in the case of landlocked economies. Recently maturing South Asian firms are also not likely to have wide visibility in the region, owing to status quo bias ("sticky" global value chains) and even reputational bias of low quality that may persist from decades earlier.

Lack of bilateral trust is a problem but appears to be related to knowledge connectivity. When entrepreneurs were asked how much trust they have in people from various countries on a scale of 1 to 4 (highest), the average bilateral score was 2.58, (between having "not that much" and "some" trust). The South Asian trust scores show much variance across bilateral pairs. Bhutan is the most trusting country, whereas India, Sri Lanka, and Bangladesh are the most trusted countries. There is a high, positive correlation between knowledge connectivity and bilateral trust scores, suggesting that bilateral mistrust is related to lack of knowledge and people-to-people interactions. The relationship could also go in the other direction, such that bilateral trust enhances belief in the quality of information and would improve perceptions of knowledge connectivity. The average bilateral score within the region is not much lower than the 2.84 score reported by Europeans. However, these scores may not be strictly comparable, given that even though the survey question is the same, the European score was recorded for a random sample of the general public as opposed to this survey's sampling of the business community.

Regional Pioneers and the Determinants of Investment Entry: Which Firms Succeed and Which Firms Do Not?

An empirical estimation of a South Asian firm's entry decision to a particular destination facilitates the characterization of pioneer investors. The determinants of entry for production investments, services investments, and trade-supporting services investments are estimated separately. Information, networks, and trust are analytically separated from traditional trade costs related to trade policy, trade facilitation, and transportation infrastructure. Information and networks are analyzed as primarily affecting the firm's fixed entry costs of investing in a particular destination. The estimation is based on a flexible framework of a firm's international engagement decision. Different engagement options have varying sunk entry costs, fixed costs, and trade costs. Sunk costs include market research, acquisition of knowledge of government regulations, and due diligence, and are unrecoverable fixed costs if the investment is not made. Two types of variation in sunk costs are important for this framework.

First, sunk entry costs vary across engagement modes. Sunk costs are related to the fixed costs of the engagement and are ranked such that the entry costs of exporting are lower than the entry costs of investing. Further, entry costs for a trade-supporting investment (such as a representative office) are lower than for other types of investment (such as a factory or hotel). These points can be summarized thus:

$$\textit{Fixed Entry Costs}^{\textit{EXPORT}} < \textit{Fixed Entry Costs}^{\textit{TRADE-SUPPORTING FDI}}$$
$$< \textit{Fixed Entry Costs}^{\textit{PRODUCTION OR SERVICES FDI}}$$

Second, sunk costs vary across firm-destination pairs for the same engagement mode, which is how information barriers and differences in access to information across firms are introduced. All else equal, firms with better knowledge connectivity to a particular destination will have lower entry costs. These points can be summarized thus:

$$\textit{Fixed Entry Costs}^{\textit{NETWORKED OR HIGH-KNOWLEDGE-CONNECTIVITY FIRM}}$$
$$< \textit{Fixed Entry Costs}^{\textit{UNNETWORKED OR LOW-KNOWLEDGE-CONNECTIVITY FIRM}}$$

The key findings are the following:

Pioneer investors are high-productivity, large firms with investible surplus funds. High-productivity, large firms are the ones that invest abroad. They have the volume of production that provides the funds to incur the sunk costs of entry. This finding applies to all types of investments. The higher the sunk costs, the higher would be the level of firm productivity needed to cover the sunk costs (thereby restricting the activity to a few large firms). Most of the investment is financed through internal funds and funds from within a conglomerate. Additional financing from home commercial banks is important only for production investment.

Pioneer investors are located nearby. Lowering traditional trade costs (using distance as a proxy) induces investment entry. Theoretically, the direction of the relationship is ambiguous: high trade costs reduce the incentives for vertical investment but increase incentives for horizontal investments that help avoid these costs. The finding of a negative empirical relationship between trade costs and investment suggests the dominance of vertical investments (that is, those that need trade costs to be low to be profitable). From an investment perspective, this finding validates the trade and transportation infrastructure and trade facilitation initiatives that seek to reduce trade costs. Investments in physical connectivity are important. Trade costs continue to be important, controlling for exporting, which suggests that the distance variable is likely capturing the importance of communications costs and digital connectivity for investment. The importance of distance is significantly greater for services investments compared with goods production (agriculture and manufacturing) investments, which is consistent with findings on the greater importance of cultural sensitivity in provision of services compared with goods.

Pioneers are well-networked abroad. Regional pioneers have information networks abroad, and these networks make investing more inclusive. Firms with founders or chief executive officers with ethnic or visible social networks abroad tend to have a higher probability of investing. Networks allow for variation in sunk entry costs across firms, implying that the additional information that firms possess reduces entry costs by reducing information frictions and uncertainty. Networks tend to be more important for services and trade-supporting services investments. Again, this evidence is consistent with the finding that cultural sensitivity is more important for services industries.

For services investments, the presence of a network tends to be more important than productivity improvement. Networks make the investing activity more inclusive, given that lower-productivity, networked smaller firms may also invest abroad, thus widening the pool of potential investors. Case study evidence supports this result, with almost all pioneers having an ethnic or social link to the first OFDI destination.

Pioneer investors are exporters. Learning through exporting increases the likelihood of investing abroad. In a dynamic setting with uncertainty, the entry costs incurred during the exporting exercise enable the acquisition of market knowledge and the formation of business networks, thereby reducing the higher entry costs of investing in the following period and increasing the likelihood of investing. Exporting also makes investing more inclusive, because again it is not only the largest firms that can afford to incur the sunk entry costs of investment. Smaller firms with experience in exporting would also be able to do so because the entry costs of investment facing them are lower. This finding further validates the importance of reducing trade costs: lower trade costs would increase FDI by making export experimentation to learn about foreign markets less costly.

Investors are followers of pioneers in their conglomerate or business group. In addition to learning through their own experiences, follower firms can learn from pioneering firms that have already invested. Information spillovers from pioneer firms within a business group reduce the entry costs of related follower firms, even in different sectors. Thus, conglomerates perform not only a financing function but also an information-sharing role in stimulating OFDI.

Unrelated follower firms are less likely to succeed due to "sticky knowledge." Sticky knowledge is one explanation for the "case of the missing herd" in South Asia. In theory, the information spillover from pioneer activities should reduce entry costs for competitor follower firms and induce a herd effect or cascade after the entry of the pioneers. Although follower firms gain awareness from the experiences of national (and global) competitors, there does not appear to be enough knowledge flow to reduce the entry costs sufficiently to spur investment. The report argues that sticky knowledge prevents transfers from pioneer firms to unrelated home follower firms in the same industry, accounting for the missing herd. Sticky knowledge may be due to motivational barriers to sharing information as well as knowledge barriers.

Investing entrepreneurs have higher risk appetite. Higher risk appetite of the entrepreneur is associated with higher likelihood of investment entry. The risk appetite of the entrepreneur was measured by whether the founder belonged to a business community or a well-known business family, and the results indicate a positive relationship between investment and risk appetite. The intuition is that a person raised in a household in which family businesses routinely succeed and fail is more likely to be open to taking risks.

South Asian investors take a gradualist path. South Asian investors' behavior is consistent with investors that face high uncertainty, have scarce capital, are new to investing overseas, and are risk averse. Investors invest gradually following different dynamic paths of learning. Firms can learn from their own experience as well as from the experiences of other related and unrelated firms. First, there is a firm's own learning through lower-fixed-entry-cost engagements, such as exporting or nonequity engagements (for example, management contracts and franchising). Even within different forms of investing, a firm may start with an investment with a low fixed cost (for example, opening a trade-supporting office to learn about the market and build relationships with industry and government) before proceeding to invest in a factory with higher fixed costs. Second, in addition to learning through their own experience, firms can learn from other pioneers, given that information spillovers from pioneers reduce the entry costs of follower firms. The information flows from related firms within a business group or conglomerate are relatively smooth and lead to related-firm entry at the same destination, either in a different sector or in another activity along the same value chain. Knowledge flows from pioneers to competitors at home may be "stickier" and reduce entry costs only marginally.

The region as a springboard. On average, 65 percent of firms (by number) first invested within the region, and 28 percent of these firms that first invested in a South Asian country went on to invest outside the region. The finding provides suggestive evidence of the region being used by some firms as an experiential investment platform to launch into global markets. The finding is consistent with the aggregate data on FDI *values* that shows much higher shares for extraregional investments.

Policy and Operational Implications

The findings of the report provide important new, actionable implications for policy interventions and investments. These recommendations are organized around enhancing knowledge connectivity, boosting physical connectivity and digital connectivity, establishing regulatory and promotional policies for OFDI, implementing IFDI promotion strategies, incorporating emerging global business practices into policy making, and identifying national policy reforms that may have regional implications. These policy recommendations apply globally but may be applied regionally to address frictions in regional engagement. They are also valid in the post-COVID-19 world, with greater emphasis in some areas.

ENHANCING KNOWLEDGE CONNECTIVITY

Lack of knowledge is often underrated as a source of friction and high costs. This report argues that focusing on knowledge connectivity, separate from other forms of traditional connectivity, is essential, because policies that reduce information frictions differ substantially from policies that reduce traditional trade costs. These information frictions reflect the high costs of search, matching, and contracting across borders and the high costs or market failures of the provision of channels or technologies to alleviate these frictions. The common determinants of the different modes of international engagement imply that addressing informational barriers would support intraregional investment as well as trade.

Policy interventions that address information and coordination failures can be extremely useful for potential regional investors. Some firms may suffer from being late entrants (and are hence unknown to the wider business community) and their more recent maturation to global competitiveness. Other competitive regional firms that are already linked to global value chains may resist incurring the sunk costs and switching costs associated with new partnerships (a "status quo" bias). Structural features of the private sector, such as prevalence of family firms and diversified business groups, may create an atmosphere in which information is generally shared more cautiously and is restricted to a select group.

The survey suggests that useful network development interventions could include support for regional and international business associations, industry meetings, match-making events, and investment missions abroad. Industry associations could also tap an industry veteran for guidance and mentoring. Network development is important, given that entrepreneurial activities are relatively new to significant segments of South Asian society. Cross-border women's networks would help businesses led by women to develop cross-border activity and partnerships and to identify unique challenges to women's participation and advancement and collectively develop solutions. They may be useful given evidence that suggests women are less likely to proactively network because of, among other things, different beliefs about appropriate networking norms. Additionally, individuals may be more at ease networking with others of the same gender.

Information-enhancing policy initiatives, such as web portals, could provide the initial foundation for dynamic activities to support information exchange and updating and network formation, including deepening industry-specific portals and guidance. The most important type of information support requested by the survey respondents related to market opportunities abroad. The next three equally valuable types of information requested were legal and management support, information on conducting business abroad, and experiences of previous investors. Knowledge intermediaries, such as consulting firms that provide high-quality information on overseas markets and regulations, would be useful in this context. Investors and potential investors identified business travel and tourism as important sources of awareness about regional business opportunities, making air connectivity vital for information exchange and relationship-building. Following COVID-19, regional air travel may become more important relative to global travel, at least in the near term, which will help regional networking and relationship building.

Information dissemination, knowledge building, and network development increase inclusivity and democratize participation in regional engagements by reducing the fixed entry costs associated with new markets and new partnerships. Greater ethnic and social networks of regional pioneers enhanced inclusivity in investing beyond the few largest and most efficient firms; similarly, information support and network-building interventions may further diffuse the opportunities for international engagement to a broader set of firms and entrepreneurs. Human capital development that includes greater exposure to entrepreneurial activities and risk management is also important to expand the use of the opportunities provided by information support.

BOOSTING PHYSICAL AND DIGITAL CONNECTIVITY

Investments in transportation infrastructure and trade facilitation (including interoperability of different national digitization initiatives) would help increase both trade and investment. Some valuable initiatives include progress on electronic data interchange and risk-based management systems at seaports and land borders, development of ports and inland waterways as well as transnational highways, and improvements in air connectivity. Many of these initiatives, while valid for global trade, will have a significant impact on intraregional trade. Countries can also build on the positive steps that some of them have implemented in the context of the pandemic, such as accepting electronic copies of trade documentation, to increase automation of border management processes. Electronic national single windows that do exist in the region need to be interoperable between trading partners to fully realize efficiency gains and boost global and regional trade. Extending digital acceptance of sanitary and phytosanitary documents (given the high share of vegetables and food stuffs in intraregional trade) will have positive region-specific effects.

REGULATORY AND PROMOTIONAL POLICIES FOR OFDI

Outward investment is the new frontier of foreign investment policy for emerging market economies. Gradually relaxing regulatory controls on OFDI or being more open to approving applications is important from both a competitiveness standpoint and the need to be agile in crisis situations, even for smaller economies. Relaxation of policy controls could be pursued within an integrated macroeconomic management framework and appropriate reporting by firms. Policy may be finessed based on private sector response.

Active support for OFDI could be restricted to information support and network formation abroad, but without creating new institutions. The institutional structure governing OFDI varies across countries and is fragmented compared with IFDI. Currently, most approvals are processed by a department of the central bank, whereas promotional support is divided across various institutions. Information and network support for OFDI could be incorporated within trade promotion agencies and inward investment promotion agencies without the need to create new institutions. This approach conserves fiscal resources made even more scarce by the need to cope with the pandemic, but also allows an integrated approach to trade and inward and outward foreign investment promotion.

IMPLICATIONS FOR INWARD FOREIGN INVESTMENT POLICY AND PROMOTION

Given the role of sunk costs in investing, smaller countries may find it practical to target affiliates of global firms in larger South Asian countries (that have already incurred the high entry costs). The inference is that investors are more likely to invest in a second South Asian economy because the entry costs would be lower, reflecting learning through prior investments in a regional neighbor. Given the highlighted lack of awareness in the region of globally competitive South Asian firms, governments may also consider seeking out and courting these firms for IFDI. The gradual approach of some investors and the potential importance of small investments requires a sophisticated incentive structure that accommodates these new entrants.

Government initiatives for inward investment facilitation may be viewed as reducing entry costs, both directly and in accessing information about procedures. Thus, initiatives such as faster and one-stop clearances, simplification of administrative procedures, and greater use of information and communication technology would reduce entry costs and encourage FDI inflows. Countries could also build on digitization initiatives, such as those relating to investment approvals and facilitation, initiated during the pandemic.

Targeting high-quality and high-visibility foreign capital is important because firms that are industry leaders and engage for the long term can attract other investors; governments will also seek FDI that has the potential for technology diffusion and engagement with local firms. Global site selection firms, which act as knowledge brokers to large multinationals, could also be targeted to enhance country visibility. Also, countries that have not made systematic efforts to bring in FDI may need to signal their intention to attract and retain value chain leaders with sustained efforts, including courtship of investors by the highest levels of government.

INCORPORATING EMERGING BUSINESS PRACTICES INTO GOVERNMENT POLICY

Government policy will benefit from an understanding that the distribution of firms within an economy is skewed, with a cluster of large, high-performing firms driving national and cross-border activity. While promoting competition, firm entry, job creation, and support to small and medium enterprises, governments, at the same time, should not constrain the growth of high-performing firms. Such an approach would also benefit from corporate firms being mindful of their role in national development. Governments are also urged to be aware of evolving business strategies, such as "asset-light" approaches, which may provide benefits similar to those from FDI without involving the traditional flows of capital across borders. Such interactions, such as the recent growth in intellectual property licensing, should be encouraged and facilitated and may require, for example, additional access to finance for local partners.

THE IMPACT OF UNILATERAL NATIONAL REFORMS ON REGIONAL ENGAGEMENT

Policies that support greater internal integration, an improved investment climate, financial sector reform, entrepreneurship education, trade policy reform, and competition within a country are likely to support regional engagement. For example, the adoption of the unifying Goods and Services Tax by the Indian government in 2017 is likely to encourage South Asian exporters and investors, given that the various taxes in different states and additional charges to cross state lines previously in effect were viewed as multiple fixed entry costs.

COVID-19 AND IMPLICATIONS FOR POLICY PRIORITIZATION

The global pandemic and induced recession heighten the importance of reforms in general but also have implications for policy prioritization that will vary by country. It is possible that in the post-COVID-19 scenario, regional engagement will gain increasing importance. Regional investment may rise relative to global investment because of increasing trade costs and reduced knowledge connectivity arising from a relative reduction in air travel from distant partners. This effect may be reinforced by structural changes in value chains that encourage regionalization and reshoring or nearshoring by lead firms from advanced economies, thereby making South Asian regional value chains more important. Also, global lead firms seeking to diversify their production locations and not rely only on China can also create more opportunities for attracting global investment in South Asia. Another factor is the importance of services in the global recovery and the large services sector in the region. Moreover, regional trade can also help provide trade buoyancy and substitute for lackluster growth in world trade, especially when the region is dynamic and can look forward to many decades of catch-up growth.

Three policy reforms are linked to issues that seem to be growing in importance in the post-COVID-19 world. First, regulatory reform of OFDI policies and knowledge-connectivity interventions may be viewed as increasing the ability of national firms to gain global competitiveness and resilience. Second, timely and targeted inward investment promotion is critical to attracting global firms seeking new locations to diversify their supply chains. Third, because health security and other trade costs have increased during the pandemic, it has become important to accelerate trade facilitation reforms to keep overall trade costs in check, which is important for maintaining trade flows as well as investment.

Finally, to ameliorate the disruptions of COVID-19 and the inevitable future pandemics and disruptions, three factors could receive greater prioritization. First, investments in digital capabilities for both governments and firms need to be prioritized as digital platforms, and digitalization more broadly, gain a larger role in communications and the conduct of business. Second, several business sectors—including health care, pharmaceuticals, medical equipment, e-commerce, education (including information technology–enabled education), and information technology–enabled services, to name a few—are likely to increase their weight in national and global economies, and governments should ensure that they do not stifle their growth through undue regulatory barriers, including those related to trade and investment. Third, government resilience and crisis-response capabilities could receive greater weight in investment destination decisions. The latter will involve both immediate logistical responses to support business continuity and longer-term fiscal responsibility that facilitates government action under crisis situations.

Concluding Remarks

Despite COVID-19-related setbacks, South Asia is likely to recover its position as one of the fastest-growing regions in the world, and the potential for shared prosperity through greater engagement remains a missed opportunity, with growing costs. This report analyzes issues facing South Asian investors from a global perspective while distilling key regional implications. The contribution of the analysis to regional engagement comes from focusing on investment and information barriers; highlighting regional opportunities, successful regional pioneers, and the availability of a wide range of engagement options; and spotlighting severe distortions in many outward investment policy arrangements. The report argues for a more integrative approach to global competitiveness that involves trade and both inward and outward FDI. Similarly, it argues that policy actions on connectivity should specifically address knowledge connectivity and digital connectivity in addition to physical connectivity.

In the data collected for this report, 63 percent (by number) of first investments were in the region. Thus, the basis for a deeper level of regional engagement exists, fueled by the links between trade, investment, and connectivity. Building on this foundation can help South Asian countries bridge the gap between current and potential opportunities for regional engagement, increase global competitiveness, and diversify the risks that have become embedded in the global environment.

Trade and FDI will continue to be critical for growth and development in the post-COVID-19 world. In South Asia, low levels of intraregional trade and investment indicate the presence of significant unexploited development potential. Moreover, regional value chains and regional trade may possibly become relatively more important in the post-COVID-19 environment, boosting the importance of reforms and investments that would unlock regional trade and investment. Whichever direction the post-COVID-19 world takes, the above-noted messages on trade and investment remain valid, and the associated policy reforms merit consideration.

Notes

1. The data used here are from the IMF's Coordinated Direct Investment Survey. Alternative data from UNCTAD show similar results for South Asia's share of world IFDI stock, at 1.3 percent for 2015, 1.38 percent for 2016, 1.38 percent for 2017, and 1.44 percent for 2018. A comprehensive discussion of foreign investment data is given in chapter 3, box 3.2.
2. The report uses the World Bank's income classification valid for the period July 1, 2019–June 30, 2020. Mauritius graduated into high-income country status on July 1, 2020.

Reference

Kathuria, Sanjay, ed. 2018. *A Glass Half Full: The Promise of Regional Trade in South Asia.* South Asia Development Forum. Washington, DC: World Bank.

CHAPTER 1

The State of Play in South Asia

Introduction

South Asia has been among the fastest-growing regions in the world over the past decade. This high-growth region offers dynamic new consumer markets as well as opportunities for production partnerships along regional value chains. However, intraregional trade is very low, suggesting that regional spillovers from individual country growth are muted. Many studies suggest that current intraregional trade is well below expected levels, resulting in significant forgone opportunities for consumers, exporters, and producers in the region.[1] Given that trade is a conduit for growth, job creation, and poverty reduction, it is important to understand and address the factors contributing to the current suboptimal levels of engagement.

History matters here, as does geography. This largely integrated region—directly integrated under colonialism or allied through other arrangements—saw its constituent nations pursue development mostly disengaged from each other after the British departure in 1947–48, except for landlocked countries and their neighbors.[2] Import-substituting industrialization strategies under highly restrictive trade programs and state-led development reinforced this trend. At the same time, advanced economies started liberalizing their markets. By the time liberalization strategies took hold in South Asia in the late 1980s and early 1990s (and in 1977 in Sri Lanka), intraregional trade as a share of total trade had fallen from about 12 percent in 1951 to 3 percent in 1990.[3] All regional economies were low-income countries at the time, with limited production profiles and consumer markets. Thus, liberalization did not go far toward developing regional engagement in the next decade. Instead, trade and investment links were predominantly with the United States, Europe, Japan, and the East Asian Tigers.

However, beginning in the 1990s and especially since 2000, the rising demand for goods and services from the expanding middle classes in South Asia has created significant opportunities for trade and investment expansion and diversification. Similarly, the region offers many opportunities for generating production efficiencies along value chains in partnership with regional players. Countries in the region now have greater differences in their endowments than a few decades back and have gained comparative advantages in a varied set of goods and services. Each country has a set of globally competitive firms. They have emerged relatively recently but at different times in each country.

Three types of trade costs have been identified as key obstacles to the development of intraregional trade. These frictions include trade policy restrictions (tariffs, nontariff measures, and services trade barriers), inadequate transport and logistics infrastructure, and inefficient trade facilitation. They have specific regional effects due to discrimination in policy or implementation, and compositional effects resulting from the products traded (for example, highly protected agri-food) and the modes of transport (land) used by regional traders. Recognizing the importance of reviving neglected connectivity after decades of disengagement, national governments, along with development partners, have prioritized the trade facilitation and connectivity agenda. However, hysteresis effects have played their part, with investments in transport infrastructure and trade facilitation, as well as some preferential tariff liberalization to least-developed economies, having a less-than-expected response.

Thus, promoting engagement within the region today, in the first instance, is not about creating preferences in favor of regional partners. It is first about removing de jure and de facto discrimination among regional partners. Recent work highlights the benefits of regional engagement through the complementarity between regional and global integration (Bown et al. [2017] on Latin America) and the technology diffusion and learning associated with greater connectivity with technologically advanced neighbors (Gould [2018] on Europe and Central Asia).[4] Elements of both arguments emerge from this report but are not the driving justification for attention to regional considerations.

This report explores two understudied factors that may be key to unlocking the potential of regional trade—intraregional investment and knowledge connectivity. Much has been written about the low levels of intraregional trade and trade costs in the region. Much less has been written about intraregional investment, the trade-investment nexus, and investors in South Asia. The relative scarcity of such analysis is driven largely by the absence of aggregate bilateral foreign investment data for emerging economies until recently, the exclusion of small economies from global data sets, statistical capacity issues in some countries, and the lack of transparent procedures with which to explore firm-level data obtained by statistical agencies for research purposes. The importance of foreign direct investment (FDI) flows has been recognized by the rise of multinational enterprises from advanced economies that coordinate global value chains through a web of equity and nonequity relationships across the globe. For example, the sales of overseas affiliates of US multinational enterprises are three times greater than exports from the United States (Antràs and Yeaple 2014). More recently, multinational firms from emerging economies have been on the increase.

In addition to the study of trade frictions, there is growing recognition of the importance of knowledge and information frictions for trade, which may be even more important than typical trade frictions for developing economies (Atkin and Khandelwal 2019). Frictions in knowledge connectivity reflect the high costs of search and matching across borders and the high costs or market failures in the provision of channels to alleviate these frictions. There is only a nascent understanding of how these frictions work and how to quantify the power of information and remedial actions to address these frictions. Some consideration is also extended to behavioral aspects of potential entrepreneurs that might impede the use of information.

This report aims to bring new insights to the analysis of South Asian regional engagement through its focus on South Asian multinational enterprises and the role of knowledge connectivity in South Asia. Amid the challenges of reengagement within the region, pioneering regional entrepreneurs have charted innovative paths to regional engagement. What are the drivers leading these firms to invest? Which firms are successful and which firms are not? What are the main constraints and the consequent implications for policy and for the private sector? These are the central questions addressed in this report.

This analysis of FDI in South Asia comes in the wake of a widely followed 2018 trade report, *A Glass Half Full: The Promise of Regional Trade in South Asia* (Kathuria 2018). This report is a natural complement to the trade report.

The analysis in this report is at the intersection of several strands of literature. It combines recent developments in the international economics literature on trade and multinational enterprises with insights from international strategic management. It also incorporates the importance of networks, culture, and aspects of behavioral economics. It uses both aggregate bilateral data and firm-level data. The bilateral data are from an underutilized aggregate global database of inward and outward direct investment stocks. To investigate the relationship between investment and information barriers, this report embarked on an extensive data-collection exercise that provided detailed information on 1,274 firms and entrepreneurs across all eight countries in the region. This firm-level survey enabled rich diagnostic and econometric exercises to be undertaken, which were combined with aggregate national data analysis and distillation of case studies of regional pioneers.

The report explores intraregional investment within a unifying approach to international engagement that involves firm choices across both equity (investment) and nonequity modes (such as trade and licensing) to serve foreign markets or source globally. A framework of heterogeneous firms in which productivity drives self-selection of firms into export and investment is used to provide an analytical lens with which to examine case studies and discipline the empirical analysis. Intraregional investment is thus explored in the context of the *outward* direct investment behavior of South Asian firms across the world and contributes to the work on emerging market multinationals.

This report provides the first comprehensive landscape of bilateral investment flows in the South Asian region. It also documents the policy environment both at home and abroad for potential investors, highlighting distortions in the overlooked outward investment program and region-specific policies that, on balance, likely reduce investment flows.

The survey instrument was informed and enhanced by intensive case studies of pioneer South Asian firms. Thus, the report attempts to provide a holistic view of the main factors that determine global engagement by South Asian firms. The survey covered firms in all countries—large, small, and fragile—in a consistent framework. It sought to collect data on family firms and private business groups, which are important in the South Asian private sector landscape but are not disposed to public provision of data. It was able to capture different types of investments, including trade-supporting investments such as representative offices, which are sometimes overlooked but could lead to greater investments. The survey facilitated the compilation of original bilateral indicators of knowledge connectivity, networks, and trust, as well as entrepreneur characteristics, which are vital to the study.

The report establishes the importance of knowledge connectivity for intraregional investment and identifies policies for addressing information barriers and network frictions. It highlights the distortions in the overlooked outward investment programs and identifies region-specific inward FDI (IFDI) and outward FDI (OFDI) policies that, on balance, may inhibit intraregional investment. Although intraregional investment is low, the report identifies a variety of outward investments in different industries, across different bilateral pairs, for different motivations, and with varying start-up costs. It documents new value chain–based micro foundations in support of liberalization of outward investment policies, enhancing the case for OFDI reform even for small economies and those with balance-of-payments concerns. Given the trade-investment nexus, greater knowledge connectivity and reforms in the investment program would likely increase trade. In the context of low information connectivity and trust, FDI offers the best opportunity for developing regional value chains, which would increase trade.

The report argues for a more integrative approach to the international competitiveness of firms, involving not only trade and IFDI but also OFDI. It concludes that these reforms in OFDI policies and interventions to address knowledge connectivity would increase inclusivity of opportunity among domestic firms and would most benefit the country when government and firms act as partners in development

The rest of this chapter reviews fundamental aspects of South Asia that are relevant for understanding intraregional investment. First, some unique factors affecting regional dynamics are discussed. Second, a profile of the relatively weak IFDI landscape of South Asia is provided. Intraregional investment is briefly considered from the more familiar IFDI perspective before the rest of the report launches into an outward investment perspective. The chapter also highlights recent growth in both intraregional investment and intraregional exports, and the emergence of regional investment pioneers. The subsequent section highlights the relevance of the report for South Asia's development. Specifically, it sets up the ensuing FDI analysis in the context of the South Asian trading landscape before a formal framework is established in the following chapter. The last section outlines the structure of the report.

Factors Influencing Regional Dynamics

Some of the key underlying factors that could affect economic engagement between countries in the region are highlighted in this section. These factors are important for trade, and, given the trade-investment nexus, would be expected to affect FDI and connectivity (see annex 1A and figure 1A.1).

Size asymmetry. The Indian economy accounts for 80 percent of regional output; it is almost nine times the size of Pakistan's, the next biggest economy. The size asymmetry is reflected in trade flows as well as in bargaining power and negotiating capacity and requires sensitivity to small-economy perspectives.

No high-income economies. Four of the eight countries (Afghanistan, Bangladesh, Bhutan, and Nepal) are classified as least developed (by the United Nations), with one being a fragile economy (Afghanistan). India and Pakistan, the largest economies, graduated from low-income country status only a decade ago.

High natural trade costs. Three of the countries are landlocked (Afghanistan, Bhutan, and Nepal) and rely on transit trade. The North Eastern Region of India is almost landlocked (figure 1A.1) and is connected to mainland India (through West Bengal state) by a narrow pass that is 21–40 kilometers in width and is called the Siliguri Corridor, or the "Chicken's Neck." Two high-elevation Himalayan countries (Bhutan and Nepal), with terrain similar to that in some parts of India and Pakistan, also face naturally escalated trade costs.

India's central location. India shares a land or marine border with all the countries except Afghanistan. The bilateral distance between some country pairs can be substantial.

Shared roots. The region shares many common characteristics of culture, religion, language, peoples, and history, combined with a strong sense of national identity and high diversity in ethnicity and local languages. These features were heightened by migratory patterns under the British Raj and in the aftermath of nation creation. Afghanistan has extraregional connections to Central Asia and the Islamic Republic of Iran.

A trust deficit. Cross-border security and land boundary and political issues at the national and subnational levels, as well as concerns about migration and water sharing, have perpetuated mistrust and hindered trade and economic engagement. Cross-border business activity has not been immune to intergovernmental frictions and issues.

Weak Track Record on Global Inward FDI

Inward flows of FDI are important for host developing economies as a direct source of external capital and foreign exchange, for the potential technology and knowledge spillovers that may occur, and for the market access they offer for new exports. IFDI is also considered the more stable form of capital inflows compared with portfolio investment flows. Policy makers in emerging markets liberalized their incoming foreign investment programs amid the tightening of commercial bank lending in the 1980s. FDI is more likely to expand national gross capital formation if it does not crowd out domestic investment and comes as new "greenfield" investment, as opposed to an acquisition of a local firm (a "brownfield" investment), which essentially reflects a transfer of capital ownership.

The potential externalities, especially those related to knowledge transfers, provide an economic rationale for some governments to offer special incentives to foreign investors relative to national investors. This knowledge refers to production processes, managerial and organizational practices, logistics, and information about exporting. Knowledge diffusion may result from direct training, employee turnover, and demonstration effects. Evidence of positive knowledge spillovers is mostly seen in the improved productivity of a multinational enterprise's network of suppliers. The impact on directly competing national firms is mixed, stimulating investment in local firms closer to the technology frontier and leading to contraction and exit of less competitive firms. The impact of FDI on exports is channeled through increases in productivity and access to foreign markets. In some cases, foreign multinational firms have the capacity to affect the entire comparative advantage of an economy, as in the well-known cases of Intel in Costa Rica and Samsung in Vietnam. In addition to direct job creation, multinational firms tend to pay higher wages.[5]

Key features of South Asia's performance on IFDI are highlighted in the next paragraphs and figures.

South Asia shows weak performance relative to low- and middle-income economies in other regions in attracting global FDI (figure 1.1). The region was home to only 1.3 percent of the global stock of IFDI of US$39.5 trillion in 2017,[6] despite producing more than 4 percent of global gross domestic product (GDP). Most foreign investment flows are between high-income economies. Middle-income and low-income economies, as shown in figure 1.1 (non-high-income economies in the figure), receive only 19 percent of all IFDI stock, of which 46 percent is situated in East Asian non-high-income economies.

Most IFDI to low- and middle-income economies (91 percent) comes from high-income economies. The main sources of IFDI are *regional* high-income economies for East Asia and Pacific (64 percent) and for Europe and Central Asia (71 percent) (blue-shaded regions in figure 1.1), but *extraregional* high-income economies for the other low- and middle-income regions (green-shaded areas are larger than blue-shaded areas). The highest value of IFDI from low-and middle-income regions (sum of orange- and red-shaded areas) is in East Asia and Pacific (US$162 billion) and Sub-Saharan

FIGURE 1.1 **IFDI Stock in Developing Economies from Regional versus Extraregional Source Economies, 2017**

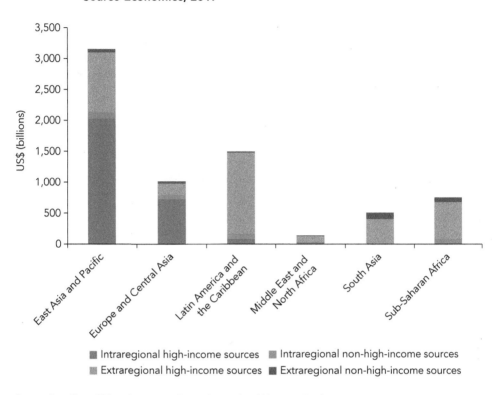

Intraregional high-income sources ■ Intraregional non-high-income sources
Extraregional high-income sources ■ Extraregional non-high-income sources

Source: Coordinated Direct Investment Survey, International Monetary Fund.

Note: High-income and non-high-income economies are defined based on an income classification valid for the period July 2019 through June 2020.

Low stock of US$3 billion of IFDI in South Asia from developing South Asian economies (orange) is barely visible in the figure. This figure can be interpreted to mean that (1) most IFDI comes from high-income economies (sum of blue and green), and (2) East Asian developing economies received more IFDI from regional economies (sum of blue- and orange-shaded regions is greater than green regions), while economies in Latin America and the Caribbean received more IFDI from extraregional economies (sum of green and red regions exceeds the size of the blue regions).

Intraregional investment share = orange region/total IFDI.

IFDI = inward foreign direct investment.

Africa (US$153 billion). South Asia has the highest amount of IFDI from *extraregional* low- and middle-income economies (red bar), reflecting investments from Mauritius (an investment hub).

In 2018, India accounted for 87 percent of South Asia's IFDI stock; South Asia in general has a low relative share of FDI to domestic output; and most FDI is in the services sector. In absolute values, South Asia's IFDI stock is estimated at US$524 billion. The IFDI stocks of Afghanistan, Bhutan, Maldives, and Nepal are valued at less than US$2 billion each. India and Sri Lanka have the highest value of FDI stock as a share of GDP, at 16.9 percent and 14.4 percent, respectively, followed by Pakistan (10.8 percent) and Maldives (9 percent). Bangladesh, Bhutan, and Nepal have IFDI stocks of 6 percent or lower, while foreign investment, at 3.1 percent of GDP, has been less important in Afghanistan (see annex 1A). In comparison, the respective figures for China and Vietnam are 20.3 percent and 26.8 percent, respectively, and 24.6 percent for Peru. Much of IFDI has been in the services sector, which dominates most of the region's economies (Gould, Tan, and Sadeghi Emamgholi 2013).

Low Intraregional Investment

This brief section on IFDI introduces intraregional investment from the more familiar IFDI viewpoint before moving specifically to the outward investment perspective in the following chapters of this report. Data used in this section are as of the end of 2017.

Intraregional investment of US$3 billion within South Asia accounts for just 0.6 percent of the total IFDI stock in the region, the lowest share of intraregional investment among developing economies (figure 1.2). Stocks of intraregional IFDI in other developing regions are 25 to 35 times larger than those in South Asia, except in the Middle East and North Africa, which recorded about US$4 billion. The highest intraregional investment, US$108 billion, was recorded by East Asian developing economies, but intraregional investment (US$81 billion) as a share of total IFDI from the world was highest in Sub-Saharan Africa. Sub-Saharan Africa's high intraregional share of inward investment reflects the role of Mauritius as an investment hub.

Intraregional investment is much higher among regions with high-income economies, as seen in figure 1.2. The shares of intraregional investment within developing economies (panel a) are substantially smaller when compared with a broader definition of each region that includes high-income economies as investment sources and destinations (panel b). In addition to data from panel a, the data in panel b reflect the large intraregional investment among high-income economies themselves, as well as the high-income economies' investment in developing regional economies (that is, low- and middle-income economies), and to a much lesser extent the investment inflows from developing regional economies to the high-income economies.

The development of regional value chains in South Asia suffers from the lack of nearby high-income economies, highlighting the role that lead firms from high-income economies play in regional value chains. High-income regional economies account for a large share of investment in developing East Asia and Pacific (64 percent) and Europe and Central Asia (71 percent). Although extraregional investment is important in Latin America and the Caribbean, it includes investment from the neighboring United States. It is no accident that these regions represent the three mature global value chain hubs around China, Germany, and the United States. The East Asia case reflects the importance of investment flows from economies such as Japan, the Republic of Korea, and Singapore for generating regional value chains. In South Asia, by contrast, foreign

FIGURE 1.2 **Intraregional Investment as a Share of IFDI from the World: Developing Economies versus All Economies, 2017**

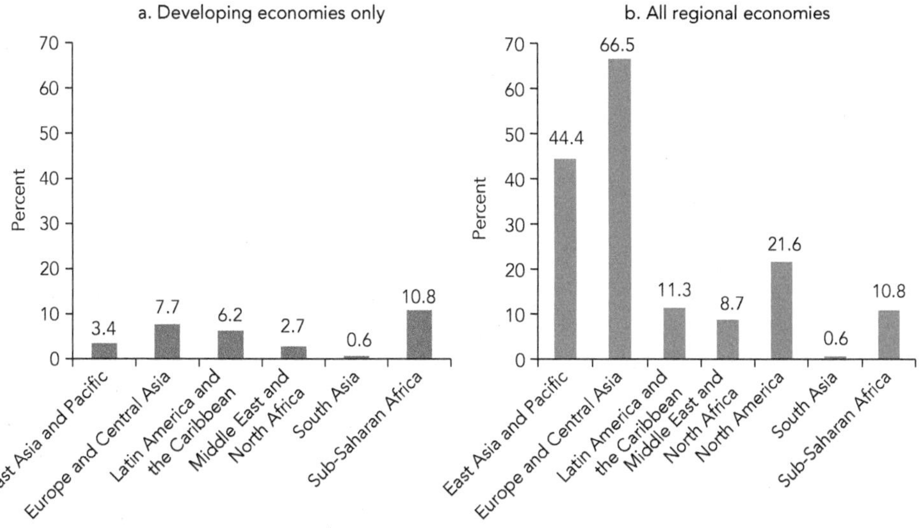

a. Developing economies only

b. All regional economies

Source: Coordinated Direct Investment Survey, International Monetary Fund.

Note: Panel a: Intraregional share of IFDI for the developing economies of a region = IFDI from all developing economies in a region to all developing economies in that region / IFDI from the world to all developing economies in that region.

Panel b: Intraregional share of IFDI for all economies of a region = IFDI from all (high-income and developing) economies in a region to all economies in that region / IFDI from the world to all economies in that region.

North America = Bermuda, Canada, and the United States.

Chile and Seychelles are the only high-income economies in Latin America and the Caribbean and Sub-Saharan Africa, respectively, according to the World Bank income classification used (valid July 2019 through June 2020). Mauritius graduated to high-income country status in July 2020.

IFDI = inward foreign direct investment.

investors have focused either on exporting to distant markets or on exploiting domestic markets. Thus, export-oriented apparel investors in South Asia sought underutilized global apparel quotas in the 1980s and 1990s, focusing on final assembly, with products destined for the European Union, the United Kingdom, and the United States. Further, most of the early multinational entrants into independent South Asia were motivated by the high trade barriers in individual countries and focused on catering to the domestic market.

A Spark of Optimism and an Opportunity to Scale Up?

Could recent acceleration in intraregional trade and investment and the emergence of pioneering South Asian investors provide some cause for optimism, in spite of the relatively weak performance reflected in the aggregate data? Is South Asia's intraregional trade on the rise? Are connectivity investments finally paying off? The intraregional export share grew during the early 2000s, only to reverse to a downward trend until 2011. After a fall in 2016, exports within the region rebounded to record levels in 2017 and 2018 (figure 1.3). This export growth in 2017 and 2018 was accompanied by a 25 percent increase in the intraregional investment stock between 2015 and 2017, albeit from a low base of US$2.4 billion.[7] About two-thirds of the FDI increase went to Bangladesh and Nepal, shared approximately equally between the two countries. Is this the trade-investment nexus at play? It may be too early to say, but the question is worth probing, especially as a post-COVID-19 (coronavirus) environment starts to transpire.

Pioneering regional firms have been successful in South Asia and beyond. The South Asian investment landscape is marked by some globally competitive firms in each country, and these firms are succeeding both within and outside the region. Early South Asian investors had a positive regional bias. One of India's earliest outward foreign investments was a manufacturing assembly plant for sewing machines developed by the Shriram Group in the Colombo suburbs of Ratmalana, Sri Lanka, in 1962. This followed the first investment in a textile factory in Addis Ababa, Ethiopia, by the Birla Group in 1960. Similarly, Pakistan's earliest outward investment was a banking branch of Karachi-based Habib Bank in Sri Lanka in 1951.

After a long dormancy, regional investment pioneers have resurfaced. Firms from different countries have invested in several sectors, motivated by varying reasons and with different capital costs. Table 1.1 provides an illustrative set of such cases. These case studies capture the experience of investors from four value chains: apparel, agri-food, automotive, and the hospitality (hotel) industry. The investors are from Bangladesh,

FIGURE 1.3 **South Asian Intraregional Exports, 1990–2018**

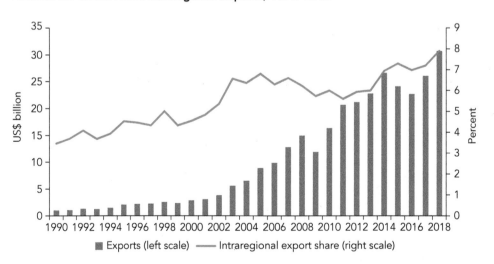

Source: Direction of Trade Statistics, International Monetary Fund.

TABLE 1.1 Case Studies in South Asian Intraregional Investment

Firm name and product	Home	Destination	Engagement type	Products and activities
Apparel value chain				
Brandix Lanka Limited	Sri Lanka	India	Export platform investment	Developed an apparel park in Andhra Pradesh. Dual role as park manager and manufacturer of weft fabric and complex intimate garments, destined for the United States.
MAS Brands Ltd.	Sri Lanka	India	Distribution investment, branding, retail investment	Introduced own "amanté" brand of brassieres in 2007, specifically suited to South Asian women. Distribution office dealt with department stores for sales. Own retail store opened in 2015.
Raymond Ltd.	India	Bangladesh, Nepal, Pakistan, Sri Lanka	Franchise	Developed its wide South Asian presence through a network of franchisees for its well-known suiting store. Fabrics are sent from headquarters.
Soorty Enterprises Pvt. Ltd.	Pakistan	Bangladesh	Trade- supporting, production investment	Opened marketing office to boost sales of denim fabric in 1992. In 2010, opened a manufacturing plant in the Comilla Export Processing Zone.
Timex Garments Pvt. Ltd.	Sri Lanka	India	Retail investment	Brand retail investment in 2011, starting in Bengaluru, for its line of women's Western wear, Avirate. Retail stores in all major cities and some Tier 2 cities. Production in Sri Lanka.
Agri-food industry				
CG Foods Pvt. Ltd. (instant noodles)	Nepal	North Eastern Region of India (NER)	Production, distribution, and retail investment	Invested in factories in NER to produce Wai instant noodles. Moved into food retailing in 2017. Started in Assam.
Dabur India Limited	India	Nepal	Production investment	Invested to produce fast-moving consumer goods and shampoos but restructured into fruit juice manufacturing. Maintains a nursery of herbal plants.

(Table continues next page)

TABLE 1.1 **Case Studies in South Asian Intraregional Investment** (*continued*)

Firm name and product	Home	Destination	Engagement type	Products and activities
Automotive value chain				
Bhutan Ferro Alloy Limited	Bhutan	India	Exporting, via related distributor	Key global exporter of energy-intensive ferrosilicon used in steel production. Sold in India through a related distribution firm to steel manufacturers of auto bodies and parts.
CEAT Limited	India	Sri Lanka	Production investment	Joint venture with management control of tire manufacturing plants in rubber-producing Sri Lanka.
Rahimafrooz Batteries Pvt. Ltd.	Bangladesh	India	Distribution investment	Export of car batteries with its own brand, Lucas and Spark, for the replacement battery market. Initially exported to India only; now includes Sri Lanka.
Hotels				
Taj Hotels and CG Hospitality Ltd.	India and Nepal	Sri Lanka	Production investment and management contracts	Taj Hotels owns and manages two hotels in Sri Lanka. Received a capital injection from CG Hospitality in 2008 to maintain operations during the height of the country's civil war.

Source: World Bank.

India, Nepal, Pakistan, and Sri Lanka. The host economies are Bangladesh, India, Nepal, and Sri Lanka.

The apparel sector includes two Sri Lankan pioneers that built brands to capture higher profit margins in the face of the phasing out of global apparel quotas in 2005. One is a brand developer and the other is a retailer selling its brand in its own stores. A third pioneer, from India, opted to provide volume and short lead times by creating an apparel park with value chain partners located in the same vicinity. The fourth is a Pakistani pioneer that set up a marketing office to sell denim cloth to Bangladeshi apparel manufacturers but wound up building its own apparel factory. The fifth is an Indian entrepreneur that has the widest reach in South Asia through the franchising of the company's custom suiting retail store, backed by the production of high-quality suiting material.

The cases from the *auto value chain* consist of the largest Bhutan ferrosilicon producer, whose output is vital for steel making in India, which goes into the production of auto bodies and auto parts. The firm's competitiveness is based on Bhutan's comparative advantage in energy-intensive manufacturing and availability of mineral deposits. Another Indian pioneer is the owner of a tire company that invests in rubber-producing Sri Lanka. The third pioneer is a Bangladeshi auto battery maker that produces for the Indian aftermarket.

The *agri-food industry* cases consist of a Nepali pioneer in instant noodles that invested in factories in the North Eastern Region of India and eventually expanded into a retail chain across all of India. The sector also includes an Indian firm that set up a juice-making factory in Nepal to serve the local market and its home market.

The *hotel industry* covers the story of a premier Indian hotel chain that invested in Sri Lanka and received a capital injection from a Nepali pioneer at the height of Sri Lanka's civil war in 2008.

Relevance of the Report

This report is relevant to South Asia's development for several reasons, from both a regional and a global perspective. First, it brings the role of knowledge connectivity and information barriers, a much-neglected issue, into the decision to export or invest. This issue has powerful policy implications. Second, it highlights the varieties of outward investment strategies and the benefits of outward investment for emerging market multinationals and draws attention to the distortions in outward investment programs. The restrictions on OFDI in many countries in South Asia restrain their dynamic firms, restrict regional value chains, and are an increasing anomaly in an era of globalization, recent setbacks notwithstanding. Third, given the trade-investment links, improving regional FDI will also improve regional trade. Improvements in trade also result from FDI's role in developing regional value chains in low-trust environments and its scope for trust-building in the longer term.

Do COVID-19 and its impact change the relevance of the report? Trade and FDI will continue to be critical for growth and development in a post-COVID-19 world. Moreover, it is possible that regional value chains will become relatively more important in the post-COVID-19 environment, boosting the significance of reforms and investments that would unlock regional trade and investment. Whichever direction the post-COVID-19 world takes, the report's messages on trade and investment remain valid and the associated policy reforms merit consideration.

CRITICAL ROLE OF KNOWLEDGE, INFORMATION, AND RELATIONSHIPS

The report incorporates knowledge connectivity and the role of information barriers into an analysis of intraregional trade and investment. Through data collected for this report, it generates its own indicators of bilateral knowledge connectivity and networks. These indicators highlight the diversity of knowledge connectivity across bilateral pairs of countries and justify the investigation into their importance for investment decision-making. Much work has been done on the roles of tariffs, paratariffs, nontariff measures, trade facilitation, and transport infrastructure as barriers to intraregional trade. Much less has been done to establish the importance of information barriers, although the existence of trade and investment promotion agencies appears to signal some appreciation of the role of information. In seeking new markets or investment destinations, firms face significant initial sunk costs, given that they do not know the market they are seeking to enter. They need to invest time and effort in gathering information about their potential markets, regulations, and partners. Understanding the role of such information costs is important because the policy remedies to address traditional trade barriers are very different from those that address informational barriers. Further, differences in knowledge connectivity across entrepreneurs effectively become a source of firm-level comparative advantage and inclusivity: smaller firms with more knowledge connectivity become more likely to be involved in multinational activity than larger firms without such connections.

Figure 1.4 presents a measure of bilateral knowledge connectivity across the 56 country pairs in the region. The measure is based on responses to questions about how well-informed South Asian entrepreneurs were of opportunities in regional economies, on a scale of 1 (lowest) to 4 (highest). An average bilateral score of 1.9 (between "not at all" and "not very well" informed) indicates low overall knowledge connectivity. These opportunities refer to both markets and firms. Figure 1.4 presents the average bilateral score by the home countries of the investors.[8] India is the most knowledgeable (higher bars in the India panel) about regional business opportunities, followed very closely by Bangladesh and Sri Lanka. India is also the most well-known (as reflected by the height of the "IND" bar in each of the other country panels). The results also indicate polarization of knowledge; that is, entrepreneurs are familiar with India and one or two nearby countries but know little about the rest of the region. For example, Bhutan's entrepreneurs know about opportunities in India and to a lesser extent in Nepal and

FIGURE 1.4 Bilateral Knowledge Connectivity in South Asia, by Home Country of Investors

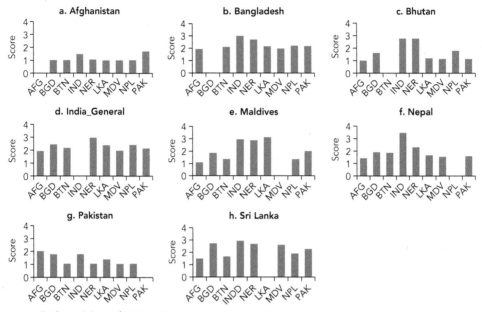

How well-informed do you feel about the opportunities abroad?
Scores range from 1 (low) to 4 (high).

Source: South Asian Regional Engagement and Value Chains Survey, World Bank.
Note: Scores are for bilateral pairs of countries with 30 or more observations. AFG = Afghanistan; BGD = Bangladesh; BTN = Bhutan; IND = India_General (India without North Eastern Region); LKA = Sri Lanka; MDV = Maldives; NER = North Eastern Region of India; NPL = Nepal; PAK = Pakistan.

Bangladesh, but know very little about Sri Lanka, Maldives, Pakistan, and Afghanistan. India is an exception in two ways—first, most Indians have balanced knowledge about their neighbors; and second, most of the neighbors are familiar with India. This finding is consistent with India's central geographical position in the region.

ANACHRONISTIC RESTRICTIONS ON OFDI AND NEW VALUE CHAIN ARGUMENTS TO SUPPORT LIBERALIZATION

Many countries in the region place strong restrictions on outward flows of capital, including direct investment. Because this study uses an outward investment perspective on intraregional investment, it highlights the issues in the neglected policy landscape for outward investment. The study surveys the policy landscape for outward investment and brings forward new arguments from a firm and value chain perspective to the typically macroeconomic debate as to why stringent restrictions on OFDI may have outlived their useful life. OFDI has several key benefits:

- All countries have growing numbers of efficient firms with global ambitions. Allowing such firms to make investment choices in a relatively unconstrained setting will not only help their competitiveness but will also be useful for their respective countries. The benefits of lifting restrictions apply equally to firms in small economies and would help generate equality of opportunity across regional firms.[9]

- OFDI allows firms to pursue more profitable activities along the value chain when these segments, such as retail, are across borders.

- OFDI allows firms to expand the scale and scope of output, which is particularly relevant for firms in small economies attempting to cater to the demands of global buyers.

- OFDI not only brings learning to the host country; it also induces reverse learning, which filters back to the parent firm and country. This knowledge includes learning about markets and processes as well as building relationships with clients and suppliers.

- With OFDI, firms can directly buy technology or brands by investing in relevant firms abroad.

- Firms may reduce vulnerabilities along the value chain by securing ownership abroad of vital raw materials.

- Through their ownership or own development of an activity abroad, firms can boost competitiveness by eliminating markups in foreign-based chain activities where market power prevails.

TRADE IMPERATIVE

Low intraregional investment and polarized knowledge connectivity are important elements in understanding the low level of intraregional trade. Intraregional trade in South Asia is the lowest among the world's regions. Intraregional exports were US$31 billion in 2018, constituting 7.9 percent of total regional exports. Given that the region's imports are 1.7 times its exports, the intraregional share of imports is only 4.7 percent of imports, making overall intraregional trade (including imports and exports) 5.9 percent of total world trade. Table 1.2 presents intraregional trade flows for 56 bilateral trade relations. Given the size asymmetry, many national trade values may not be large and many bilateral trade flows may seem small in absolute value terms. However, from the perspective of a small country, this value is often a large share of total trade.

Incentives for regional trade engagement vary among countries, but the logic of regional trade in South Asia is growing ever stronger for all countries. Landlocked countries need to cooperate with contiguous countries to negotiate transit trade agreements to access ports. For India, the virtually landlocked North Eastern Region provides a significant reason for cooperation, especially with Bangladesh (figure 1A.1). The large and growing gap between current and potential trade (with actual trade being only one-third

TABLE 1.2 South Asian Intraregional Goods Exports and Imports, 2018 (US$ millions)

Exporter (source) ↓	Destination (importer)										South Asia Region as export market (%) ↓
	AFG	BGD	BTN	IND	MDV	NPL	PAK	LKA	SAR	WLD	
AFG		0.11		315		0.01	202		517	716	**72**
BGD	3		4	793		43	69	20	932	31,448	**3**
BTN		7		490		15	0.12		513	541	**95**
IND	726	**8,789**	647		218	**7,225**	**2,386**	**4,442**	24,434	320,142	**8**
MDV	0.13	3		8			0	22	33	205	**16**
NPL	0.00	11	1	416	0		0.29	0.10	428	757	**57**
PAK	1,232	746	0	377	6	2		367	2,730	23,193	**12**
LKA	0	129	0.01	748	107	9	79		1,074	11,308	**9**
SAR	1,962	9,686	652	3,147	331	7,293	2,737	4,852	**30,661**	388,310	**7.9**
WLD	8,268	58,169	766	489,750	2,464	9,993	62,739	21,166	653,315	19,180,641	
SAR as import source (%) →	**23.7**	**16.7**	**85.2**	**0.6**	**13.4**	**73.0**	**4.4**	**22.9**	**4.7**		

Source: Direction of Trade Statistics, International Monetary Fund.
Note: This table should be read as, for example, Afghanistan's exports to India are valued at US$315 million, while the country's total exports are US$716 million. Exports to South Asia are worth US$517 million, which constitutes 72 percent of its total exports. Afghanistan imports goods with a total value of US$8,268 million, of which US$1,962 comes from South Asia. This amounts to 23.7 percent of Afghanistan's imports. Numbers in bold are trade relationships of more than US$1 billion. AFG = Afghanistan; BGD = Bangladesh; BTN = Bhutan; IND = India; LKA = Sri Lanka; MDV = Maldives; NPL = Nepal; PAK = Pakistan; WLD = world.

of estimated potential trade), the trade tensions in the global environment, and the relatively strong growth of South Asia render the regional market highly attractive (Kathuria 2018). Among the bilateral trade relationships, India-Pakistan trade shows the largest gap between current and potential trade. Bangladesh-India and Bangladesh-Pakistan trade are also substantially below potential. The suboptimal levels of trade engagement imply significant welfare losses for consumers, exporters, and producers.

The report considers the complex relationship between trade and investment across space and time. South Asia is lagging relative to the world in the contribution of goods exports to national income (World Bank 2019), and foreign investment could address this situation. IFDI may stimulate exports through productivity increases and access to export markets. Outward trade-supporting investments are expected to increase exports of goods by increasing learning about markets and building stronger relationships with clients. Similarly, outward distribution investments by manufacturers would increase goods exports. Over time, trade and investment are connected through a learning mechanism in which a firm may enter a market first using an entry strategy that has relatively low capital costs (exporting) and later adopt the most expensive investment option. Annex 1B briefly examines the trading landscape in South Asia and foreshadows the type of FDI and the likely direction of FDI in the region; for example, key traded goods and services trade flows can provide good indications of potential FDI.

Developing Regional Value Chains

Regional engagement is enhanced through the trade-investment-connectivity-trust–regional value chains nexus. The low level of trade is reflected in the lack of a network of regional value chains, which could provide a dynamic impetus to trade, as in East Asia. South Asia exhibits only pockets of evidence of regional value chains, the most visible being in the apparel sector and the auto industry. The entire value chain for apparel is available in the region, yet apparel manufacturers source extensively from East Asia. Cotton and yarn come from India and Pakistan, and fabrics are made in India, Pakistan, and, to a lesser extent, Bangladesh and Sri Lanka. Design capability is growing in India, Pakistan, and Sri Lanka; trade logistics and network coordination are strong in Sri Lanka; and manufacturing takes place in Bangladesh, India, Nepal, Pakistan, and Sri Lanka. Bangladesh is the second-largest exporter of apparel in the world after China. Moreover, the region's economies have specialized within the sector, with Nepal and Sri Lanka having niche markets in pashmina shawls and complex intimate apparel, respectively. Bangladesh focuses on casual wear, and Pakistan specializes in denim and has a strong related industry of home textiles. Protection of the manufacture of human-made fibers has resulted in low-quality materials in the region, leading to substantial imports from China in addition to other inputs. Much of the intraregional FDI in this sector is associated with the emergence of regional value chain activity.

In the context of low-trust environments and difficulty in the enforcement of contracts, ownership through FDI offers the best option for developing regional value chains, albeit through intrafirm activity across borders. Such FDI activity has been seen in the apparel value chain, with Bangladesh being the largest recipient of FDI. Regional trade has been volatile, especially for some bilateral trade relationships, including drops in the absolute value of exports (not just in export shares), as seen in figure 1.3. FDI may go a long way toward reducing uncertainty and bringing more stability to trade transactions through regional value chain development.

Reducing the Trust Deficit

The report analyzes links between FDI and trust, the latter being in short supply in South Asia. Trust in business relationships has become an increasingly important determinant of global business activity because complex transactions within value chains cannot be fully specified in standard transactional contracts. Higher bilateral trust is positively linked with FDI and trade flows (Da Rin, Di Giacomo, and Sembenelli 2019; Guiso, Sapienza, and Zingales 2009).[10] Moreover, once FDI occurs, because FDI is a stable and long-term commitment to economic engagement, it in turn helps enhance trust between countries through deeper people-to-people interactions. The report generates a measure of bilateral trust in South Asia using the same question asked of Europeans in the European Commission's Eurobarometer surveys. It identifies bilateral trust deficits and surpluses in South Asia and explores the link between trust and knowledge connectivity.

The Region as a Springboard

Neighbors tend to provide grounds for experimentation for exporters and investors and then a springboard for global engagement. South Asia's tariffs have come down since 1990 (though they are still the highest among developing regions), so the region could potentially play this role. Because entry costs into regional economies tend to be lower, many firms use their region as a learning platform and a springboard to global markets. This is evidenced in developing countries' exporting more sophisticated products first to other developing nations before facing more challenging markets and demanding consumers. In addition, as the ratio of foreign trade costs to domestic trade costs falls, value chain activities first become more regional and thereafter move to more global settings (Antràs and de Gortari 2020). Although earlier work (Yatawara 2013) finds that the South Asia Region was the first market for only 28 percent of goods exports, the findings of this report suggest that almost two-thirds of (the number of) investments are first placed within the region. Thus, continued increases in connectivity, including knowledge connectivity, and policy reform would help South Asian countries expand both exports and investments regionally and globally.

BROADER CONTRIBUTIONS AND LIMITATIONS

The general contributions of the report relate to the understanding of emerging market multinational enterprises; the highlighting of overlooked outward investment programs, their distortions, and new potential gains from reform; and the importance of information frictions and the compilation of indicators of knowledge connectivity and social capital. Some key findings about investment decision-making result from the application of insights from the international trade literature to the investment literature, such as knowledge connectivity and exporting (Dickstein and Morales 2018) and sequential exporting (Albornoz et al. 2012). The literature also confirms some relationships seen in the trade literature for investment, such as the greater importance of trade costs for services exports compared with goods exports. The report contributes to the nascent work on information frictions, establishing the importance of knowledge connectivity for investment participation and showing how it can be even more important than productivity for some investments. It also adds to recent work on the dynamic relationship between exports and investment (Conconi, Sapir, and Zanardi [2016], using Argentinean data).

The empirical results show that reduced trade costs are important for investment directly (a theoretically ambiguous relationship) as well as indirectly, through increased learning about investment potential by export experimentation. Further, the importance, based on regression analysis, of visible ethnic or social networks (based on founder background) for investment entry is an uncommon finding. When entrepreneurs are asked to rank important factors in decision-making, they tend to rank ethnic networks low. This low rating likely occurs because entrepreneurs highlight the business case for investments, but at the same time network links provide an inherent knowledge or subconscious confidence to proceed with the investment. In addition, these networks are more important for services investments.

Another important contribution is the inclusion of firm-level "frictions" that are important in the private sector landscape, such as the prevalence of business groups, conglomerates, and family firms. The results point to business groups as an organizational structure that can capture pioneer firms' knowledge spillovers for other related firms or incubated new firms. It also contributes to recent work that recognizes the importance of including entrepreneur characteristics in firm-level analyses.

Although the report offers an innovative approach and findings, it also has limitations. For the aggregate FDI data, the analysis does not make adjustments for the role of investment hubs or calculate the ultimate destination of investments. However, it does draw attention to the extent of outward investment from South Asia that goes to investment hubs (44–72 percent). Further, ultimate investor estimates from UNCTAD (2019) for IFDI are used to show that intraregional investment is only marginally underestimated in the unadjusted data.

By choosing to include all South Asian countries and unlisted firms (such as family firms not required to provide information), typically available variables used in advanced-economy firm-level studies of multinational enterprises were not available for analysis. Thus, the report does not emphasize the precision of the specific magnitude of the coefficients estimated. Instead, it relies on the sign of the coefficients and the relative size of coefficients. It is hoped that this report will inspire further work that uses more detailed firm-level financial information to provide a greater degree of precision in estimates for individual countries.

Plan of the Report

This report is structured as a single document with the separate chapters to be read sequentially. However, efforts have also been made to make each chapter self-contained.

Chapter 2 develops a flexible conceptual framework for regional and international engagement. It draws from the latest international economics literature on trade and investment, as well as strategic management literature, to gain an understanding of regional economic engagement. It incorporates a value chain approach by considering the separate activities involved in delivering a product or service to the consumer. It facilitates an analysis of catering to external markets as well as global sourcing of goods and services. The framework also allows simple illustrations to be provided for a range of substitutable equity and nonequity strategies with which entrepreneurs can enter foreign markets. These strategies vary in their sunk entry costs, fixed costs of operations, and trade costs. The framework then incorporates information frictions, networks, learning, culture, and behavioral economics to guide the analysis in the study. Variation in the sunk entry costs at the firm level drives the dynamics of this report.

Chapter 3 highlights outward investment from South Asia using aggregate national bilateral data, firm-level survey data, and case studies of regional pioneers. It profiles South Asian total outward investment in the world and within the region using an augmented aggregate bilateral data set that is currently underutilized. Next, it outlines the policy environment faced by outward investors at home (domestic OFDI policy) and abroad (foreign IFDI policy). It then analyzes OFDI using the firm-level data obtained from the South Asia Regional Engagement and Value Chain Survey, which was carried out in all eight economies of South Asia, covering 1,274 firms. Supplemented with case study evidence, the many opportunities and motivations for such regional outward investment are outlined and the variety of paths that pioneering entrepreneurs have selected are highlighted using the framework of chapter 2.

Chapter 4 focuses on information, networks, learning, and relationships. First, through the data-collection process, it estimates the level of bilateral knowledge connectivity, networks, and trust in South Asia. It then incorporates these notions of information, networks, and learning into a standard estimation of the determinants of firm-level outward investment along the lines of the framework developed in chapter 2. This estimation enables the firms that succeed and those that do not to be characterized.

Chapter 5 distills the policy implications from the evidence provided in chapters 3 and 4. It offers policy and other interventions that could enhance regional and global engagement opportunities for South Asian firms. The main recommendations are split into two categories: enhancing connectivity and policy reforms. The former set of recommendations includes knowledge connectivity and network formation as well as physical and digital connectivity. The latter set includes investment policy reform of both outward and inward investment programs. It also suggests that government policies should be updated in line with the latest developments in business practices, and that other unilateral national policy reforms could boost regional engagement. The implications of the COVID-19 pandemic for regional engagement and policy prioritization are also considered.

Annex 1A: Underlying Profiles of South Asian Economies

TABLE 1A.1 **Profile of South Asian Economies, 2019**

Aspect of profile	Afghanistan	Bangladesh	Bhutan	India	Maldives	Nepal	Pakistan	Sri Lanka
GDP (current US$, billions)	19.3	302.6	2.5	2,869	5.6	30.6	278.2	84.0
GDP per capita (current US$)	507	1,856	3,316	2,100	10,627	1,071	1,285	3,853
GNI per capita (current US$, Atlas method)	530	1,940	3,140	2,120	9,680	1,090	1,410	4,020
Land area (km²)	652,860	130,170	38,140	2,973,190	300	143,350	770,880	61,864
Population (millions)	38.0	163.0	0.8	1,366.4	0.5	28.6	216.6	21.8
Aged population (% of working population) (world: 13.6%)	4.8	7.7	8.9	9.5	4.8	8.9	7.1	16.6
Median age (world: 29.6 years)	17.2	25.7	25.7	26.8	28.6	22.2	21.8	32.3
Life expectancy at birth (years)	–	72.5	70.2	68.6	77.3	70.3	66.5	75.3
Human capital index (0–1, best)[a]	0.39	0.46	–	0.48	–	0.50	0.39	0.59
Schooling, age 15+, total (years)[b]	3.7	5.9	–	5.2	6.0	4.0	5.5	11.1
Schooling, age 15+, female (years)	1.8	5.7	–	4.1	5.9	3.6	4.3	11.1
Agriculture, value added (% of GDP)	25.8	12.7	15.8	16.0	5.2	24.3	22.0	7.4
Industry, value added (% of GDP)	14.1	29.6	36.1	24.8	11.7	13.3	18.3	27.4
Services, value added (% of GDP)	55.5	55.5	55.5	55.5	55.5	55.5	55.5	55.5
Exports of goods and services (US$, billions)	1.8	46.4	0.9	528.3	3.9	2.7	28.2	19.4
Exports of goods and services (% of GDP)	9.3	15.3	34.0	18.4	69.0	8.7	10.1	23.1
Imports of goods and services (US$, billions)	7.4	64.9	1.3	606.4	4.4	14.2	56.5	24.6
Imports of goods and services (% of GDP)	38.3	21.4	50.4	21.1	78.0	46.3	20.3	29.2
Remittances inflows (US$, billions)	0.8	18.4	0.1	83.3	0.004	8.2	22.2	6.7
Remittances inflows (% of GDP)	4.3	6.1	2.2	2.9	0.1	26.9	8.0	8.0
FDI, net inflows IFDI (US$, millions)	119	3,613	6	42,156	539	67	1,737	1,614

(Table continues next page)

TABLE 1A.1 Profile of South Asian Economies, 2019 *(continued)*

Aspect of profile	Afghanistan	Bangladesh	Bhutan	India	Maldives	Nepal	Pakistan	Sri Lanka
FDI, net inflows IFDI (% of GDP)	0.6	1.3	0.2	1.5	10.1	0.2	0.6	1.8
FDI, net outflows OFDI (US$, millions)	41	23	–	11,446	–	–	–	68
FDI, net outflows OFDI (% of GDP)	0.20	0.01	–	0.41	–	–	–	0.08
IFDI stock (US$, millions)	572	16,032	138	458,595	477	1,743	34,061	12,757
IFDI stock (% of GDP)	3.1	5.9	5.6	16.9	9.0	6.0	10.8	14.4
OFDI stock (US$, millions)	658	758	3	77,153	275	101	1,163	1,627
OFDI stock (% of GDP)	3.6	0.3	0.14	2.8	5.2	0.4	0.4	1.9
Ease of Doing Business 2020 rank (1–190, worst)	173	168	89	63	147	94	108	99
Trading across Borders (DB) score (1–100, best)	30.6	31.8	94.2	82.5	55.9	85.1	68.8	73.3
Logistics Performance Index (1 to 5, best)	1.95	2.58	2.17	3.18	2.67	2.51	2.42	2.60
Marine Connectivity–Liner Shipping Index, 1 to 100, best	–	13.3	–	55.5	7.4	–	34.1	62.1
Visa-free travel (number of countries) (world median: 97)[c]	26	41	53	58	85	38	32	42
GATT/WTO entry (year)	2016	1972	n.a.	1948	1983	2004	1948	1948
EU trade preferences	EBA	EBA	EBA	GSP	n.a.	EBA	GSP+	GSP+
Transition to middle-income status (year)[d]	n.a.	2015	2007	2008	1994 (2011)	2020	2009	1998 (2019)

Source: World Bank data.
Note: Italics are used for 2018 data. — = not applicable; n.a. = not available. DB = Doing Business; EBA = Everything But Arms; EU = European Union; FDI = foreign direct investment; GATT = General Agreement on Tariffs and Trade; GDP = gross domestic product; GNI = gross national income; GSP = Generalized System of Preferences; GSP+ = Generalized System of Preferences Plus; HCI = Human Capital Index; IFDI = inward foreign direct investment; OFDI = outward foreign direct investment; WTO = World Trade Organization.
a. The HCI calculates the contributions of health and education to worker productivity. The index score ranges from 0 to 1. The highest score of 0.88 was obtained by first-ranked Singapore and may be interpreted as meaning that a child born today can expect to be 88 percent as productive as a future worker would be if that child received complete education and full health care. Data pertain to 2018.
b. Barro-Lee educational attainment 2010, rev. 2018.
c. Henley Passport Index. Visa-free travel is defined as no visa required, or no prior government approval required (for example, visa on arrival, a visitor's permit, or Electronic Travel Authority). An e-visa required prior to travel does not qualify.
d. In 2011, Maldives graduated from lower-middle-income to upper-middle-income status and from least developed country status, which is based on income, human capital, and vulnerability. Maldives had a transition period of three years and lost GSP+ preferences in 2014. Sri Lanka moved into upper-middle-income status in World Bank fiscal year 2020, starting July 1, 2019, but dropped down for the period July 1, 2020, through June 30, 2021. Nepal graduated from low-income status on July 1, 2020.

FIGURE 1A.1 Geographic Profile of South Asia

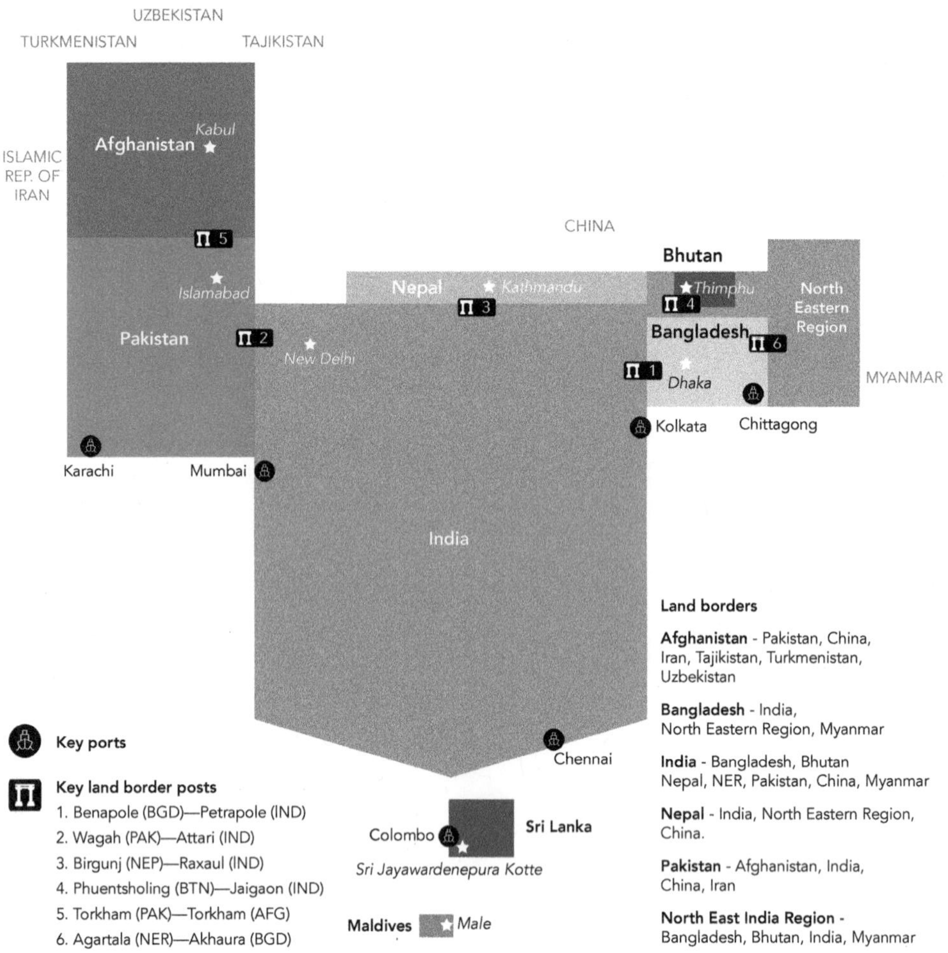

Source: World Bank.

Note: Bhutan and Maldives not to scale. AFG = Afghanistan; BGD = Bangladesh; BTN = Bhutan; IND = India; LKA = Sri Lanka; NER = North Eastern Region; NPL = Nepal; PAK = Pakistan.

Annex 1B: The South Asian Trade Landscape: Foreshadowing the Trade-Investment Nexus

Some fundamental economic features of South Asian economies are provided in annex 1A. Statistics presented in values and as shares of GDP highlight the asymmetry issues discussed in the chapter. Some common features among the South Asian economies (as reflected in shares of GDP) include a large services sector, the importance of remittances inflows to the region, low FDI, and lower goods-to-services export ratios compared with other regions (except Bangladesh). For Bhutan, Maldives, and Sri Lanka, this low ratio reflects the importance of tourism. Electricity exports are very important for Bhutan. Products from all countries except India have preferential access to the EU market. South Asian citizens, however, face difficult access to travel markets because of low visa-free travel ability. Trade facilitation and logistics performance have been traditional limitations among South Asian economies, but most have made improvements recently. There are variations in marine connectivity, with strategically located Sri Lanka performing well. Most economies have had cumbersome investment climates, which India is starting to improve, moving up from the rank of 130 out of 189 countries in the overall ease of doing business in the *Doing Business* 2016 report to 63 out of 190 in the 2020 rankings. Pakistan has also made improvements, moving from the rank of 138 to the rank of 108 over the same period.

Trade, trade costs, and foreign investment are closely interrelated. IFDI affects trade through impacts on productivity and access to foreign markets. Trade outcomes may indicate the scope of profitable outward investments and provide a basis for understanding the potential intraregional investment landscape. Four types of investments are considered—production investments (agriculture and manufacturing), services investments, trade-supporting investments (representative offices), and turnkey investments with some equity. The trade-investment relationships are formalized in chapter 2. The following sections review some stylized facts about intraregional trade in South Asia (see Kathuria [2018] for details) and some intuitive expectations of investments that may follow.

KEY MARKETS: POTENTIALLY ATTRACTIVE FOR HORIZONTAL INVESTMENTS, AS WELL AS DISTRIBUTION AND TRADE-SUPPORTING INVESTMENTS

Key markets for traded goods and services are possible locations for different types of investments: production investments that can cater to these markets and avoid trade costs (horizontal investments); wholesale or retail distribution services investments to better control distribution and marketing; and trade-supporting investments to learn about markets and build relationships with clients and suppliers.

India is the dominant South Asian trading partner for all countries in South Asia except Afghanistan and Pakistan, where it is the second-largest South Asian trading partner, after Pakistan and Afghanistan, respectively. Sri Lanka also plays an important role in trade with Maldives, being its largest export market and second-largest import source. Table 1.2 shows that there are only five cells in the trade matrix that are greater than US$1 billion, with India's exports to Bangladesh leading, at US$8.8 billion in 2018. The others are India's exports to Nepal, Sri Lanka, and Pakistan, and Pakistan's exports to Afghanistan.

Landlocked countries trade the most with their contiguous neighbors, with India being the dominant trading partner in exports and imports for Bhutan and Nepal.

Afghanistan trades heavily with its neighbors, particularly with the Islamic Republic of Iran (especially on the import side), followed by Pakistan, China, and the nearby Central Asian republics Turkmenistan, Kazakhstan, and Uzbekistan.

The key export markets for the nonlandlocked countries are the European Union and the United States. The European Union tends to be relatively more important for all countries, with a more substantial difference seen for Bangladesh, Maldives, and Pakistan. The importance of the European Union reflects the provision by the European Union of duty-free, quota-free preferences to the least developed countries under the Everything But Arms arrangement, and preferences to Pakistan and Sri Lanka under the Generalized System of Preferences Plus program (in effect, only India gets excluded from such trade preferences). East Asia is the dominant source of imports for South Asia, with China accounting for more than 10 percent of imports for all the economies except Bhutan and Maldives.

The diaspora and migrant workers represent important export markets for goods and services. The South Asian diaspora is large, with 36.5 million migrants, of which 10.8 million are Indian. India has the largest number of migrants in the world, and Bangladesh and Pakistan are in sixth and eighth positions, respectively. The top three destinations for South Asian migrants are Saudi Arabia, the United Arab Emirates, and the United States, with 5.5 million, 4.6 million, and 2 million migrants, respectively. (The Islamic Republic of Iran comes in third officially, but this primarily only reflects movement of people from Afghanistan.[11]) An intraregional diaspora also exists, as do intraregional migrant workers.

MAIN TRADED GOODS: OPPORTUNITIES FOR PRODUCTION COOPERATION

Key goods traded provide additional information on potential investment opportunities along the value chain to reduce costs through specialization (vertical investments) or to move to segments with higher profit margins.

The top intraregional goods exports are textiles and apparel, motor vehicles, and vegetables and food products. The key exports with a positive regional bias are motor vehicles and vegetables and food products. The shares of these exports to the region were more than double those of the relevant export shares to the rest of the world (table 1B.1). Textiles and apparel exports were 24 percent of exports to the region, a similar share as to the rest of the world. However, this figure is double the export share from 2011, when textiles and apparel exports accounted for only 12.2 percent of exports to the region. India successfully exports motor vehicles despite high import duties in the region.

Electricity trade has grown, especially with Indian investments (first public, then private) in Bhutan's hydropower production; India's investment in hydropower has now extended to Bangladesh and Nepal. This is a case where foreign investment explicitly preceded trade.

Textiles and apparel are South Asia's largest exports to the world, amounting to 26 percent of total exports from South Asia. Textiles and apparel are followed by stone and glass, chemicals, fuels, and vegetables.

SERVICES TRADE FLOWS ARE PARTICULARLY INDICATIVE OF INVESTMENT POTENTIAL

Services trade flows help strongly identify potential areas of investment because suppliers and consumers need to be in close physical contact ("the proximity burden" of services trade). About 59 percent of services are supplied through commercial presence. Commercial presence is particularly important for financial services, construction, telecommunications, recreational services, and distribution services (WTO 2019).[12]

Trade in services such as *tourism* is important for many economies, especially Bhutan, Maldives, Nepal, and Sri Lanka. Intraregional tourism has grown, with the largest number of tourists in Sri Lanka and Bhutan coming from India. Bangladesh is the dominant source of tourist arrivals in India, and Sri Lanka is among India's top 10 sources. Medical tourism from Afghanistan to Peshawar, Pakistan, and New Delhi, India, is strong, as is the flow from Maldives to Sri Lanka. Bangladesh is India's largest source of medical tourists. Religious tourism within the region is also important. Resort hotel tourism in Maldives relies on EU and US tourists and is priced significantly higher relative to the rest of the region.

Intraregional labor services. Bhutan's and Maldives' small sizes create a need for migrant workers supplied by intraregional labor services. The dominant sources of workers have been Nepal (for Bhutan) and Bangladesh and Sri Lanka (for Maldives). Bangladesh uses skilled labor from Sri Lanka and India, and India uses workers from Nepal and Bangladesh. The much larger extraregional and intraregional labor flows have generated an industry of recruitment services, usually housed in the home country, that exports the labor.

Financial services for remitting money. Remittances are an important source of foreign exchange, except for Bhutan and Maldives, which are importers of labor. These remittances are significantly larger than FDI inflows for most of the economies (table 1A.1). These remittances have created demand for financial services that intermediate the transfer of funds. For Nepal, remittances are several multiples of FDI inflows or of exports of goods and services. The remittances reflect the flow of migrant workers, mostly to the Middle East and South Asia. Although India receives the largest amount of remittances in absolute terms (US$69 billion in 2018), Nepal is the most dependent on remittances (28 percent of GDP). For Bangladesh, Pakistan, and Sri Lanka, remittances are equivalent to more than 5 percent of GDP.

Transshipment services. The Port of Colombo in Sri Lanka is an important transshipment hub for Indian products. Bangladesh relies more on the Port of Singapore.

The port city hubs of Dubai and Singapore play a role in facilitating regional trade as transshipment and commercial hubs as well as conduits that reduce the high transaction costs of direct bilateral trade. The United Arab Emirates is important for receiving exports from India and Afghanistan and for sourcing of imports for Pakistan and Maldives. Singapore is an important import hub for Maldives and Bangladesh.

INTRAREGIONAL TRADE COSTS ARE HIGH: TRADE COSTS ARE IMPORTANT FOR INVESTMENT BUT AMBIGUOUS IN DIRECTION

Low intraregional trade has been primarily attributed to high trade costs, broadly interpreted (Kathuria 2018). In addition to natural factors, intraregional trade costs are driven by the proliferation of regulatory barriers and other nontariff measures, high tariffs and paratariffs on goods of high relevance for trade in the region (by their exclusion from trade agreements), services trade restrictions, inefficient trade facilitation, and the poor state of transport and logistics infrastructure. Early arguments based on similarity of endowments and low purchasing power have become less relevant (Yatawara 2013).

Trade costs have a direct effect on investment, but the direction of the relationship is ambiguous and depends on the type of investment. High tariffs or trade costs may induce a one-time horizontal investment to circumvent the costs, or they may discourage investment in vertically integrated industries that would involve products being frequently subjected to high tariffs or trade costs, given that vertical investments operate with multiple border crossings within a value chain framework.

Discrimination and compositional effects of intraregional trade costs. Trade costs have a disproportionately negative impact on intraregional trade compared with extraregional trade, arising from the nature of the goods traded, the modes of transport used in the region, and the unpredictable implementation of trade rules and regulations. Disentangling these forces is not easy.

Compositional effects are relevant for trade in agri-food products, which are generally subject to heavy food safety regulatory measures. And food and vegetable products are disproportionately important in South Asian regional trade (table 1B.1). Additional uncertainty in the sector arises because government trading agencies are active in food staples trade, and governments use export restrictions and import tariffs to stabilize food prices. In addition, limitations in transport and logistics infrastructure become regionally biased when much of regional trade is land based, and not just for landlocked countries. Thus, inefficiencies in customs clearance at land border posts and neglected roadways from these posts have disproportionately adverse impacts on intraregional trade costs. For example, 75 percent of trade between India and Bangladesh goes through the Benapole (Bangladesh)–Petrapole (India) land border posts (see figure 1A.1). For landlocked Bhutan and Nepal, 98 percent (99.3 percent of trade with India) and 87 percent of trade, respectively, is through land routes.[13] In addition, compared with seaports, land border posts are less likely to have testing laboratories nearby, and any required testing would involve extra days of travel time to the closest laboratory.

Discriminatory policies are most apparent in the India-Pakistan trade relationship (see Kathuria [2018] for more details). Before 2019, India had provided most-favored-nation status to Pakistan (in 1996); Pakistan had not reciprocated. In addition, Pakistan permitted only 138 products to be traded via the Wagah-Attari border; all other trade products used the sea route. Nevertheless, before 2019, 17 percent of India-Pakistan trade took place through this land border post (Taneja, Bimal, and Sivaram 2018). In 2019, trade relations between the two countries deteriorated further, with India rescinding Pakistan's most-favored-nation status and imposing a 200 percent duty on all products not eventually destined for export markets.[14] Six months later, Pakistan banned all new trade transactions with India, although transit trade to Afghanistan was not to be disrupted.[15]

Trade policy and trade agreements. Alternatively, investors may choose regional locations that have preferential market access to destinations of interest or invest based on scope for tariff arbitrage.

It is beyond the scope of this report to cover all the trade agreements in South Asia, but a few points may be made. The main regional free trade agreement (FTA) is the South Asian Free Trade Agreement (SAFTA), which was signed in 2006. Afghanistan, Bangladesh, Bhutan, Maldives, and Nepal receive additional preferences as least developed nations. In 2012, India completed a phased duty-free tariff preference program for all least developed countries, which was expanded in 2014. Afghanistan and Bangladesh have benefited from this program. Bangladesh also received specific preferences related to apparel (ready-made garments). A series of transit and trade agreements in 2015 and 2018 have advanced Bangladesh-Indian cooperation. See table 1B.2.

India-Bhutan and India-Nepal trade, currency, and labor relations. Bhutan and Nepal do not use SAFTA preferences for trade with India; they have separate trade treaties with India that give them deeper advantages. Beyond these preferences, trade costs are lowered by additional factors. The Nepali rupee has been pegged to the Indian rupee at 1.60:1 since 1992. The currency exchange of the Indian rupee to the Bhutanese ngultrum is 1:1. The Indian rupee is widely circulated in several countries in South Asia, although it is not legal tender. Treaties of friendship allow for labor flows from Bhutan and Nepal to India, and in general, reciprocity has been provided.

Other important agreements are the India–Sri Lanka FTA, which was operationalized in 2000; the Pakistan–Sri Lanka FTA, which was signed in 2005, but without much impact; and the Afghanistan-Pakistan Transit and Trade Agreement, which was signed in 2011 (see Ahmed and Shabbir [2016] for Afghanistan-Pakistan trade).

TABLE 1B.1 Sector Shares of Exports to South Asia and the Rest of the World, 2015

Product description	(1) Composition of exports to SAR (%)	(2) Composition of exports to non-SAR (%)	(3) Intraregional exports (% exports to world), by sector
Animal	1.1	3.5	2.3
Vegetable	13.7	6.4	13.6
Food products	5.6	2.0	17.5
Minerals	2.6	0.8	19.1
Fuels	8.5	9.9	6.0
Chemicals	8.5	10.4	5.7
Plastic or rubber	3.9	2.6	10.0
Hides and skins	0.4	1.7	1.8
Wood	1.6	0.6	16.8
Textiles and clothing	24.1	25.7	6.5
Footwear	0.3	1.3	1.5
Stone and glass	1.2	13.6	0.7
Metals	6.2	6.7	6.4
Machinery and electricity	6.5	6.7	6.7
Transportation	14.7	6.3	14.7
Miscellaneous	1.4	2.6	3.7
All HS6 codes	100.0	100.0	6.9
Raw materials	15.3	7.4	13.2
Intermediate goods	35.7	28.4	8.5
Consumer goods	32.1	53.0	4.3
Capital goods	16.9	11.2	10.1
WTO H1 agricultural	25.7	10.5	15.3
WTO H1 industrial	74.3	89.5	5.8
WTO H1 petroleum	7.0	9.7	5.1

Source: World Bank data.
Note: Exports *ijk* for exports of country *i*, to destination *j*, of sector *k*, where *i* = SAR , and *j* = SAR, Non-SAR, or World.
Column 1 = Export SAR,SAR *k* / Σ *k* Export SAR,SAR (Composition of exports to SAR); Column 2 = Export SAR,Non-SAR *k* / Σ *k* Export SAR,Non-SAR (Composition of exports to non-SAR); Column 3 = Export SAR,SAR *k* / Export SAR, World *k* (Intraregional exports as a share of total exports, by each sector). Data for 2015 are the latest data available at the disaggregated level for Bangladesh. H1 = HS 1996 version with data from 1996; HS6 = Harmonized System at 6-digit level; SAR = South Asia; WTO = World Trade Organization.

TABLE 1B.2 **South Asian Intraregional Trade Agreements**

Preference provider	Afghanistan	Bangladesh	Bhutan	India	Maldives	Nepal	Pakistan	Sri Lanka
Afghanistan							T	
Bangladesh			B	T B		P B		
Bhutan								
India	L	L T B	L T B		L	L T B		X
Maldives								
Nepal		B	B	B				
Pakistan	T							X
Sri Lanka				X			X	

Source: World Bank.
Note: All nations belong to the South Asian Free Trade Agreement. B = BBIN (Bangladesh, Bhutan, India, Nepal) Motor Vehicle Agreement, not yet operationalized, and Bhutan has deferred implementation; L = unilateral duty-free imports provided by India to least developed countries; P = preferences for selected products; T = transit and trade agreements; X = bilateral free trade agreement.

Notes

1. A World Bank study (Kathuria 2018) estimates intraregional trade is one-third of its potential based on a gravity model of bilateral trade. Bilateral predictions of trade flows are estimated based on simple characteristics such as distance, economic size, contiguity, and other standard variables. See Kathuria (2018, box 1.1) for a summary of the gravity modeling approach, estimates of the trade gap, and references to some of the other studies.

2. Note that Maldives gained independence in 1965 and did not pursue protectionist trade policies.

3. Indian liberalization reforms began gradually in the early to mid-1980s, but the dramatic liberalization in 1991 is typically identified as the major reform date. See World Bank (2004) for 1951 data.

4. Gould (2018) highlights the multidimensionality of the connections—trade, investment, migration, information and communication technology, and air connectivity—and their greater positive impact on growth collectively.

5. For more on the impact of foreign investors on host communities, see Aitken and Harrison (1999); Amighini, McMillan, and Sanfilippo (2017); Anderson, Larch, and Yotov (2017); Baum, Pundit, and Ramayandi (2017); Harrison and Rodriguez-Clare (2010); and Javorcik (2004).

6. The data used here are from the IMF's Coordinated Direct Investment Survey. Alternative data from UNCTAD show similar results for South Asia's share of world IFDI stock, at 1.30 percent for 2015, 1.38 percent for 2016, 1.38 percent for 2017, and 1.44 percent for 2018. A comprehensive discussion of foreign investment data is given in chapter 3, box 3.2.

7. IFDI stocks reflect accumulated changes in FDI inflows plus changes in valuation and currency fluctuations. Therefore, the first difference in IFDI stocks is not used as an estimate of FDI inflows.

8. There are eight investor home economies but nine investment destinations because the North Eastern Region of India (NER) was treated as a separate destination due to its remoteness. There were no investors from NER.

9. The literature documents the importance of large firms ("superstars") in trade and production, and their impact on aggregate trade fluctuations, on aggregate welfare, and even on a country's comparative advantage (Bernard et al. 2018; Freund and Pierola 2015; Gabaix 2011). In this context, OFDI can enable firms in small economies to grow and become more competitive.

10. For more on the trust deficit in South Asia, see Kathuria (2018, overview and chapter 1).

11. United Nations Population Data on migrant stocks, 2017. Migrants are defined as residents born in different countries, while the diaspora refers to migrants and their offspring born in the reporting country.

12. Estimates of services provision by mode in 2017 are cross-border transactions (27.7 percent), consumption abroad (10.4 percent), commercial presence abroad (58.9 percent), and presence of individuals abroad (2.9 percent) (WTO 2019).

13. Bhutan Trade Statistics 2018, and Nepal Department of Commerce.

14. Notification No.05/2019-Customs, Department of Revenue, Ministry of Finance, New Delhi, February 16, 2019.

15. SRO 927(I)/2019 and SRO 928(I)/2019, Ministry of Commerce, Islamabad, August 9, 2019, applying to imports and exports, respectively. SRO-977, on September 2, 2019, allowed the pharmaceutical industry to import raw material, medicines, and medical devices regulated by the Drugs Regulatory Authority of Pakistan.

References

Ahmed, Vaqar, and Saad Shabbir. 2016 "Trade & Transit Cooperation with Afghanistan: Results from a Firm-Level Survey from Pakistan." Sustainable Development Policy Institute, Islamabad.

Aitken, B., and A. E. Harrison. 1999. "Do Domestic Firms Benefit from Direct Foreign Investment? Evidence from Venezuela." *American Economic Review* 89 (3): 605–18.

Albornoz, F., H. F. Calvo Pardo, G. Corcos, and E. Ornelas. 2012. "Sequential Exporting." *Journal of International Economics* 88 (1): 17–31.

Amighini, Alessia A., Margaret S. McMillan, and Marco Sanfilippo. 2017. "FDI and Capital Formation in Developing Economies: New Evidence from Industry-level Data." Working Paper 23049, National Bureau of Economic Research, Cambridge, MA.

Anderson, James E., Mario Larch, and Yoto V. Yotov. 2017. "Trade and Investment in the Global Economy." Working Paper 23757, National Bureau of Economic Research, Cambridge, MA.

Antràs, Pol, and Alonso de Gortari. 2020. "On the Geography of Global Value Chains." *Econometrica* 84 (4): 1553–98.

Antràs, Pol, and Stephen R. Yeaple. 2014. "Multinational Firms and the Structure of International Trade." In *Handbook of International Economics*, volume 4, edited by G. Gopinath, E. Helpman, and K. Rogoff, 55–130. Amsterdam: North-Holland.

Atkin, David, and Amit Khandelwal. 2019. "How Distortions Alter the Impacts of International Trade in Developing Economies." Working Paper 26230, National Bureau of Economic Research, Cambridge, MA.

Baum, Christopher F., Madhavi Pundit, and Arief Ramayandi. 2017. "Capital Flows and Financial Stability in Emerging Economies." Economics Working Paper 522, Asian Development Bank, Manila.

Bernard, A. B., J. B. Jensen, S. J. Redding, and P. K. Schott. 2018. "Global Firms." *Journal of Economic Literature* 56 (2): 565–619.

Bhutan, Ministry of Finance. 2018. *Bhutan Trade Statistics.* Department of Revenue and Customs.

Bown, Chad P., Daniel Lederman, Samuel Pienknagura, and Raymond Robertson. 2017. *Better Neighbors: Toward a Renewal of Economic Integration in Latin America.* Latin America and Caribbean Studies. Washington, DC: World Bank.

Conconi, Paola, André Sapir, and Maurizio Zanardi. 2016. "The Internationalization Process of Firms: From Exports to FDI." *Journal of International Economics* 99 (C): 16–30.

Da Rin, Marco, Marina Di Giacomo, and Alessandro Sembenelli. 2019. "Trust and Foreign Ownership: Evidence from Intra-European Foreign Direct Investments." *Review of International Economics* 27 (1): 313–46.

Dickstein, Michael J., and Eduardo Morales. 2018. "What Do Exporters Know?" *Quarterly Journal of Economics* 133 (4): 1753–801.

Freund, Caroline, and Martha Denisse Pierola. 2015. "Export Superstars." *Review of Economics and Statistics* 97 (5): 1023–32.

Gabaix, Xavier. 2011. "The Granular Origins of Aggregate Fluctuations." *Econometrica* 79 (3): 733–72.

Gould, David Michael. 2018. *Critical Connections: Promoting Economic Growth and Resilience in Europe and Central Asia.* Europe and Central Asia Studies. Washington, DC: World Bank.

Gould, David M., Congyan Tan, and Amir S. Sadeghi Emamgholi. 2013. "Attracting Foreign Direct Investment: What Can South Asia's Lack of Success Teach Other Developing Countries?" Policy Research Working Paper 6696, World Bank, Washington, DC.

Guiso, L., P. Sapienza, and L. Zingales. 2009. "Cultural Biases in Economic Exchange?" *Quarterly Journal of Economics* 124 (3): 1095–131.

Harrison, A., and A. Rodríguez-Clare. 2010. "Trade, Foreign Investment, and Industrial Policy for Developing Countries." *Handbook of Development Economics*, 1st ed., vol. 5. Amsterdam: Elsevier.

India, Ministry of Finance, Department of Revenue. 2019. Notification No.05/2019-Customs, Department of Revenue, Ministry of Finance, New Delhi.

Javorcik, Beata S. 2004. "Does Foreign Direct Investment Increase the Productivity of Domestic Firms? In Search of Spillovers through Backward Linkages." *American Economic Review* 94 (3): 605–27.

Kathuria, Sanjay, ed. 2018. *A Glass Half Full: The Promise of Regional Trade in South Asia.* South Asia Development Forum. Washington, DC: World Bank.

Nepal, Department of Commerce. 2018. https://moics.gov.np/en.

Pakistan, Ministry of Commerce. 2019. SRO 927(I)/2019 and SRO 928(I)/2019. Islamabad.

Taneja, Nisha, Samridhi Bimal, and Varsha Sivaram. 2018. "Emerging Trends in India-Pakistan Trade." Working Paper, Indian Council for Research on International Economic Relations, New Delhi.

UNCTAD (United Nations Conference on Trade and Development). 2019. *World Investment Report 2019: Special Economic Zones.* Geneva: UNCTAD.

World Bank. 2004. "Trade Policies in South Asia: An Overview." Report 29949, vol. 2, World Bank, Washington, DC.

World Bank. 2019. *South Asia Economic Focus, Spring 2019: Exports Wanted.* Washington, DC: World Bank.

World Bank and WTO (World Trade Organization). 2019. *Global Value Chain Development Report 2019: Technological Innovation, Supply Chain Trade, and Workers in a Globalized World.* Washington, DC: World Bank Group.

WTO (World Trade Organization). 2019. *World Trade Report 2019: The Future of Services Trade.* Geneva: World Trade Organization.

Yatawara, Ravindra. 2013. "Boosting South Asian Export Performance through Regional Integration." Chief Economist's Office, South Asia Region, World Bank, Washington, DC.

CHAPTER 2

Cross-Border Engagement: An Integrated Analytical Framework

Introduction

Why do some South Asian firms engage in regional markets while others do not? What are the characteristics of these regional pioneer firms? What is the preferred mode of engagement of these firms? What is the dynamic path for these firms upon entry, and what are the implications for other firms in the same industry in their home country? The internationalization of firms has created a large literature in the international economics and international business fields. In international trade, the movement of the analytic unit from countries and sectors to firms has led to an array of models enriching the understanding of firms' foreign market entry decisions.

To move toward answering these questions, this chapter develops a simple, flexible framework with which to discuss issues related to foreign engagement entry. The framework accommodates five key priorities. First, firms may engage with foreign economies along two basic fronts—they are interested in *serving international markets*, or *global sourcing*, or both. Second, the framework applies to intermediate and final *goods and services* industries and activities. Third, the framework takes a *value chain approach*, incorporating all the activities involved in bringing a product from concept to market, including network coordination, research and development, logistics, assembly, distribution, and branding.

Fourth, a *range of engagement options* are available to firms, with varying levels of capital requirements. An analytical distinction is made between equity modes and nonequity modes of engagement. The three broad strategies or instruments of internationalization examined are trade, foreign direct investment (FDI) (equity mode), and nonequity modes (international contractual agreements such as licensing and franchise agreements).[1] For example, to serve foreign markets, firms may export, establish subsidiaries to produce and sell in foreign markets (horizontal outward FDI), or license intellectual property to foreign licensee firms to produce the firm's products for a royalty payment associated with the use of the firm's brand, technology, or other proprietary knowledge. Similarly, global sourcing may be achieved by importing goods and services inputs from unaffiliated foreign firms; establishing subsidiaries abroad to more efficiently produce activities along the value chain, which in turn could be imported and incorporated into the final product (vertical outward FDI); or alternatively purchasing a license for foreign technology and producing the inputs at home.

Fifth, the framework enables the incorporation of the network of relationships (social capital), culture, information frictions, and psychological issues that affect decision-making. Although the management literature (for example, Johanson and Vahlne 1977, 2009) has tackled these issues for a long time, the field of economics has only more recently incorporated them into trade and investment (Bernard and Moxnes 2018) and development thinking (World Bank 2015).

Given the broad scope of the exercise, this chapter presents a framework that will guide the analysis of firm behavior in chapter 3 and the empirical estimation in chapter 4 instead of developing a formal model that is then empirically estimated. The rest of the chapter progressively develops the building blocks of the framework and is organized as follows: The next section begins with a simple exposition of global value chain activities and outlines the various frictions involved in carrying out activities abroad. It serves as a useful tool for illustrating different modes of international engagement and the relationship between trade and investment. The following section provides a simple stylized version of international firm entry among heterogeneous firms (distinct in their productivity levels) and introduces the notion of sunk entry costs that must be incurred to enter a market, which only the more productive firms can afford. Allowing for investment to have higher entry costs than exporting implies that the most productive firms will invest, medium-productivity firms will export, and low-productivity firms will serve only home markets. The chapter then shows that allowing for variation in these sunk entry costs across different entry modes generates firm selection into a spectrum of entry modes. The last section introduces the notion of knowledge connectivity—information, networks, and learning—and how it factors into entering new markets. Variation of firm-level information about markets is incorporated into the framework as variation in the sunk entry costs across firms for a particular mode of entry.

Incorporating a Value Chain Approach

World flows of trade and investment are increasingly determined by complex production arrangements. Technological advances and government policy liberalization have created new opportunities for specialization by enabling the separability and tradability of most of the activities along a value chain needed to bring a product from conception to market. Thus, global value chains (GVCs) have developed, with chain activities based in locations where they can be most efficiently performed, coordinated by lead firms through sophisticated intrafirm and interfirm relationships (Antràs 2018, 2020; World Bank 2020).

Integrating into GVCs has been a dynamic avenue for increased competitiveness, trade penetration, job creation, and income generation in many economies. Firms could access global markets and technology by specializing in a single component or activity within these advanced production networks. Firms only need to be relatively more efficient in one activity along the value chain, instead of needing to have a comparative advantage in producing a final good. Firms based in low- and middle-income economies in geographical proximity to the three global production hubs (China, Germany, and the United States) involved in the trade of parts and components have benefited substantially. Association of Southeast Asian Nations (ASEAN) economies have grown by developing a "factory Asia" in China, Japan, and the Republic of Korea. Mexico has benefited from a United States–centric "factory North America," while "factory Europe," led by Germany, has stimulated many neighboring Eastern European economies, such as the Czech Republic, Hungary, and Poland.

Is there scope for a "factory South Asia," with India acting as a hub for the development of a regional value chain that would benefit itself and its neighboring economies?

A simple, integrated framework of multinational enterprise (MNE) decision-making within a GVC is useful for organizing thinking about the links between trade and FDI. Consider four important cross-border participation decisions:

- *Production location decision*—where to locate and number of locations

- *Market decision*—what markets to serve and products to supply

- *Sourcing decision*—what intermediate goods and services to source and their origin

- *Ownership decision*—what activities to perform inside firm boundaries (at home or abroad)

To illustrate the separability and tradability of activities, allow a value chain to have four parts: (1) headquarters services, including network coordination, research and development, design, and branding; (2) intermediates production; (3) assembly activity; and (4) distribution and retail sales (see figure 2.1). All these activities may be carried out in one location, but they are most likely carried out most efficiently in different locations and involve selling in foreign markets. Fragmenting the value chain across national boundaries would involve incurring certain fixed costs of entry (discussed in the next section) and variable frictional costs. These frictional costs include headquarters governance or input transfer costs associated with network coordination, monitoring, and technology transfer, as well as foreign marketing costs associated with adapting a product or advertising campaign to the destination market. Trade costs are also incurred to bring intermediates to the assembly location and final product to the consumer market location. The trade costs include transportation costs and border clearance costs such as tariffs and nontariff measures.

The ownership decision, sometimes called the "internalization" or "make-or-buy" decision, entails determining which chain activities to conduct within the boundaries of the firm and which should be done through contracting with outsiders (at home or abroad). High transaction costs tend to gear a firm toward ownership and include situations in which there are difficulties in establishing complete contracts that cover all contingencies and where customized (relation-specific) investments are needed.[2] In the face of incomplete contracts, ownership provides a source of bargaining power when unforeseen contingencies are encountered. The ultimate sourcing, assembly, market, and ownership decisions are the outcomes of a profit-maximization and strategic-goal-optimization strategy.

Business relationships along the value chain have become increasingly important, and relational contracting has been growing. Production along value chains has created complex arrangements across international partners, which have been a challenge for contracting. It has expanded the extent of the "incompleteness"—the inability to incorporate everything that can ever happen—of the standard transactional contract. Thus, firms have opted for relational contracts—informal agreements sustained by the value of the future relationship—which overcome the inefficiencies associated with incomplete transactional contracts. GVCs may involve sharing proprietary knowledge on the part of the lead firm and customized (relation-specific) investments on the part of the partner firm. Thus, relationships and trust have become very important, albeit with some variation by industry (see Gould 2018; Kukharskyy 2016; Malcomson 2012).

FIGURE 2.1 Multinational Location Options and Frictions

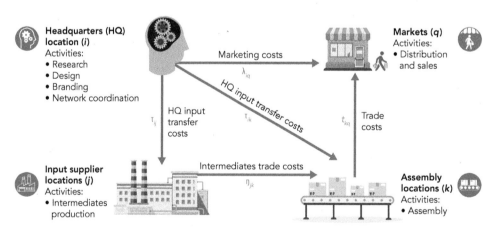

Source: Adapted from Head and Mayer 2019.

Value chain positioning matters. Structural transformation of economies is not always accompanied by higher productivity (Rodrik, McMillan, and Sepúlveda 2016). Thus, improving livelihoods may not necessarily be about moving to different value chains but instead to different segments of the value chain with higher value added or higher profit margins, as represented in Stan Shih's "smile curve" (World Bank and World Trade Organization 2019). For example, in the apparel sector, the profit margins are much higher in retail than in manufacturing, which is typically the activity developing economies dominate.

The framework given in figure 2.1 facilitates better understanding of the complex interfirm and intrafirm relationships that prevail in global value chains. Box 2.1 provides a simple illustration of different types of trade (including trade in services) and investment strategies that can be used to serve home and foreign markets. These strategies include exporting, traditional horizontal investment, vertical investment, export

---

BOX 2.1 Internationalization Strategy Options for Serving Consumer Markets at Home and Abroad

The various avenues for serving the home and foreign markets, using the framework given in figure 2.1, are illustrated and discussed here. Global firms have a variety of options for setting up their value chains to serve a particular market, and the ultimate strategy reflects the outcome of comparing relative profits. Increasingly complex firm strategies have made traditional classifications of investment type more difficult and less useful. The relationship between trade and investment flows across different multinational enterprise (MNE) strategies addressing the substitutability and complementarity of exporting and foreign direct investment (FDI) is schematically represented in figure B2.1.1. Assume there are three countries, and that the goal is to serve the home and one foreign market (F2). The services trade flows from headquarters are omitted to avoid clutter.

Exporting. A simple classic exporter scenario involves intermediates production and assembly at home. Products are sent to a foreign market (F2) distributor (square distribution activity), incurring a trade cost. This involves no FDI.

Traditional horizontal FDI. The firm chooses to save on trade costs by replicating the production process in the foreign consumer market (F2), rather than by exporting from home. A firm faces the proximity-concentration trade-off, that is, a firm weighs the net savings in trade costs (incorporating additional production costs abroad) from FDI against the net gains of scale economies from single-location production at home (and having to pay export trade costs). This type of FDI is sometimes associated with "market-seeking FDI," as in the case of tariff-jumping FDI, and would result in FDI replacing export flows and being a substitute for trade.

Traditional vertical FDI. A firm minimizes costs by production fragmentation, setting up different stages of production in different countries according to comparative advantage. To invest in vertical FDI, the cost advantage in producing intermediates abroad would have to be greater than the sum of new trade costs of importing intermediates and the coordination costs of multinational production λ associated with dealing with a fragmented production process. This is the efficiency-seeking FDI or resource-seeking

(Box continues next page)

BOX 2.1 Internationalization Strategy Options for Serving Consumer Markets at Home and Abroad *(continued)*

FIGURE B2.1.1 Internationalization Options for Serving Consumer Markets at Home and Abroad

---- Intermediates trade cost ⎯⎯ Final goods trade costs

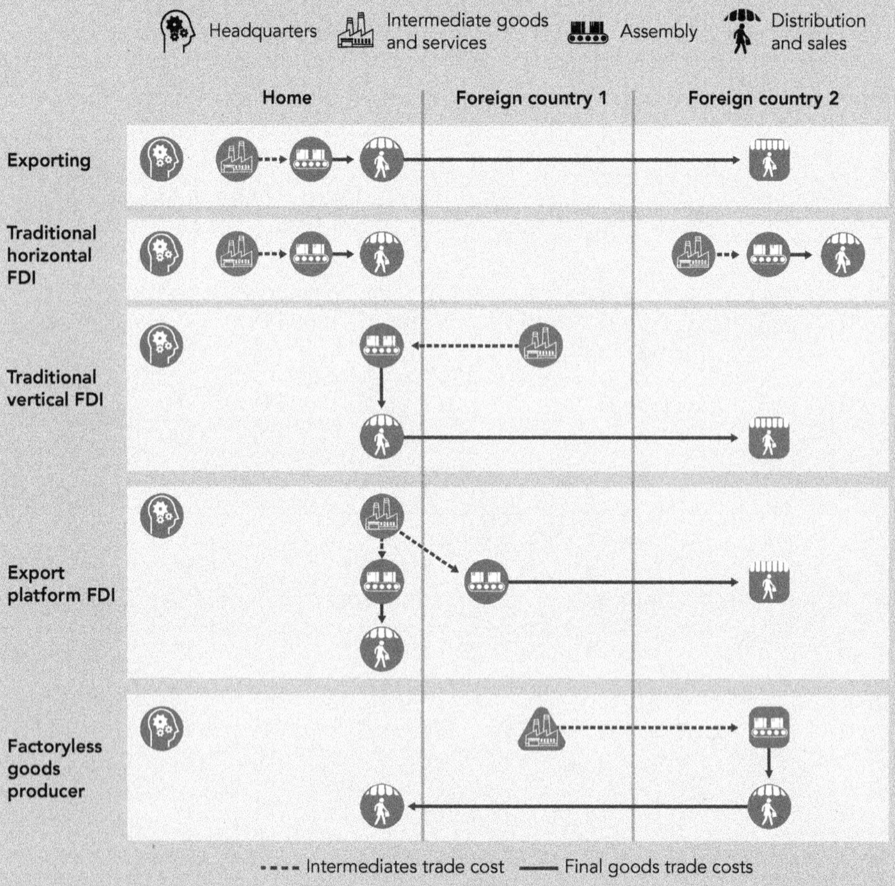

Source: World Bank.

Note: To avoid clutter, input transfers from headquarters to all other activities at home and abroad are not illustrated. FDI = foreign direct investment. The shapes around the activities reflect nationality of ownership: the circle represents ownership by the home firm, the triangle represents ownership by the foreign firm from foreign country 1, and the square represents ownership by the foreign firm from foreign country 2. For example, home country ownership in foreign country 2 is represented by the circles surrounding the intermediate production, assembly, and distribution activity icons in foreign country 2.

FDI associated with global value chains (GVCs). For example, Intel is mainly engaged in vertical FDI, with the skilled labor–intensive part of the production process (for example, wafer production) located in developed countries and the unskilled labor–intensive part

(Box continues next page)

BOX 2.1 Internationalization Strategy Options for Serving Consumer Markets at Home and Abroad *(continued)*

(for example, assembly and testing) located in developing countries. All production facilities are fully owned by Intel. Vertical FDI complements trade and is associated with increased exports of final goods (because of more competitive costing) and imports of intermediate goods and services for production.[a]

Export platform FDI. A firm fragments production by setting up final goods assembly operations in a foreign market (F1) to serve a third market (F2), with no sales in the FDI host country. The cost competitiveness may reflect horizontal reasons dominated by low trade costs between the host country (F1) and the final consumer market (for example, a free trade agreement between F1 and F2), or be driven by efficiency considerations (vertical) of the platform location. Platform FDI is associated with higher final goods exports of the global firm, but these exports would be originating from the foreign location and home exports would now be only intermediates.[b]

There are implications associated with the ownership issue and nonequity relationships. The GVC network is a complex mix of affiliates and arms-length suppliers with differing contracting strategies. Typically, arguments in favor of keeping activities within the boundaries of the firm through FDI are based on (1) the high transaction costs in the contracting environment and (2) the need for relationship-specific investments to be made by the foreign contracting party. The contracting of arm's-length input suppliers from F1 in a complex strategy could be readily represented by an F1-national's ownership of intermediates (a triangular "intermediates" icon) in the export platform FDI scenario. The net trade implications of nonownership versus ownership in a complex strategy are ambiguous, but they are likely to be more similar if multinational production frictions are lower.

The importance of nonequity relationships has increased. Lower multinational production costs (through better intellectual property protection), services trade, and sophisticated contracting could be a substitute for FDI. As a result, some analysts highlight the importance of the trade-investment-services–intellectual property nexus.[c]

Factoryless goods producers and GVC coordinators. The strategies that lead to factoryless goods producers and GVC coordinators are prevalent in some GVCs and arise when firms outsource their production activities to contract manufacturers while keeping all necessary research and development, design activities, marketing, and branding in house. For example, Nike does not own any of the hundreds of contracted clothing and shoe producers across the world that assemble its products.

a. In this context, gross exports data may reflect double-counting of intermediate products trade because they enter as imported components and thereafter are part of the embedded value in final goods exports.

b. This kind of FDI is associated with MNEs' investing in peripheral member countries of a preferential trade agreement (with relatively lower factor prices) to serve the richer economies within the union, as with FDI in the European Union's late entrants from Eastern Europe (Tintelnot 2017). Similarly, apparel investors based in India, Pakistan, and Sri Lanka produce certain basic product lines in Bangladesh where labor is cheaper and access to the European Union is duty free, while other more skill-intensive product lines are produced in the investor's home country.

c. For example, the initial management know-how that spurred the Bangladeshi apparel industry developed from a technical partnership between the local firm Desh Garments and a Korean garment manufacturer, Daewoo Corporation: Daewoo provided technical training to Bangladeshi workers and managers and marketing services in exchange for a share of the sales.

platform FDI, and "factoryless" goods producers. The factoryless strategy captures the preference of some manufacturing firms to pursue "asset-light" approaches in which the manufacturing of inputs and final assembly are contracted outside firm boundaries, restricting firm activities to research, design, and marketing. The relationship between trade and investment is also readily visualized, highlighting the complexities of understanding whether trade and investment act as substitutes or complements. The rest of this chapter develops 12 propositions that highlight the implications of this framework.

Proposition 1. The value chain approach highlights the goods and services activities that are involved in getting a product from concept to market. The separability and tradability of these activities allow for greater specialization and competitiveness but involve fixed entry costs and variable frictional costs of international engagement.

Proposition 2. The complexity of value chain activities has enhanced the value of business relationships and trust. It has led to the growth of relational contracting, in which contracting parties behave in an expected manner to sustain the relationship in the long term, although such behavior is not explicitly stipulated in a transactional contract.

Proposition 3. Value chain positioning matters because the level of value added and profit margins vary with different activities along the chain.

Proposition 4. A value chain approach provides insights into understanding the trade-investment nexus.

Foreign Market Entry Decision

Antràs and Yeaple's (2014) framework, which uses firm heterogeneity in productivity and a monopolistic competition industrial structure along the lines of Melitz (2003), is used to study export performance and multinational activity. The focus is on analysis of the entry decision to serve foreign markets.[3] It relies on recent literature that studies heterogeneous firms and their decisions to export (reviewed by Melitz and Redding 2014), source globally (Antràs, Fort, and Tintelnot 2017), and invest abroad (reviewed in Antràs 2016; Antràs and Yeaple 2014). The approach illustrated in figure 2.1 is simplified such that the production of intermediates and assembly are bundled into one production activity within a two-country framework. A flexible framework that covers different modes of market entry is developed to guide the study of firm behavior, but the econometric analysis in chapter 4 focuses on the investment decision abroad. The literature on exporting is significantly more mature and is adapted to study investor dynamics in chapter 4.

These are the key drivers of foreign market entry for heterogeneous firms:

- *Firm differences in productivity,* ϕ_i. Productivity differences reflect differences in cost structure and potential profits. Higher productivity is associated with greater revenue and larger firm size.

- *Sunk (fixed) entry costs of foreign market entry, f_x, where x is the entry mode.* A firm that exports or invests abroad faces sunk costs of foreign market entry relating to information acquisition; due diligence; consumer market research; regulatory research; entry location analysis; research on government incentives; search and matching costs for partners, such as distributors, along the relevant segment of the value chain; and contracting costs. Sunk costs are one-time fixed costs that cannot be recovered if the firm decides not to enter. They are assumed to be similar per destination across firms in the benchmark framework.

- *Fixed costs in the destination market, F_x, where x is the entry mode.* Based on the entry mode, foreign firms may face additional fixed costs in the destination country. These costs do not vary with export volume. Exporters that have secured distributing partners abroad may have zero additional fixed costs (as in the classic model of exporting with foreign distribution partners, illustrated in box 2.1). MNEs that set up manufacturing firms incur the fixed costs of setting up plants in the foreign country. Alternatively, firms may incur the costs of setting up small offices to facilitate trade, termed trade-supporting investment. Further, exporters may engage in distribution FDI. Exporters that act as their own wholesalers must develop a system of warehouses, and those that act as retailers incur the additional costs of setting up storefronts.

Summing sunk and other fixed costs together—following Conconi, Sapir, and Zanardi (2016)—let the combined

Fixed entry costs of entry mode x, $f_x = f_x + F_x$ = sunk entry costs + other fixed costs.

- *Variable trade costs, t.* These costs cover transportation, tariffs, and nontariff measures, as well as broader trade costs related to trade facilitation, border management, and time.

The basic setup of the model is as follows: A domestic firm in operation bears no internal trade costs when the firm sells only in the home country. If the firm chooses to export, however, it bears additional fixed entry costs f_{EX} in each foreign market, and an international trade cost, t. On the other hand, if it chooses to serve a foreign market through foreign direct investment (horizontal FDI), it incurs no variable trade costs but bears higher fixed costs f_{FDI} in every foreign market. Firms that serve foreign markets also cater to the domestic market. The fixed entry costs f_{EX} may be interpreted as the sunk costs of gathering information on consumer markets and government regulations. The fixed costs f_{FDI} include these sunk costs, the duplicate fixed (sunk) production costs embodied in f_Z at home, as well as the additional sunk and fixed costs of forming a subsidiary in a foreign country.

The exporting decision. Faced with the sole option of exporting or not, profit-maximizing domestic firms facing a common level of fixed entry costs of exporting, f_{EX}, self-select into exporting because only the more productive firms would find it profitable to pay these sunk entry costs (figure 2.2, panel a). Because more productive firms produce more output, this sorting pattern also implies that exporters are larger than firms that only serve the domestic market. Better-performing, larger firms (above a threshold productivity $\phi_{EX}{}^*$) benefit from the market expansion effects of trade that allow scale economies to be exploited, while lower-productivity firms contract and cater only to the domestic market, and very-low-productivity firms exit. Thus, trade leads to a reallocation effect, wherein production is more concentrated in better-performing firms. Lower sunk entry costs and lower trade costs are associated with greater exporting. Similarly,

FIGURE 2.2 Relationship of Productivity to Serving Foreign Markets by Exporting and Investing Abroad

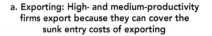

a. Exporting: High- and medium-productivity firms export because they can cover the sunk entry costs of exporting

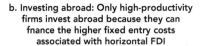

b. Investing abroad: Only high-productivity firms invest abroad because they can finance the higher fixed entry costs associated with horizontal FDI

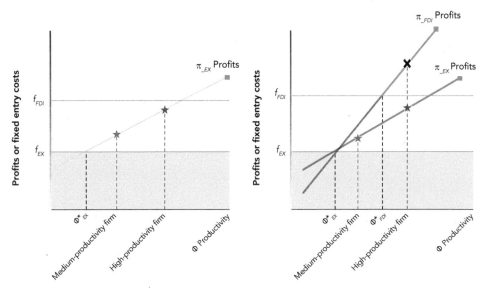

Source: A highly simplified version of a diagram given by Helpman, Melitz, and Yeaple 2004.
Note: Panel a. The upward-sloping line π_{EX} represents expected gross profits under exporting. The line is orange above f_{EX} and respective productivity ϕ^*_{EX} (the survival productivity cutoff), representing positive net profits. Firms with productivity above ϕ^*_{EX} export. Both the medium-productivity firm and the high-productivity firm find it profitable to export. Profits for the high-productivity firm are higher because it produces more output. Lower sunk entry costs and lower trade costs lead to more exporting. Lower sunk entry costs shift the profit function to the left. Lower trade costs lead to a steeper profit function. In both cases, the result is a lower survival productivity cutoff, expanding the set of potential exporters.
Panel b. The upward-sloping line π_{FDI} represents expected gross profits under horizontal FDI. It is steeper because it involves zero trade costs. The line is green above the higher fixed entry costs of investment, f_{FDI}, and respective productivity ϕ^*_{FDI} (the survival productivity cutoff), representing positive net profits. Firms with productivity above ϕ^*_{FDI} invest. In this scenario, only the high-productivity firm serves the foreign market through investing. This firm receives higher profits than under exporting (marked by "**X**"). The medium-productivity firm serves foreign markets by exporting.
FDI = foreign direct investment.

global sourcing will involve sunk fixed entry costs and variable trade costs, and only the more productive firms will be able to incur these costs.[4]

The exporting versus horizontal FDI decision. Horizontal FDI involves setting up production and distribution structures abroad. Given that multinational production involves the trade-off of higher fixed entry costs $f_{FDI} > f_{EX}$ to save on trade costs, the profit function under FDI will be steeper because of the elimination of the trade costs. As a result, the survival productivity cutoff for investing abroad will be much higher than for exporting, $\phi_{FDI}^* > \phi_{EX}^*$ (Helpman, Melitz, and Yeaple 2004). Thus, only the most productive firms will find it profitable to invest abroad. In considering the export-versus-FDI option, the firm assesses profitability by looking at the proximity-concentration trade-off of incurring the higher fixed costs of operating abroad and not having to incur trade costs. The profitability of high-productivity firms is higher under FDI compared with the exporting scenario (figure 2.2, panel b). It follows that the most productive firms serve the foreign market via subsidiary sales (OFDI); medium-productivity firms serve the foreign market via export; and still-lower-productivity firms serve only the domestic market. This framework is useful for analyzing the provision of both goods and services products.

Lowering fixed entry costs of investment creates more multinationals. However, the relationship between trade costs and foreign investment is more complex, because lower trade costs have an ambiguous effect on investment (Alfaro and Chen 2019; Anderson and van Wincoop 2004). They decrease the likelihood of incurring capital costs abroad (horizontal FDI) to avoid these now-low variable trade costs (via the proximity-concentration trade-off) but increase the incentive to invest abroad to gain competitiveness in chain activities (vertical FDI).

Based on the analysis above, three further propositions are developed:

Proposition 5. High-productivity, large firms self-select into exporting and sourcing inputs globally because these activities involve upfront sunk entry costs, and their sales volumes permit them to cover these fixed costs.

Proposition 6. Only the most productive firms self-select to serve foreign markets by investing abroad, owing to the higher fixed entry costs. The resultant sorting pattern implies that medium-productivity firms will export, and lower-productivity firms will serve only domestic markets.

Proposition 7. Higher productivity and lower fixed costs of entry are associated with more multinational activity. Trade costs have an ambiguous impact on FDI.

Toward a Spectrum of Engagement Modes: Variation of Entry Costs across Modes

This framework can be applied more broadly to analyze results in the presence of additional choices in the mode of entry. In the traditional business literature, entry mode choice is a trade-off between resource commitment and control. Within this structure, to consider firm behavior with exporting, FDI, and licensing options to serve foreign markets, it would be useful to break down the fixed entry costs into sunk entry costs and other fixed costs. In the classic case of exporting to a foreign distributor, the strategy involves a sunk entry cost, zero fixed costs abroad, and positive trade costs. A horizontal investment abroad, involving the replication of production and distribution abroad, involves a sunk entry cost related to due diligence and a high fixed cost associated with building a factory, which is offset by zero variable trade costs. The licensing option involves a sunk cost of finding a suitable partner abroad with which to share intellectual property such as a brand or technology, low trade costs (no goods trade costs but some services export trade costs and monitoring and maintenance costs), and zero fixed costs at the destination market. In this case, the fixed costs are borne by the foreign partner, which is assumed to be able to serve the market with lower fixed costs than could the home investor (if they had invested abroad), based on the partner already having operations or superior local knowledge of operating in the foreign environment. The fixed costs in the destination by the home firm in each mode may be represented by $0 = F_{EX} = F_{LIC} < F_{FDI}$.

The ordering of sunk entry costs is not as straightforward, but it is likely that the different sunk entry costs reflect the level of risk involved in each form of engagement. Given that a horizontal investment involves the high capital cost of building a plant, the extent of due diligence and information gathering would be significantly higher than that of exporting, $f_{EX} < f_{FDI}$. It is not so obvious that the sunk entry costs of all nonequity modes of entry are greater than those of exporting. However, consider that the due diligence required for licensing would involve not only consumer market research for assessing profitability but also more intense diligence on finding a trustworthy partner and high contracting costs to minimize the risk of intellectual property appropriation by the partner. The implication that these costs would be higher than the sunk costs of exporting are borne out by empirical work by Briggs and Park (2013). The sunk costs would then be ranked $f_{EX} < f_{LIC} < f_{FDI}$, and the combined fixed entry costs, f_x, would be ranked

$$\textit{Fixed Entry Costs}^{\textit{EXPORT}} < \textit{Fixed Entry Costs}^{\textit{LICENSING}} < \textit{Fixed Entry Costs}^{\textit{FDI}} \qquad (2.1)$$

The ordering of trade costs is $t_{EX} > t_{LIC} > t_{FDI}$. It follows that the expected profit curve would be steepest for FDI and shallowest for profits under exporting, resulting in this ordering of survival productivity cutoffs: $\phi_{EX}^* < \phi_{LIC}^* < \phi_{FDI}^*$. This result would produce the same type of sorting by productivity as before, where the most productive firms invest abroad, the next range of firms license intellectual property, followed by those that export, with the least-productive firms serving only the domestic market.

The bargaining between licensor and licensee on profit sharing is not readily captured in this framework, but it still provides intuitive results based on productivity and the fixed entry costs, especially for capital-intensive services industries such as hotels.[5]

Intermediaries. The recent analysis of trade with intermediaries is also related to this work, given that specialized trading firms (intermediaries) may reduce the sunk costs of exporting (particularly to specific markets), thus allowing previous nonexporting firms to export indirectly (Ahn, Khandelwal, and Wei 2011). Intermediaries based at home provide low fixed entry costs of indirect exporting f_{IE}, with $f_{IE} < f_{EX}$, but charge a fee that increases the marginal cost of foreign distribution, λ. They charge this fee for aggregating the output of small firms, matching buyers abroad with the relevant exports, and guaranteeing quality to foreign buyers. Thus, for a given product, the indirect export price is greater than the direct export price, which results in lower revenues from indirect exporting relative to direct exporting, in the presence of elastic demand. Similarly, investment intermediaries reduce the fixed costs of FDI entry. Investment intermediaries may pool capital from different sources or provide consultancy services related to the consumer market or site selection abroad.

Value chain activities and a spectrum of fixed entry costs. By splitting apart the activities of the value chain, far more opportunities for international engagement become available. Firms may invest abroad in only one part of the value chain instead of replicating all activities abroad, as assumed in horizontal FDI. The wide range of capital requirements and skill requirements for activities along a value chain expands a firm's inclusivity in access to global markets. For example, consider that an exporter pays a variable marketing cost or distribution cost, λ_{EX}, if it uses a local agent and has zero fixed cost of distribution. Alternatively, the exporter could incur a fixed cost of setting up a distribution network, F_M, such that $0 = F_{EX} < F_M < F_{FDI}$, and incur sunk entry costs, f_M, such that $f_{EX} < f_M < f_{FDI}$; then the variable distribution costs, λ_{EX}, would be zero, or effectively the same as for a local distributor. This creates the familiar proximity-concentration trade-off between the resulting fixed entry cost of marketing FDI, f_M, $f_{EX} < f_M < f_{FDI}$ and variable foreign marketing distribution costs λ_{EX}:

$$\textit{Fixed Entry Costs}^{\textit{EXPORT}} < \textit{Fixed Entry Costs}^{\textit{DISTRIBUTION FDI}} < \textit{Fixed Entry Costs}^{\textit{FDI}} \quad (2.2)$$

A standard firm-sorting equilibrium according to productivity would arise, with survival cutoff productivity ranked $\phi^*_{EX} < \phi^*_M < \phi^*_{FDI}$ from lowest to highest. The most productive firms will pursue horizontal FDI (essentially both production and distribution FDI), whereas firms with medium productivity, ϕ_M, which are above survival productivity cutoff, ϕ^*_M, but below the productivity cutoff, ϕ^*_{FDI}, could invest abroad in distribution services only. Firms with productivity below ϕ^*_M would be classic exporters if they cover the sunk costs of exporting. As before, larger firms with more exports care more about variable costs. They would be more willing to trade the fixed capital cost of setting up a distribution center for lower variable distribution costs abroad. In so doing, they capture the profit margins of wholesalers, gain better feedback from consumers, and have better control of their distribution and replenishment strategies. Sales and profits will be higher than under exporting, but lower than under horizontal FDI.

The logic presented above may be extended to illustrate a spectrum of entry options and respective magnitudes of fixed entry costs that a firm faces when it seeks to serve foreign markets. As listed in table 2.1, the sunk entry costs would be lowest if there were intermediaries at home—local firms or affiliates of a foreign customer firm or foreign trading firm. E-commerce has also brought down the cost of export entry. However, as the fixed costs of entry expand, the exporter firm receives greater control of its chain activities and has greater scope to adjust prices, adjust markups, and be responsive to consumers. This approach also broadens the scope for analyzing the relationship between exports and foreign investment in serving the foreign market, where horizontal FDI may be associated with lower exports but the vertical FDI associated with input sourcing would complement exports. Here, vertical FDI—in the form of trade-supporting FDI, distribution FDI, or retail FDI—complements exports and leads to progressively higher foreign sales.

Based on the analysis given above, further propositions are developed:

Proposition 8. Trading intermediaries and investment intermediaries may help smaller firms by reducing the fixed costs of trading and investing, respectively.

Proposition 9. Firms with medium levels of productivity may invest in a single value chain activity abroad that requires lower fixed entry costs compared with horizontal FDI.

TABLE 2.1 Serving Foreign Markets: Alternative Modes in Rising Order of Fixed Entry Costs (1 Low–9 High)

	Indirect exporting
1	Intermediaries at home
	Direct exporting
2	Sales through digital platforms or e-commerce
3	To foreign distributor or agent
4	To foreign client firm
5	To foreign client firm with licensing of brand for retail investment
6	With own marketing office abroad (trade-supporting services FDI)
7	With own wholesale distribution abroad (wholesale services FDI)
8	With own wholesale and retail distribution abroad (wholesale and retail services FDI)
	No exporting
9	With own production and distribution abroad (horizontal FDI)

Source: World Bank.
Note: FDI = foreign direct investment.

Information, Networks, and Learning: Variation of Entry Costs across Firms

Although the basic framework is intuitive, it also seems likely that the export or investment decision is driven not just by the variation in how efficiently production at home is organized but also by differences in how well foreign markets are understood. This variation in information about destination markets among firms is captured here through heterogeneity in sunk entry costs among firms. The sources of the variation may reflect the level of embeddedness of the firm in the destination market or sector globally, the existing networks in the destination market, and tacit knowledge of the market or the business operating environment. These issues highlight the importance of "social capital," that is, the value of social networks and relationships in conducting business. Networks may provide access to information and influence and to finance and potential assistance in hard times, and may lower search and other transaction costs through greater inherent trust. With networks, it is not just "who you know" that matters but "who and what who you know knows." The greater the networks of your connection, the greater the value of that relationship. Thus, although productivity is important, a less efficient firm with family connections in the destination market may export or invest, while a higher-productivity firm without such connections may not (see Boisso and Ferrantino 1997; Jackson 2011; Rauch and Trindade 2002).

Modeling the variation in firm-level information on destination markets through fixed entry costs is validated by extensive work on exporting. The importance of fixed entry costs of exporting, although prone to overestimation, has been confirmed in various studies (Das, Roberts, and Tybout 2007; Dickstein and Morales 2018). It is well-accepted that the studies reflect imperfect information. Authors have extended the standard framework to allow for product-specific fixed entry costs (for multiproduct firms) and market-specific fixed entry costs, which are, on average, higher for advanced markets. The impact of fixed entry costs on firm entry is confirmed by the fact that the increases in exports that follow lower sunk costs tend to be through new firm entry (the extensive margin) rather than through an increase in export value of existing exporters (the intensive margin).

The identification of firm-market fixed entry costs is an important consideration for South Asian firms, where years of regional nonengagement have led to narrow and shallow business networks in some country pairs. However, given the prevalence of diverse communities and the migration that occurred particularly around the time of partition, it is highly likely that there are large differences among national firms in knowledge connectivity (and hence sunk entry costs) compared to communities and markets across national boundaries.

The approach used here is consistent with the work of Wagner and Zahler (2015), which allows for random entry costs and shows that a less productive firm with a lucky draw of a low fixed entry cost could enter a new destination ahead of a more productive firm with an unlucky draw of a high fixed entry cost. Empirical work (Castro et al. 2016) for Chile has found heterogeneity in fixed export costs across firms. The work also found that the export decision incorporates both fixed export costs and productivity, allowing for the presence of high-productivity nonexporters (facing high fixed export costs) and low-productivity exporters (facing low fixed export costs). Additional work tries to capture variation in the available information across firms and finds that larger firms have more information than small firms, regardless of export experience (Dickstein and Morales 2018).[6]

Variation in uncertainty at the firm level is related to variation in information and the level of connectedness. In its simplest form, uncertainty can be reduced by obtaining information, implying that firms that face high uncertainty about a destination face high sunk fixed entry costs to resolve this uncertainty. There are different types of uncertainty—demand, policy, exchange rate, political, security—and they all can apply to the host or the home country. Interest in uncertainty has increased because of the growth in trade policy uncertainty since the global financial crisis of 2008, along with the ability to create empirical proxies for uncertainty using panels of firm-level outcomes, online news databases, and surveys. Measures of country- and global-level policy uncertainty using textual analysis of newspapers have proved accurate in capturing relevant events (Baker, Bloom, and Davis 2016). Many studies find evidence that high policy uncertainty at the country level undermines economic performance because firms delay or forgo investments and hiring, productivity-enhancing factor reallocation is slowed, and consumption expenditures are delayed (Bloom 2014; Caldara et al. 2019).

Other work has estimated uncertainty variation at the firm level, measured as political risk using textual analysis of firm investor updates (Hassan et al. 2019) and as the absolute value of foreign sales forecast errors (Chen et al. 2020). Firms may respond passively to uncertainty through the real options approach,[7] which causes firms to assume a "wait and see" attitude and postpone their investment decisions. Alternatively, or additionally, they may take an active approach by engaging in activity to reduce firm-level uncertainty, for example, increasing lobbying in the United States (Hassan et al. 2019; Kost 2019) and entering foreign markets to acquire information and resolve uncertainty (Chen et al. 2020).

The role ascribed here to firm-level knowledge connectivity is captured in other fields using different terminology. The business management literature argues that a firm that intends to engage in foreign activities suffers a knowledge deficit about the foreign market, its players, and the rules (implicit and explicit) of the operating environment—sometimes called a liability of foreignness (Johanson and Vahlne 2009). A related management concept that gets at varying degrees of foreignness is psychic distance, which refers to the factors that make it difficult to understand foreign environments, including differences in language, culture, business practices, and industrial development. Regional engagement will require knowledge acquisition and learning about regional markets to overcome uncertainty and better understand the opportunities those markets offer. The extent of this required learning will depend on the psychic distance between the home and foreign firms or markets. In this situation, experience is the key source of learning.

In network theory, which views markets as networks of relationships between firms, the liability of foreignness is replaced by a liability of outsidership. In this framework, internationalization success depends on the firm's relationships and networks in the destination country or the industry globally—its insidership. Thus, foreign firms may face a liability of outsidership that may be overcome if they are well connected. Networks provide a source of knowledge that may reduce uncertainty in foreign markets, foster trust in relationships, increase awareness of opportunities, and induce quicker commitment abroad, as in the case of "born global" firms (Madsen and Per 1997).

Based on the analysis above, the final three propositions are developed:

Proposition 10. Lowering sunk entry costs will increase international entry by firms.

Proposition 11. Given the rich diversity of communities and migration in South Asia, there are likely to be large differences among national firms in knowledge connectivity compared to businesses and communities across national boundaries.

Proposition 12. Information-enhancing, uncertainty-reducing, transaction-cost-lowering, connection-building networks, as well as inherent knowledge, reduce sunk entry costs. Learning may be viewed as the reduction of sunk entry costs over time through experience.

Concluding Remarks

This chapter has developed key elements of a simple framework that guides the ensuing analysis of international engagement by firms. First, the value chain approach highlights the various frictions that accompany international engagement. It also provides an intuitive means of conceptualizing different forms of international engagement and the relationship between trade and investment. Second, the framework of firm entry with varying fixed entry costs and trade costs enables analysis of exporting-versus-investing options and enables analysis across a spectrum of entry modes. The most productive firms can afford to cover the highest fixed entry costs, but there are also intermediate options between exporting and direct horizontal investment. Third, knowledge connectivity (the level of information and networks in a destination market) across firms may be readily incorporated into sunk entry costs for a particular entry mode. Higher knowledge connectivity reduces sunk entry costs, which is important because, given intraregional migration, there is likely to be significant variation in knowledge connectivity and social capital across firms and entrepreneurs relating to markets in South Asia.

The next chapter provides a comprehensive picture of intraregional investment in South Asia using an outward investment lens. It analyzes underutilized aggregate bilateral investment data and firm-level data collected specifically for this report, as well as case studies of regional pioneers. The types of investments, the sector of origin, the motivation for engagement, and the modes of engagement are covered. The entry strategies of regional pioneers are discussed specifically using the framework illustrated in box 2.1. The econometric estimation of the firm investment entry decision given in chapter 4 is based on the framework discussed here.

Notes

1. Technically, trade is a nonequity mode of internationalization, but it is treated separately for analytical purposes and because the term "nonequity modes" is typically used to refer to international contractual agreements. These international contractual agreements may be classified as trade in services. For example, the receipt of fees for licensed intellectual property is classified under services trade in a country's balance of payments accounts.

2. For example, a component supplier may have to invest in machinery that is appropriate only for production for one particular lead firm, making the new investment not useful in fulfilling orders for other clients.

3. The greater focus on exporting as opposed to global sourcing here is due to data limitations that prevent symmetric empirical analysis on importing in chapter 4.

4. Global sourcing models (Antràs, Fort, and Tintelnot 2017) are often not modeled exactly symmetrically to exporting. Through competition effects, the costs of imported inputs fall as the number of sourcing partners increases.

5. Although this case may apply to capital-intensive services sectors such as hotels, it may be different for knowledge-intensive services industries. In services industries such as consulting and software services, the fixed cost of investing, F_{FDI}, is quite low, and trade costs are also low. The sunk cost of investing, which would involve standard due diligence, could be lower than the sunk cost of licensing, where it is difficult to find trustworthy capable partners and contracting is complicated. In this case, for low trade costs t_{LIC}, the most productive firms will serve markets by licensing, and the medium-productivity firms will serve foreign markets through investment (Bhattacharya, Patnaik, and Shah 2012).

6. Although the focus in this section is on sunk fixed costs of entry, networks and social capital may also reduce variable costs of production, such as through smoother labor market relations abroad and better navigation of the foreign bureaucracy.

7. A real option provides management the right, but not the obligation, to undertake business decisions or investments.

References

Ahn, Jae Bin, Amit K. Khandelwal, and Shang-Jin Wei. 2011. "The Role of Intermediaries in Facilitating Trade." *Journal of International Economics* 84 (1): 73–85.

Alfaro, Laura, and Maggie Chen. 2019. "Transportation Cost and the Geography of Foreign Investment." In *Handbook of International Trade and Transportation*, edited by Bruce Blonigen and Wesley Wilson, 369–407. Cheltenham, UK: Edward Elgar Publishing.

Anderson, J. E., and E. van Wincoop. 2004. "Trade Costs." *Journal of Economic Literature* 42 (3): 691–751.

Antràs, Pol. 2016. *Global Production: Firms, Contracts, and Trade Structure.* Princeton, NJ: Princeton University Press.

Antràs, Pol. 2018. "Global Value Chains: The Economics of Spiders and Snakes." 2018 Ohlin Lecture, Stockholm School of Economics, Stockholm, October 15.

Antràs, Pol. 2020. "Conceptual Aspects of Global Value Chains." *World Bank Economic Review* 34 (3): 551–74.

Antràs, Pol, Teresa C. Fort, and Felix Tintelnot. 2017. "The Margins of Global Sourcing: Theory and Evidence from U.S. Firms." *American Economic Review* 107 (9): 2514–64.

Antràs, Pol, and Stephen R. Yeaple. 2014. "Multinational Firms and the Structure of International Trade." In *Handbook of International Economics,* volume 4, edited by G. Gopinath, E. Helpman, and K. Rogoff, 55–130. Amsterdam: North-Holland.

Baker, S., N. Bloom, and S. J. Davis. 2016. "Measuring Economic Policy Uncertainty." *Quarterly Journal of Economics* 131 (4): 1593–636.

Bernard, Andrew, and Andreas Moxnes. 2018. "Networks and Trade." NBER Working Paper 24556, National Bureau of Economic Research, Cambridge, MA.

Bhattacharya, Rudrani, Ila Patnaik, and Ajay Shah. 2012. "Export Versus FDI in Services." *World Economy* 35 (1): 61–78.

Bloom, Nicholas. 2014. "Fluctuations in Uncertainty." *Journal of Economic Perspectives* 28 (2): 153–76.

Boisso, Dale, and Michael Ferrantino. 1997. "Economic Distance, Cultural Distance and Openness in International Trade: Empirical Puzzles." *Journal of Economic Integration* 12 (4): 456–84.

Briggs, Kristie, and Walter G. Park. 2013. "There Will Be Exports and Licensing: The Effects of Patent Rights and Innovation on Firm Sales." *Journal of International Trade and Economic Development* 23 (8): 1112–44.

Caldara, D., M. Iacoviello, P. Molligo, A. Prestipino, and A. Raffo. 2019. "The Economic Effects of Trade Policy Uncertainty." *Journal of Monetary Economics* 109 (January): 38–59.

Castro, Luis, Ben G. Li, Keith E. Maskus, and Yiqing Xie. 2016. "Fixed Export Costs and Export Behavior." *Southern Economic Journal* 83 (1): 300–20.

Chen, Cheng, Senga Tatsuro, Sun Chang, and Zhang Hongyong. 2020. "Uncertainty, Imperfect Information, and Expectation Formation over the Firm's Life Cycle." CESifo Working Paper 8468, CESifo, Munich.

Conconi, Paola, André Sapir, and Maurizio Zanardi. 2016. "The Internationalization Process of Firms: From Exports to FDI." *Journal of International Economics* 99 (C): 16–30.

Coyle, Diane, and David Nguyen. 2019. "No Plant, No Problem? Factoryless Manufacturing and Economic Measurement." Discussion Paper ESCoE DP-2019-15, Economic Statistics Centre of Excellence, London.

Das, S., M. J. Roberts, and J. R. Tybout. 2007. "Market Entry Costs, Producer Heterogeneity, and Export Dynamics." *Econometrica* 75 (3): 837–73.

Dickstein, Michael J., and Eduardo Morales. 2018. "What Do Exporters Know?" *Quarterly Journal of Economics* 133 (4): 1753–801.

Dunning, John H. 2000. "The Eclectic Paradigm as an Envelope for Economic and Business Theories of MNE Activity." *International Business Review* 9 (2): 163–90.

Fontagné, L., and A. Harrison, eds. 2017. *The Factory-Free Economy: Outsourcing, Servitization, and the Future of Industry*. Oxford: Oxford University Press.

Gould, David Michael. 2018. *Critical Connections: Promoting Economic Growth and Resilience in Europe and Central Asia*. Europe and Central Asia Studies. Washington, DC: World Bank.

Hassan, T. A., S. Hollander, L. van Lent, and A. Tahoun. 2019. "Firm-Level Political Risk: Measurement and Effects." *Quarterly Journal of Economics* 134 (4): 2135–202.

Head, Keith, and Thierry Mayer. 2019. "Brands in Motion: How Frictions Shape Multinational Production." *American Economic Review* 109 (9): 3073–124.

Helpman, E., M. Melitz, and S. Yeaple. 2004. "Export versus FDI with Heterogeneous Firms." *American Economic Review* 94 (1): 300–16.

Jackson, Matthew O. 2011. "An Overview of Social Networks and Economic Applications." *Handbook of Social Economics*, edited by J. Benhabib, A. Bisin, and M. O. Jackson, 511–85. Amsterdam: North Holland Publishing.

Johanson, J., and J. E. Vahlne. 1977. "The Internationalization Process of the Firm: A Model of Knowledge Development and Increasing Foreign Market Commitments." *Journal of International Business Studies* 8 (1): 23–32.

Johanson, J., and J. E. Vahlne. 2009. "The Uppsala Internationalization Process Model Revisited: From Liability of Foreignness to Liability of Outsidership." *Journal of International Business Studies* 40 (9): 1411–31.

Kost, Kyle. 2019. "Trade Policy Uncertainty, Investment, and Lobbying." Unpublished manuscript, University of Chicago.

Kukharskyy, B. 2016. "Relational Contracts and Global Sourcing." *Journal of International Economics* 101 (C): 123–47.

Madsen, T. K., and S. Per. 1997. "The Internationalization of Born Globals: An Evolutionary Process?" *International Business Review* 6 (6): 561–83.

Malcomson, James. 2012. "Relational Incentive Contracts." In *Handbook of Organizational Economics*, edited by R. Gibbons and J. Roberts, 1014–65. Princeton, NJ: Princeton University Press.

Melitz, Marc J. 2003. "The Impact of Trade on Intra-Industry Reallocations and Aggregate Industry Productivity." *Econometrica* 71 (6): 1695–725.

Melitz, Marc J., and Stephen J. Redding. 2014. "Heterogeneous Firms and Trade." In *Handbook of International Economics*, vol. 4, edited by G. Gopinath, E. Helpman, and K. Rogoff, 1–54. Amsterdam: Elsevier.

Rauch, J. E., and V. Trindade. 2002. "Ethnic Chinese Networks in International Trade." *Review of Economics and Statistics* 84 (1): 116–30.

Rodrik, Dani, Margaret McMillan, and Claudia Sepúlveda. 2016. "Structural Change, Fundamentals and Growth: An Overview." In *Structural Change, Fundamentals and Growth*, edited by M. McMillan, D. Rodrik, and C. Sepúlveda. Washington, DC: International Food Policy Research Institute.

Tintelnot, F. 2017. "Global Production with Export Platforms." *Quarterly Journal of Economics* 132 (1): 157–209.

Wagner, Rodrigo, and Andrés Zahler. 2015. "New Exports from Emerging Markets: Do Followers Benefit from Pioneers?" *Journal of Development Economics* 114 (C): 203–23.

World Bank. 2015. *World Development Report 2015: Mind, Society, and Culture.* Washington, DC: World Bank.

World Bank. 2020. *World Development Report 2020: Trading for Development in the Age of Global Value Chains.* Washington, DC: World Bank.

World Bank and World Trade Organization. 2019. *Global Value Chain Development Report 2019: Technological Innovation, Supply Chain Trade, and Workers in a Globalized World.* Washington, DC: World Bank Group.

CHAPTER 3

Spotlight on Outward Foreign Investment and Foreign Direct Investment Policies

Introduction

Multinational firms based in developing economies are an important and growing phenomenon in the foreign investment landscape. These so-called Southern multinationals have found that outward foreign direct investment (OFDI) is an important strategy for gaining competitiveness.[1] In post–global recession China, OFDI has become an important component of a strategy to increase the returns on its international assets, compared with traditionally held, low-yielding international reserves (Aizenman, Jinjaarak, and Zheng 2017). This report builds on other research undertaken to improve the understanding of these multinational enterprises from emerging economies (Dixit 2011; Gomez-Mera et al. 2015; Perea and Stephenson 2018), which is important because most theories of multinational enterprises are based on the behavior of multinationals originating from advanced economies.

An outward investment perspective is taken to study South Asian intraregional investment. OFDI involves cross-border investment in which the investor or parent company is a resident entity, whereas inward FDI (IFDI) involves investment when the parent company is a nonresident entity (see box 3.1). This is in line with the study's approach to investigating firm decision-making over a range of globalization options—trade, other nonequity modes, and direct foreign investment abroad. In this framework, inward investment would be a joint decision with a foreign firm, and thus is not the focus of this study. The OFDI approach also provides an opportunity

---

BOX 3.1 Defining Inward and Outward Foreign Direct Investment

Inward foreign direct investment (IFDI), also called direct investment in the reporting economy, includes all asset and liability transfers between a resident firm and nonresident parent, and also nonresident fellow (related) enterprises if the ultimate controlling parent is nonresident.

FDI net inflows are the value of inward direct investment made by nonresident investors in the reporting economy. Made up of equity, reinvested earnings, and intrafirm debt, net inflows can take a positive or negative value.

Outward foreign direct investment (OFDI), also called direct investment abroad or "overseas investment" in the reporting country, includes all assets and liabilities transferred between resident parent direct investors and their nonresident direct investment enterprises, and fellow (related) enterprises, if the ultimate controlling parent is resident.

FDI net outflows are the value of outward direct investment made by the resident investors of the reporting economy to external economies. Made up of equity, reinvested earnings, and intrafirm debt, net outflows can take a positive or negative value.

Source: IMF 2013.
Note: Implementation of the Balance of Payments Manual 6th Edition methodology has brought changes to the definition of direct investment by making it consistent with the Organisation for Economic Co-operation and Development's benchmark definition of foreign direct investment, notably the recasting in terms of control and influence, treatment of chains of investment, and fellow enterprises, and presentation on a gross asset and liability basis as well as according to the directional principle.

---

to study emerging market multinationals from a South Asian perspective. These multinationals are expected to perform better than their counterparts from high-income economies in less transparent business environments, given their own experience in low-quality governance environments at home, and by making use of the benefits of potentially existing ethnic and linguistic networks (Dixit 2011). In the framework laid out in chapter 2, emerging market multinationals entering other developing economies would be expected to have lower entry costs and lower variable costs relative to other multinationals. With regard to the frictions along value chains represented in figure 2.1, emerging market multinationals would have lower costs of technology transfer, of product adaptation to markets, and of marketing.

The lack of official bilateral FDI data for developing economies prevented such an analysis from being conducted previously. A similar situation still prevails for bilateral services trade flows. The analysis in this chapter overcomes data limitations in three ways. The chapter uses the International Monetary Fund's Coordinated Direct Investment Survey (CDIS) data, a relatively recent endeavor that captures both the inward and outward bilateral stock of FDI. The use of the CDIS data overcomes the exclusion of small and fragile South Asian economies from global data sets with the use of mirror data. Second, given the data issues involved in identifying bilateral movements from aggregate foreign investment flows (see box 3.2), and the need for firm-level data to understand multinational behavior, the South Asia Regional Engagement and Value Chain Survey was implemented across all eight countries in South Asia to capture relevant firm-level information. Third, deep case studies were developed with the cooperation of regional investment pioneers to gain an understanding of the decision-making process of pioneering firms and entrepreneurs. This chapter provides a comprehensive portrait of intraregional investment in South Asia using these sources.

The region exhibits low levels of outward investment and the lowest level of intraregional investment relative to other low- and middle-income economies in other geographic regions. India is the largest intraregional investor, but its investment in other South Asian countries accounts for only 2 percent of total Indian OFDI and amounts to about a fifth of Indian investments in Sub-Saharan Africa. Sri Lanka and Bangladesh are the largest recipients of South Asian investment. Much of South Asian OFDI, both in absolute terms and relative to the global average, goes to investment hubs. Singapore, Mauritius, the United Arab Emirates, and Hong Kong SAR, China, account for 50 percent of OFDI stock from South Asia. When other investment hubs are included, the share rises to 77 percent.

The outward investor perspective also makes possible a rare focus on OFDI policies in South Asia. The usual emphasis on traditional advanced economy multinationals and the consequent neglect of OFDI policies (generally liberal in the home country of traditional multinational enterprises) has led to attention on restrictive IFDI policies in developing economies, a potential destination for these traditional multinational enterprises. This report, on the other hand, highlights the largely restrictive, discretionary, and nontransparent OFDI arrangements in South Asia, apart from India and to a lesser extent Sri Lanka. It also highlights the lingering remnants of region-specific OFDI and IFDI policies in South Asia that are likely to stymie investment in net terms.

The experiences of regional pioneers in South Asia highlight the opportunities that outward investment offers for emerging market firms. The report shows that although small, South Asia has a varied and rich outward investment landscape in the types of investment, sectors of origin, and modes of engagement, with varying initial capital costs. It also highlights the different drivers of OFDI and identifies new value chain–based motivations for emerging market multinationals. For example, OFDI allows firms to achieve higher profit margins along a value chain when the associated activities are located across the border, to cater to buyers' higher volume and product scope requirements, to increase learning and build relationships with clients and suppliers, and to buy technology, brands, or other intellectual property when developing them at home may be capability constrained or take too much time. These new value chain–based benefits of OFDI heighten the need for policy reform in South Asia.

BOX 3.2 Issues with Global Foreign Direct Investment Data

Making use of global foreign direct investment (FDI) data is complicated. A 10 percent ownership threshold is established for these capital flows, embedding a notion of ownership and control, to distinguish them from foreign portfolio investment. FDI is reported as a *flow* over a period, as well as a *stock* reflecting historically accumulated flows at a given time. The most widely used global direct investment data are from the International Monetary Fund's (IMF's) balance of payments data on direct investment flows in the IMF International Financial Statistics along with the data on flows and stocks of IFDI and OFDI collected by the United Nations Conference on Trade and Development (UNCTAD). The distinction between IFDI and OFDI relates to the nonresidency and residency of the parent firm, respectively. IFDI (or just FDI) typically refers to investments made by a nonresident parent company (or company with a nonresident parent). OFDI refers to investments abroad made by resident parent firms (see box 3.1).

Definitional and classification issues. The definitional issues pose problems in two ways for national data. First, institutional investors could buy more than 10 percent of firm shares but impart no technology or managerial skills that are typically associated with FDI. Second, there is plenty of scope to misclassify investments, as has been well documented for India (Rao and Dhar 2018).

Bilateral data availability for developing economies. Bilateral data on developing economies had been absent from the analysis until recently.[a] Researchers used fDi Markets data (www.fDimarkets.com), owned by the *Financial Times* newspaper, which compiles bilateral data based on newspaper announcements of investments across borders in various industries. However, the data on investment levels and job creation are based on approvals or pronouncements as opposed to realized outcomes. UNCTAD introduced a bilateral data set that deals with actual flows, but it is available only up to 2012.

Prevalence of investment hubs inhibits the understanding of bilateral FDI flows. The issue with even using reliable bilateral FDI flows data from the balance of payments accounts is that the data show only capital movement without information on the final destinations or the original source of investment funds. Multinational firms use strategies that involve indirect routes to investment via investment hubs for various reasons, including tax optimization. A combination of banks, law practices, accounting firms, and other financial specialists design offshore structures for their corporate clients to maximize profits.

Investment hubs tend to be low-tax territories with many bilateral preferential tax and investment agreements, and offer sophisticated financial and legal services and strict confidentiality laws. This combination has led them to become avenues for tax and regulatory evasion. (See annex 3A on the role of Mauritius in India's cross-border investments.) Some have argued that investment hubs offer scope for legitimate tax planning (Hong and Smart 2010), and that the revenue erosion effect is smaller than the efficiency effect of reducing investment entry costs and stimulating investment by more firms (as in the framework in chapter 2). The current thinking appears to be that the tax evasion costs combined with the potential flow of illicit funds require reform in these investment hubs and financial centers, which are sometimes referred to as tax havens. Consequently, many nations have now joined the Organisation for Economic Co-operation and Development's (OECD's) Common Reporting Standard and the OECD–G-20 Base Erosion and Profit Shifting initiative.[b]

(Box continues next page)

BOX 3.2 **Issues with Global Foreign Direct Investment Data** (continued)

Thus, investment hubs complicate the identification of true sources of investment, including domestic sources in the case of roundtripping (see box 3.3). Researchers have worked meticulously on individual country data to decipher original sources of investment funds. "Ultimate investor" country data are reported by 14 developed economies. Recent work by Casella (2019) provides a probabilistic estimate of "ultimate investor" bilateral IFDI stock, identifying the actual source country of investors from investment hubs for 2017.

Using the IMF's CDIS data. The IMF's Coordinated Direct Investment Survey (CDIS) data (which provide updated bilateral data only on the stock of direct foreign investment) help to discern the state of intraregional investment in South Asia. The data start in 2009 for a sample of 92 (IFDI) and 62 (OFDI) countries and reach a sample of 111 (IFDI) and 80 (OFDI) in 2017. The CDIS also reports mirror data separately, in the same conceptual way that missing-reporter trade data are constructed from trading partner data. That is, missing-reporter outward investment bilateral data may be reconstituted by using inward FDI data from all the counterpart countries. The reporter data and mirror data have had stark differences on occasion (as is common with trade data). Negative values are also reported and reflect disinvestment. The CDIS data are augmented in this report by using a combination of reporter and mirror data. Missing-reporter data or suppressed confidential data are replaced by mirror data whenever possible, and vice versa for missing mirror data (see appendix A for details on data augmentation).[c] The benchmark OFDI figures are calculated using mirror data supplemented by reporter data when needed because record keeping on IFDI tends to be better than that on OFDI, especially for developing economies. Further, two South Asian countries (Bhutan and Nepal) do not report OFDI data, while two others (Afghanistan and Maldives) do not report any data. In addition, an important hub, the United Arab Emirates, reports neither IFDI nor OFDI data. Thus, mirror data are important for capturing the activities of these countries.[d]

a. Organisation for Economic Co-operation and Development (OECD) and Eurostat data included bilateral FDI statistics for members of the OECD and the European Union (and some other large middle-income economies).

b. The following 38 jurisdictions have made commitments to the OECD on transparency and information exchange for tax purposes: Andorra, Anguilla, Antigua and Barbuda, Aruba, The Bahamas, Bahrain, Belize, British Virgin Islands, Cayman Islands, Cook Islands, Cyprus, Dominica, Gibraltar, Grenada, Guernsey, Isle of Man, Jersey, Liberia, Liechtenstein, Malta, Marshall Islands, Mauritius, Monaco, Monserrat, Nauru, Netherlands Antilles (Curaçao and St. Maarten after 2010), Niue, Panama, Samoa, San Marino, Seychelles, St. Lucia, St. Kitts and Nevis, St. Vincent and the Grenadines, Turks and Caicos Islands, the US Virgin Islands, and Vanuatu. Other localities that have been termed tax havens (Gravelle 2015) include Costa Rica; Hong Kong SAR, China; Ireland; Luxembourg; Macao; Maldives; the Netherlands; Seychelles; Singapore; Switzerland; Tonga; and Vanuatu. In 2017, the EU's list of noncooperative jurisdictions for tax purposes (the blacklist) additionally included American Samoa, Fiji, Guam, Oman, Trinidad and Tobago, the United Arab Emirates, and the US Virgin Islands. The list is reviewed twice a year, and economies have been removed from the list. The 12 economies on the blacklist at the beginning of 2020 were American Samoa, Cayman Islands, Fiji, Guam, Oman, Palau, Panama, Samoa, Seychelles, Trinidad and Tobago, US Virgin Islands, and Vanuatu (https://ec.europa.eu/taxation_customs/tax-common-eu-list_en#heading_0).

c. This analysis calculates four augmentations separately: (1) using reporter OFDI data as the base, missing data augmented by mirror data; (2) using mirror OFDI data as the base, missing data augmented by reporter data; (3) using the maximum value when two values are available; and (4) using the minimum value when two values are available. See appendix A for details.

d. The downside is that the Afghanistan-Maldives investment relationship is omitted in both directions, as is Bhutanese and Nepali outward investment to Afghanistan and Maldives. However, the values of these four relationships are likely to be very close to zero.

The rest of the chapter is organized as follows: The next section documents the flow of aggregate outward investment from developing economies and benchmarks South Asian outward investment and intraregional investment against other developing regions. The following section analyzes the policy environment investors face both at home (for OFDI) and abroad (for IFDI). OFDI policies are discussed in more detail, given that these policies are rarely spotlighted. As with trade policy, discussed in chapter 1, discriminatory factors against some neighbors are identified in both OFDI and IFDI policies, as are restrictive home policies. The chapter then proceeds to characterize outward investment at the firm level using outward investment survey data collected from an original survey of 1,274 South Asian firms (the South Asian Regional Engagement and Value Chains Survey) and the experiences of pioneering regional entrepreneurs. It highlights the opportunities in the region and outside. It also looks at the varying motivations for OFDI and the many paths firms have taken for the types of investment they have chosen and the sectors in which they operate. This analysis sets up the econometric analysis of firm-level outward investment entry that follows in chapter 4.

Outward FDI and Intraregional Investment: Evidence from CDIS and UNCTAD Data

Emerging market multinationals have become more important. Multinational firms have traditionally been a phenomenon of the high-income economies of Europe, Japan, the United Kingdom, and the United States, but the number of emerging market multinationals has been growing. Since about 2003, these newcomer multinational firms have led to growth in OFDI from developing economies (figure 3.1).

However, some statements about their importance, rising to 30 percent of world outward investment flows, may be exaggerated or at least need qualification. First, the relative magnitudes differ for FDI stock versus FDI flows data. OFDI flows data (dashed lines in figure 3.1) better capture the recent rising trend of developing country OFDI and tend to result in higher estimates than stock data (solid lines) because they do not incorporate the dominant past performance of advanced economy multinationals as OFDI stock data do. Second, the often-referenced UNCTAD investment data (and UNCTAD's annual World Investment Reports) use a broad definition of "developing" economy that includes high-income economies of East Asia (for example, the Republic of Korea and Singapore), the Middle East (for example, Saudi Arabia and the United Arab Emirates), Africa (Seychelles), and Latin America (Chile). The United Nations (UN) definition is substantially different from the traditional World Bank (WB) classification of developing economies as middle-income and low-income economies. Comparing the estimates of developing economy OFDI represented by the orange (WB) and blue (UN) lines shows that the UN definition leads to an estimate that is 12–13 percentage points higher.

FIGURE 3.1 **Developing Economy Share of World OFDI Flows and Stocks**

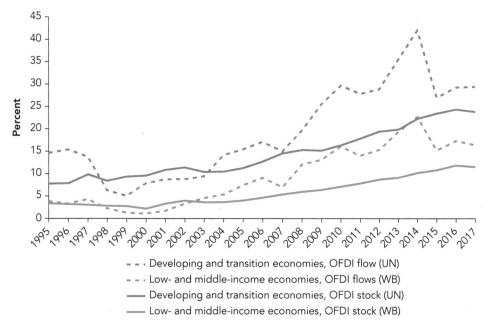

Source: UNCTAD 2019b.
Note: The United Nations definition of developing economies includes high-income economies such as Saudi Arabia and Singapore. The orange lines marked "WB" refer to developing economies (low- and middle-income economies), as defined by the World Bank in its income classification for the period July 2019 through June 2020. OFDI = outward foreign direct investment; UN = United Nations; WB = World Bank.

Third, these "high-income developing economies" actually account for the bulk of OFDI, on average, by "developing" economies (UN definition) since 1990. Further, a significant portion of OFDI from "high-income developing economies" is from Hong Kong SAR, China; Singapore; Taipei, China; and Korea—once termed the Four Asian Tigers. Finally, the "developed" high-income economy multinational practice of using investment hubs in "developing high-income economies" such as Singapore and in middle-income economies such as Mauritius to route their capital also dampens the larger role of emerging market multinationals suggested by standard data (see box 3.2 on data issues related to investment hubs).

According to the UNCTAD classification, developing economy OFDI flows increased from 8 percent in 2000 to 29 percent of world OFDI flows in 2017. The OFDI stock data show a rise from 10 percent in 2000 to 24 percent in 2017. Compared with UNCTAD's classification, the World Bank classification suggests a lower starting point, a higher growth rate, and 2017 values that are about half the magnitude. OFDI for low- and middle-income economies shows a sharp rise in flows, from 1 percent in 2000 to 16 percent in 2017, and stocks rose from 2 percent to almost 12 percent during the same period. Growth in stocks is driven by middle-income countries, with low-income countries contributing less than 0.5 percent of developing economy OFDI. About 75 percent of low- and middle-income economies' OFDI stocks and flows are from the BRICS economies (Brazil, the Russian Federation, India, China, and South Africa).

South Asia's share of world OFDI stock (0.3 percent) is low compared with that of other developing regions, as reflected in the IMF's CDIS augmented bilateral investment stock data in figure 3.2. The augmented CDIS data generate lower estimates of the share of world OFDI attributed to low- and middle-income economies, about 6 percent of the total US$39.5 trillion OFDI stock in 2017, compared with 10.8 percent using UNCTAD data under the World Bank's country classification. South Asia's share of global OFDI is only higher than that of the developing economies of the Middle East and North Africa (0.1 percent). Greater OFDI shares are registered in East Asia and Pacific (2.4 percent of world OFDI), Europe and Central Asia (0.9 percent), Latin America and the Caribbean (1.1 percent), and Sub-Saharan Africa (1 percent). See box 3.3 for a historical perspective on OFDI in South Asia.

FIGURE 3.2 Outward FDI Stock from Developing Economies to the World, 2017; Regional versus Extraregional Destination Economies

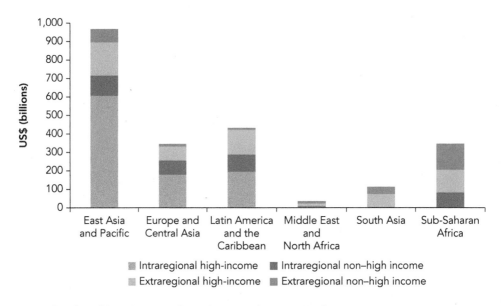

Source: Coordinated Direct Investment Survey, International Monetary Fund.
Note: Chile and Seychelles are the only high-income economies in Latin America and Sub-Saharan Africa, respectively. Developing economies refer to low- and middle-income economies and are defined here as non-high-income economies, based on an income classification valid for the period July 2019 through June 2020. For July 2020 through June 2021, Mauritius is classified as a high-income country. This figure conveys that (1) East Asian developing economies had the most OFDI (height of bars); (2) most OFDI goes to high-income economies (sum of light shades of blue and orange), except for Sub-Saharan Africa; and (3) developing economies of East Asia and Pacific, Europe and Central Asia, and Latin America and the Caribbean invested relatively more within the region compared with outside (sum of light and dark blue–shaded areas is greater than the sum of the light and dark orange–shaded areas). The other regions invested relatively more outside the region. Intraregional investment share = dark blue region/total OFDI. The low intraregional OFDI stock of US$3 billion in South Asia (dark blue) is barely visible in the figure.

BOX 3.3 South Asian Outward Investment: A Historical Perspective

Indian overseas investment in the pre-independence era was related to trading and financing opportunities from the mass migrations that resulted from the colonial economic system and famine-related impacts in the late nineteenth century. Earlier, merchant migrant networks had developed along trade routes to establish control over information and credit within communities. With migration came more substantial opportunities to cater to the diaspora, particularly in East Africa, Southeast Asia, and Sri Lanka (then Ceylon). For example, in 1937 a member of the South Indian Chettiar banking community opened branches of the Indian Overseas Bank simultaneously in India, Malaysia, and Myanmar (then Burma) to meet the needs of overseas Indians in Southeast Asia. Similarly, the Bank of Baroda (established in 1908) in Gujarat state opened offices in Kenya and Uganda in 1953. Bank branches expanded along the emigrant trail. Before independence, there was no outward foreign direct investment (OFDI) in manufacturing, but there are indications of Indian ownership of Burmese rice mills and saw and timber mills in 1930. This was not technically OFDI, given that Burma was part of the British Raj (1824–1937) during this period, and likely reflected the successful movement of the Chettiar community from traditional money-lending activities to nontrading activities. In the early 1950s, Jain merchants from Palanpur, Gujarat—a community well known in the gem trade—set up wholesale operations in the diamond business in Antwerp, Belgium. These Indian firms then outsourced the cutting and polishing of rough diamonds from Southern Africa to India, a business that continues to thrive today.

In the post-independence period, Indian OFDI in manufacturing developed in response to regulatory barriers (licensing requirements for large firms and reservation of products for small firms).[a] Indian firms managed overseas investments in the face of the restrictive Foreign Exchange Regulation Act 1973 through joint ventures with host nationals (often of Indian descent), borrowing from foreign banks and the capitalization of exports. (The capitalization of exports refers to equity contribution abroad by exporting machinery and equipment from India.) The first manufacturing OFDI recorded was a joint venture by the family-run Birla Group, which set up a textile mill in Ethiopia in 1959–60.

The major traditional merchant communities hailed from Gujarat and Sindh in western India, and Tamil Nadu and Kerala in the south. Muslims included Khojas, Bohras, and Memons; Hindus included Lohanas, Bhatias, Patidars, and Patels. Bhaibands and Bhatias from Sindh navigated the Persian Gulf. Chettiars of south India ventured into Burma, Malaysia, and Sri Lanka, and the Moplah/Mappila Muslims from Kerala and Tamil Nadu operated in Sri Lanka and Burma. Marakkayars ventured to Burma and southeast Asia. The Marwaris who migrated within India from Rajasthan and Bombay to Calcutta in the east had a limited transnational presence that was restricted to Burma.

Sources: Markovits 2008; Tumbe 2017.
a. This includes the Monopolies and Restrictive Trade Practices Act of 1969 reservation policy for small-scale industry, which started in 1967 with 47 products but had expanded to 800 products by 1978 and 1,000 products by 1996 (Panagariya 2008).

Most outward investment flows from developing economies go to high-income economies and almost half originate from East Asia and Pacific and 5 percent from South Asia. A few key insights are apparent from figure 3.2, which presents the breakdown by region of the total outward investment stock of US$2.2 trillion from developing economies as of the end of 2017. First, almost half of developing country outward investments come from East Asia and Pacific, with South Asia responsible for just 5 percent. Second, most OFDI goes to high-income economies (71 percent, as represented by light shaded areas of blue and orange), except for OFDI from Sub-Saharan Africa. Three, the OFDI toward high-income destinations is regionally biased, driven by the high magnitudes from East Asia and Pacific, Latin America and the Caribbean, and Europe and Central Asia. The other developing regions favor extraregional destinations. Four, the high share of OFDI from Sub-Saharan Africa to developing economies in the region and outside the region reflects Mauritius's role as an investment hub, particularly for Africa and India (see annex 3A for the Mauritius-India connection). Five, OFDI shares from developing economies to their regional partners (both high-income and developing economies) are very high at 75 percent for both East Asia and Pacific and Europe and Central Asia, and 67 percent for Latin America and the Caribbean. Lower shares of 25 percent are registered for both the Middle East and North Africa and Sub-Saharan Africa, and just 2.7 percent for South Asia.

India's share of South Asia's total OFDI stocks is greater than 94 percent (2018 data from CDIS): Maldives, however, reports a higher share of OFDI to GDP, of 5 percent. Afghanistan and India report OFDI stocks as a share of GDP of 3.6 percent and 2.8 percent, respectively, with Sri Lanka's at 1.9 percent of GDP.

South Asia's share of intraregional investment, at 2.7 percent of total OFDI, is the lowest compared with other developing regions, as well as compared with regions defined to include both high-income and developing economies as sources and destinations of investment (figure 3.3, panels a and b, respectively). Focusing on intraregional investment among developing economies (equivalent to the dark blue spaces in figure 3.2), the highest shares of OFDI are registered in Sub-Saharan Africa, Europe and Central Asia, and Latin America and the Caribbean. Alternatively, when accounting for all OFDI source economies from a region (including high-income economies) to all other economies in a region, the strong regional bias in Europe and Central Asia and East Asia and Pacific is clearly seen in panel b of figure 3.3, where intraregional investment accounts for 66 percent and 56 percent of all outward investment, respectively. These high shares reflect the development of regional value chains in these areas. These computations capture all investments between high-income economies in the region, OFDI from high-income regional economies to regional developing economies, as well as OFDI from regional developing economies to high-income and other developing economies in the region.

Investment from extraregional investors through regional investment hubs inflates the true extent of intraregional investment links. For example, the Netherlands and Luxembourg account for 41 percent of German FDI inflows, but only 16 percent of this amount is from resident investors. Similarly, Singapore has become a hub for global investors investing in the Association of Southeast Asian Nations economies, thus inflating East Asia and Pacific's true intraregional investment share. The previous overestimation of intraregional FDI is confirmed for Europe and Asia,[2] based

FIGURE 3.3 Intraregional Investment as a Share of Total OFDI, 2017; Regional Developing Economies and All Regional Economies

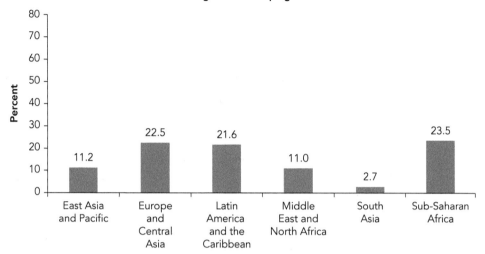

a. Regional developing economies

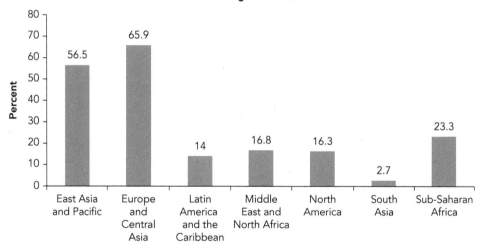

b. All regional economies

Source: Augmented Coordinated Direct Investment Survey data, International Monetary Fund.
Note: North America = Bermuda, Canada, United States. Chile and Seychelles are the only high-income economies in Latin America and the Caribbean and Sub-Saharan Africa, respectively, according to the World Bank income classification applied (July 1, 2019 through June 30, 2020). Mauritius graduated to high-income country status in July 2020. Intraregional share of OFDI in panel a = OFDI from all developing economies in a region to all developing economies in that region / OFDI to the world from all developing economies in that region
Intraregional share of OFDI in panel b = OFDI from all economies in a region to all economies in that region / OFDI to the world from all economies in that region.
OFDI = outward foreign direct investment.

on estimates of ultimate investor locations in Casella (2019). Similarly, the extent of "South-South" investment (intra-developing-country investment) drops from 46 percent to 23 percent using ultimate investor estimates, suggesting that investors from advanced economies enter developing regions through both high-income (for example, Singapore) and middle-income developing economy (for example, Mauritius) investment hubs (Casella 2019).

In contrast, for transition economies (the UN classification for low- and middle-income economies of Europe and Central Asia), the share of intragroup investment increased when based on ultimate investors, suggesting that regional investors invested through an extraregional investment hub. The reasons for such behavior include better legal and financial infrastructure in the financial centers and avoidance of discrimination based on country brand image. For example, Cyprus acts as an investment hub for investment into and out of Russia.

The largest outward investors from South Asia are India, Sri Lanka, Pakistan, and Bangladesh, with India accounting for more than 94 percent of the region's total stock of OFDI (table 3.1). India is also the largest source of intraregional investment (accounting for 72 percent of intraregional investment), while Sri Lanka and Pakistan account for 14 percent and 11 percent, respectively. The largest bilateral investments are from India to Sri Lanka, followed by India to Bangladesh and India to Nepal. The next highest are Sri Lanka's investments in Bangladesh, followed by Pakistan's investments in Bangladesh (see bold numbers in table 3.1). Intraregional investment stocks vary widely across individual countries in South Asia. Bhutan, Sri Lanka, Maldives, and Pakistan directed 15 percent or more of their OFDI within the region; the region accounted for 5 percent or less of the OFDI portfolio of the remaining countries (table 3.1, last column).

As seen in table 3.1 and figure 3.4, Sri Lanka, Bangladesh, and Nepal receive the largest shares of regional investment (42 percent, 33 percent, and 13 percent, respectively). For Pakistan and Sri Lanka, the largest regional recipient is Bangladesh (figure A.2 in appendix A, which shows individual country OFDI stocks to their largest destinations). This OFDI involved investments in apparel manufacturing for both countries, and additionally involved investments in power generation for Sri Lanka. Maldives and India are also among Sri Lanka's top investment destinations. In turn, Sri Lanka is among the top destinations of OFDI from Maldives. India is among the top investment destinations for Afghanistan, Bhutan, and Maldives, and somewhat lower in the rankings for Nepal and Sri Lanka. Not surprisingly, no regional economy is among India's top investment destinations.

India's OFDI to South Asia (US$2.2 billion) is just 2 percent of total Indian OFDI stock. Analysts have argued that Indian firms use OFDI to gain technology and brands from advanced economy markets, such as Tata Motors' purchase of Land Rover (United Kingdom). Although this is true, Indian firms have invested US$10.7 billion in Sub-Saharan Africa—almost six times their investment in South Asia. This numerical value excludes the 68 percent of total investment to Sub-Saharan Africa that goes to

TABLE 3.1 South Asian Intraregional Investment Stocks, by Country, 2017

US$ millions

Outward investor (source) ↓	Destination (host or recipient)										South Asia Region as destination (%)↓ of OFDI
	AFG	BGD	BTN	IND	MDV	NPL	PAK	LKA	SAR	WLD	
AFG		0.02	—	7.7	—	—	1.2	—	9.0	618.6	1.4
BGD	0.0	0.0	0.0	0.0	0.7	42.0	3.8	6.8	53.3	1061.9	5.0
BTN	—	0.0		0.38	—	0.01	—	—	0.38	1.1	33.8
IND	14.4	512.7	46.9		39.0	319.3	0.25	1,239.0	2,171.5	107,055.7	2.0
MDV	—	0.15	—	8.3		—	—	16.7	25.1	144.3	17.4
NPL	—	0.17	—	0.69	—		—	—	0.86	90.0	1.0
PAK	41.6	233.6	—	0	31.7	22.8		11.7	341.3	1784.8	19.1
LKA	—	265.0	—	69.8	82.0	1.4	1.3		419.5	1639.0	25.6
SAR	56.0	1,011.6	46.9	86.9	153.4	385.4	6.5	1,274.2	3,020.9	112,395.4	2.7
WLD	84.5	14,091.2	141.5	441,828.6	776.0	1,639.4	42,448.1	11,069.8	512,078.9	39,510,709.2	
SAR as source (%) →	66.3 (n.a.)	7.2 (7.3)	33.2 (33.5)	0.020 (1.64)	19.8 (n.a.)	23.5 (21.0)	0.015 (0.2)	11.5 (11.8)	0.6		

Source: Augmented Coordinated Direct Investment Survey data, International Monetary Fund.

Note: Figures in bold represent bilateral investment stocks greater than US$200 million.

Numbers in parentheses represent UNCTAD's ultimate investor estimates for inward foreign direct investment. Higher values reflect underestimates of intraregional investment arising from investment hubs, potentially reflecting both investment from regional partners and roundtripping. Thus, for India, the share of regional investors and roundtripping is estimated to be much higher, at 1.64 percent compared with 0.02 percent from the "raw" estimates.

— = not available; n.a. = not applicable; AFG = Afghanistan; BGD = Bangladesh; BTN = Bhutan; IND = India; LKA = Sri Lanka; MDV = Maldives; NPL = Nepal; OFDI = outward foreign direct investment; PAK = Pakistan; WLD = world.

FIGURE 3.4 **Intraregional Outward Foreign Direct Investment into South Asia, 2012–17**

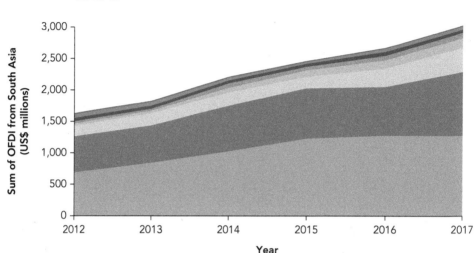

Source: Augmented Coordinated Direct Investment Survey data, International Monetary Fund.
Note: OFDI = outward foreign direct investment.

investment hub Mauritius, from where the final destination is unclear. Some analysts posit that this phenomenon points to a "less than friendly environment" in host nations toward Indian investment (Kelegama 2014), reflecting fears based on size asymmetry, as discussed in chapter 1.

Investment hubs are important destinations for South Asian economies. About 27 percent of South Asia's outward investment was destined for the 38 investment hub jurisdictions (box 3.2) listed by the Organisation for Economic Co-operation and Development (OECD) as joining its reporting standards initiative, although only 8 percent of world OFDI stock was destined for those locations. The share of investment hubs in South Asia's outward investment rises to 58 percent if the Netherlands, Singapore, and the United Arab Emirates are added to this list of investment hubs. It is clear from figure 3.5 that about 50 percent of South Asian OFDI stocks go to the four investment hubs of Singapore, Mauritius, the United Arab Emirates, and Hong Kong SAR, China. Singapore is the number one or two OFDI destination for Bangladesh, India, Maldives, Nepal, and Sri Lanka (see figure A.2 in appendix A).

Intraregional investment remains largely the same using ultimate investor estimates. The UNCTAD ultimate investor estimates calculated for inward investment suggest that investment hubs underestimate intraregional investment by just US$175 million. Data from Afghanistan and Maldives are missing, so the six-country standard intraregional

FIGURE 3.5 **Outward Foreign Direct Investment from South Asia, 2012–17**

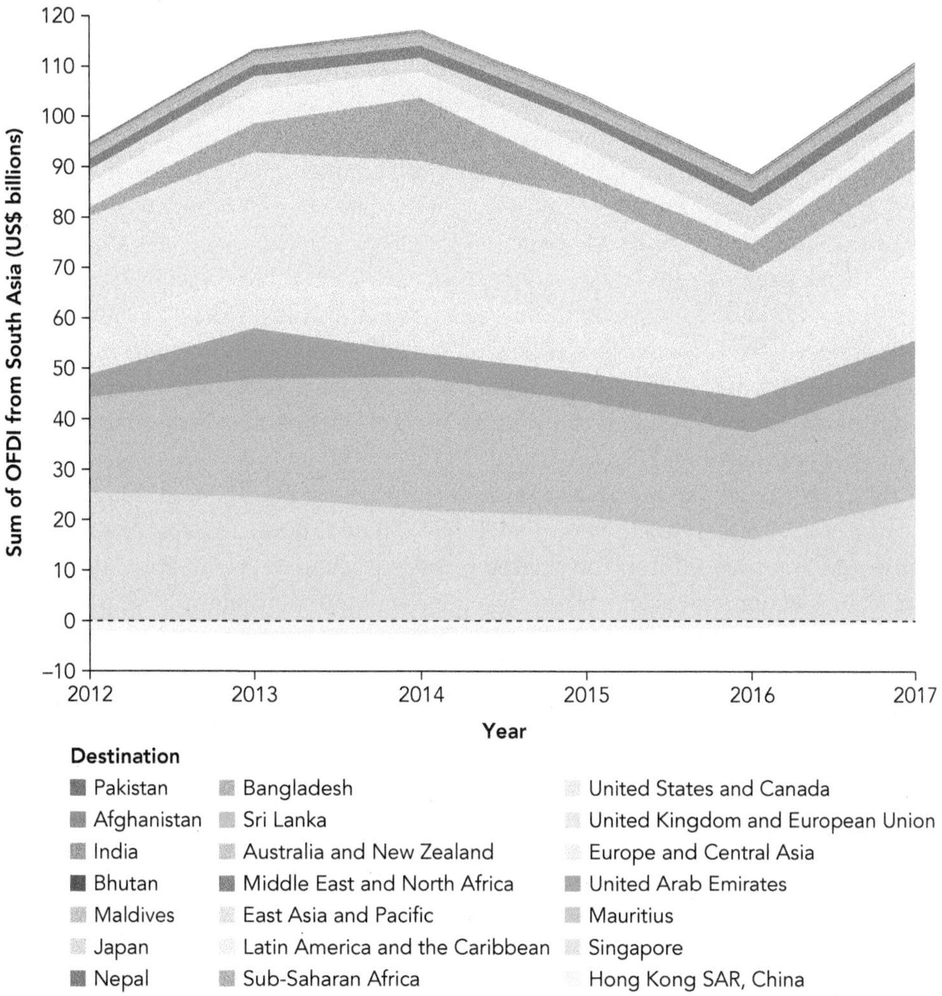
Sum of OFDI from South Asia (US$ billions)
120
110
100
90
80
70
60
50
40
30
20
10
0
–10
2012
2013
2014
2015
2016
2017
Year
Destination
Pakistan
Afghanistan
India
Bhutan
Maldives
Japan
Nepal
Bangladesh
Sri Lanka
Australia and New Zealand
Middle East and North Africa
East Asia and Pacific
Latin America and the Caribbean
Sub-Saharan Africa
United States and Canada
United Kingdom and European Union
Europe and Central Asia
United Arab Emirates
Mauritius
Singapore
Hong Kong SAR, China

Source: Augmented Coordinated Direct Investment Survey data, IMF.
Note: OFDI = outward foreign direct investment.

investment share of total IFDI would increase from 0.55 percent to 0.58 percent with the ultimate investor adjustment. A report on Nepal's FDI finds that 46 percent of the stock of inward investment came from the West Indies, mainly from the British Virgin Islands (Nepal Rastra Bank 2018).

Expatriate working populations also complicate intraregional investment estimates. As specified in box 3.1, the definition of FDI is based on transactions between residents and nonresidents, with no reference to citizenship, meaning that it is difficult to differentiate South Asian investors resident overseas from citizens. For example, South Asian investors with residency in the United Arab Emirates (where citizenship is rarely given) which invest in their country of origin cannot be separated from other investors from the United Arab Emirates which invest in the same country. Both capital flows are OFDI from the United Arab Emirates. This is not roundtripping as long as the investment capital is earned in Dubai or any place outside the national border of the destination. Similarly, an Afghan national who is resident in Dubai and investing in Pakistan would not be considered to be making an intraregional investment. It is a foreign investment from the United Arab Emirates. Roundtripping occurs when earnings by residents at home are channeled through a foreign company back to the home country as foreign capital. This issue may be one way to reconcile the US$1.8 billion OFDI by Pakistan with reports from the United Arab Emirates Land Authority, which annually reports India and Pakistan as investing US$6 billion to US$7 billion each in Dubai real estate. The discrepancy may be due to the United Arab Emirates' reporting of purchases by South Asian nationals residing and working in the United Arab Emirates; technically, this would not constitute FDI.

The use of investment hubs for tax-evasion purposes may be of diminishing concern because of the progress made by the OECD–G-20 Base Erosion and Profit Shifting initiative and improved information sharing across jurisdictions. Many economies (119) and 17 jurisdictions have signed the Convention on Mutual Administrative Assistance in Tax Matters, developed by the OECD and the Council of Europe and endorsed by the G-20 in 2009. India's and Pakistan's participation came into force in 2012 and 2016, respectively. Major financial centers participate, including those relevant to South Asia. The agreement became effective for Mauritius in 2015; Singapore in 2016; Hong Kong SAR, China, in 2018; and the United Arab Emirates in 2018. In fact, the United Arab Emirates fell into the blacklist in March 2019 but undertook remedial measures and was removed from the list in October 2019.

Policy Environment for Intraregional Investment

Understanding the policy influences on intraregional investment requires an appreciation of the policies that apply to outward investment at home and IFDI policies in the destination country.[3] At the global level, investment policy reform has traditionally focused on liberalizing the IFDI policy arrangements of developing economies. Outward FDI (OFDI) liberalization has not been prioritized in developing economies because of an insufficient number of their own multinational enterprises and concerns associated with managing the balance of payments in capital-scarce economies. However, because OFDI has become an important part of many emerging economy success stories, an examination of these policies is vital. Such an investigation is particularly important in South Asia, where restrictive outward investment arrangements and regionally biased policies affect intraregional investment. This section examines OFDI policies in South Asian countries and briefly outlines IFDI policies. Regional bias in both types of investment policies is identified. Finally, the role of international investment agreements is analyzed. As highlighted in box 3.1, IFDI policies deal with investment from a foreign parent firm or nonresident into the home (host) country, while OFDI policies deal with overseas investment from a domestic parent firm or home residents.[4] Investment policies may be separated into regulatory policies and promotional policies.

OFDI POLICIES IN SOUTH ASIA

There are no current efforts to benchmark and track the incidence and intensity of outward investment policies at the global level. The IMF's *Annual Report on Exchange Arrangements and Exchange Restrictions* (IMF 2018) provides a binary indicator variable of the presence of restrictions on outward direct investment for 192 economies. A more refined coding of the information from annual reports would be needed to generate a data set of policy changes. The existing data suggest that compared with low-income economies, middle-income economies tend to have a higher share of liberal OFDI arrangements, and this difference has been increasing slightly over time (Perea and Stephenson 2018). This finding is consistent with low-income economies' concerns about foreign exchange shortages. South Asian countries have a diverse range of policies, with India being relatively more open, followed by Pakistan and Sri Lanka. Bangladesh, Nepal, and Bhutan have very restrictive policies, and Afghanistan and Maldives have no explicit policy to track. The relevant laws and institutions are summarized in table 3.2, and the regulations are summarized in table 3.3.

India, Pakistan, and Sri Lanka

Currently, India, Pakistan, and Sri Lanka have explicit legislation permitting OFDI. Early regulations suffered from many ambiguities, and reform often involved clarifying positions. India and Sri Lanka require a prospective investor to pick an authorized dealer, typically a licensed commercial bank, to act as an intermediary

TABLE 3.2 **Laws and Institutions Related to Outward Direct Investment Policy in South Asia**

Country	Outward foreign direct investment policies	Institution
Afghanistan	None discernible	Da Afghanistan Bank
Bangladesh	Foreign Exchange Regulation Act, 1947 (amended 2015) Guidelines for Foreign Exchange Transactions, 2018, Vol. 1, Chapter 10, para. 24 (November 2017), https://www.bb.org.bd/aboutus/regulationguideline/foreignexchange/fegvol1.php	Bangladesh Bank
Bhutan	Foreign Exchange Rules and Regulations, 2013, Royal Monetary Authority, https://www.rma.org.bt/new%20regulations/Foreign%20Exchange%20Regulations.pdf	Royal Monetary Authority; Ministry of Finance

(Table continues next page)

TABLE 3.2 **Laws and Institutions Related to Outward Direct Investment Policy in South Asia** (continued)

Country	Outward foreign direct investment policies	Institution
	Regulations relating to the possession of assets and properties outside Bhutan by Bhutanese citizens, 1993, Ministry of Finance, https://www.mof.gov.bt/wp-content/uploads/2015/07/RegulationAssetsProperties.pdf	
India	Foreign Exchange Management Act (FEMA), 1999; Sections 10(4) and 11(1), 42 of 1999, https://www.rbi.org.in/scripts/NotificationUser.aspx?Id=173&Mode=0 Government of India, Ministry of Commerce Notification No. 4/1/93-EP(OI) dated August 17, 1995 Reserve Bank of India. 2019. Master Direction on Direct Investment by Residents in Joint Venture and Wholly Owned Subsidiary Abroad, Updated September 18, 2019. RBI /FED/2015-16/10, FED Master Direction No. 15/2015-16.	Reserve Bank of India
Maldives	None discernible	Maldives Monetary Authority
Nepal	Act Restricting Investment Abroad, 1964; Income Tax Act, 2002; Foreign Exchange (Regularization) Act, 2019 (1962), https://www.nrb.org.np/	Nepal Rastra Bank
Pakistan	Foreign Exchange Circular No. 12, 2001, Investment Abroad by Residents of Pakistan, http://www.sbp.org.pk/epd/2001/FEC12.htm Foreign Exchange Circular No. 11 1995, Investment Abroad by Resident Pakistanis, http://www.sbp.org.pk/epd/1995/c11.htm Foreign Exchange Circular No. 66 of 1993, http://www.sbp.org.pk/epd/1993/c66.htm	State Bank of Pakistan
Sri Lanka	Foreign Exchange Act, No. 12 of 2017 Government Gazette Notification No. 2045/56 of 17.11.2017, https://www.cbsl.gov.lk/sites/default/files/cbslweb_documents/laws/cdg/Foreign_Exchange_Act_Direction_No_14_of_2017_e1.pdf Outward Investment Account, 2011 Gazette Notification Nos. 1686/50, 1686/52, and 1686/53 dated January 1, 2011, http://www.dfe.lk/web/index.php?option=com_content&view=article&id=365&Itemid=704&lang=en	Central Bank of Sri Lanka

Sources: Bimal 2018; UNCTAD 2019a; World Bank data.

between themselves and the central bank of the home country. There is generally an automatic route and a government approval route; the automatic route does not require any prior approval from the central bank. The procedure in India is that investors fill out "Form ODI," which they take with the required documentation to the authorized dealer. In Sri Lanka, the potential investor sets up an overseas investment account at the authorized dealer once the required documentation is produced.

TABLE 3.3 **Summary of OFDI Regulatory Policies in South Asia**

Policy	Afghanistan	Bangladesh	Bhutan	India	Maldives	Nepal	Pakistan	Sri Lanka
Explicit legislation permitting OFDI		x		x			x	x
Explicit legislation banning OFDI						x		
No explicit legislation on OFDI	x				x			
Scope for automatic approval				x				x
Investors apply through authorized dealers				x				x
Investors deal directly with central bank	x		x		x	x	x	
Explicit legislation permitting representative offices abroad		x	x	x			x	x
Required repatriation of dividends		x		x			x	x
Restriction on purchases of real estate				x			x	
Destination-specific procedures exist				x				
Capital repatriation law introduced after 2014			x	x		x	x	
OFDI promotion				x				

Source: World Bank.
Note: OFDI = outward foreign direct investment.

India was earliest in the liberalization process. In 1992, India introduced an automatic route for outward investment through concessions in the Foreign Exchange Regulation Act, 1973, and an amendment to that act in 1993. In 1999, legislation more consistent with India's liberalization strategy, the Foreign Exchange Management Act, was passed. OFDI liberalization has involved increases in the dollar value of the limit for the automatic route, and then a designation of the limit as a share of the net worth of the investing firm. Within the region, India's policies are the most liberal, with automatic approvals up to 400 percent of net worth, not to exceed US$1 billion annually. Notification No. 263/2013 also made it possible for individuals to start up a company outside India under the Liberalized Remittance Scheme. Over time, the annual remittance limit under the Liberalized Remittance Scheme has gradually been raised, from US$25,000 in 2004 to US$250,000 in 2019. India restricts real estate purchases abroad but permits property development. OFDI is also not permitted in the sale of financial products linked to the Indian rupee (see box 3.4 for an outline of India's gradual liberalization of outward investment).

Sri Lanka's Foreign Exchange Act No. 12 of 2017 established an automatic route and limits for outward investment for the first time. Different dollar value limits were established based on whether the investor was an individual, a private firm, or a publicly listed company. The highest limit was US$2 million for publicly listed companies. Firms were allowed US$300,000 per year to set up and maintain offices abroad. OFDI above the stipulated limits goes through a government approval route. Outward investment accounts for the purchase of shares abroad and the setting up of overseas offices were allowed in 2011. Before this legislation, all investment proposals went through an approval process, but the central bank was generally supportive of outward investors.

Pakistan's outward investment is governed by a 2001 law that allows OFDI, but all investments are subject to approval by the State Bank of Pakistan. Applications are sent by investors directly to the State Bank of Pakistan. The law requires the investment to be "ordinarily in a similar activity" as the one in which the investor is engaged; it also requires repatriation of dividends and disinvestments and their conversion to local currency. The first regulations were set out in 1993, and then amended in 1995. In 2005, mutual funds were allowed to invest 30 percent of their aggregate funds abroad, up to a limit of US$15 million, subject to State Bank of Pakistan approval. Like India, Pakistan restricts OFDI for purchases of real estate. A proposed revision of OFDI regulations emerged in 2016, but it did not become law. This legislation would have introduced authorized dealers; allowed automatic approval for up to 50 percent of the net worth of the investor firm, as measured by the average of the past three years of tax returns; and banned real estate purchases. A capital repatriation law was introduced in 2019 to bring back capital from abroad.

India is the only country in South Asia that pursues active promotional policies supporting outward investment. Through the Export-Import Bank of India, the government provides financial support under the Overseas Investment Finance program.

BOX 3.4 Timeline of India's Gradual Path to Liberalization of OFDI

Year	Action	Amount
1992	Automatic route introduced	
	Limit for automatic approval (of which, limit for cash remittances)	US$2 million (US$0.5 million)
	Companies can raise capital in overseas markets via global depository receipts, American depositary receipts, or foreign currency convertible bonds	n.a.
1995	Fast Track Route introduced	n.a.
	Process for approvals moved to Reserve Bank of India from Commerce Ministry to get single window clearance mechanism	US$4 million
	Could not be invested in the stock market and not for real estate investments	n.a.
1997	Non-exporter exchange earners brought under fast-track route	n.a.
1999	End of OFDI neutrality condition (that is, repatriating remittances in five years as dividends)	n.a.
	Permitted value of OFDI under the automatic route was raised	Rs 1,200 million: Nepal and Bhutan
		US$30 million: other SAARC and Myanmar
		US$15 million: other countries
2000	Foreign Exchange Management Act	n.a.
	Automatic route limit raised to	US$50 million
2002	Automatic route limit raised to	US$100 million
2003	Automatic route limit raised to	100% of net worth
	Limit raised for SAARC and Myanmar (except Pakistan)	US$150 million
		Rs 7,000 million: Nepal and Bhutan
2004	Consolidate role of RBI	
	Introduced the LRS with automatic route limit	US$25,000
2005	Automatic route limit raised to	200% of net worth
2006	Under automatic route, allowed to disinvest without prior approval of RBI	n.a.
2006	Proprietary and partnership firms with export track record allowed to invest on approval	n.a.
2007	June: Automatic route limit raised to	300% of net worth
	September: Automatic route limit raised to	400% of net worth

(Box continues next page)

BOX 3.4 Timeline of India's Gradual Path to Liberalization of OFDI *(continued)*

Year	Action	Amount
	September: Automatic route under LRS raised to	US$200,000
2008	Automatic route limit raised for investment in natural resources with prior approval	up to 400% of net worth
	Raised borrowing limit	n.a.
	Real estate and banking prohibited	n.a.
	Individuals allowed to remit under the LRS	US$125,000 per year
	Indian banks can set up branches abroad; need clearance under the Banking Regulation Act, 1949, from the Department of Banking Regulation, RBI	n.a.
	Access to international financial markets progressively liberalized	n.a.
	Allowed to use special purpose vehicles to finance cross-border activity	n.a.
2012	Allowed to invest in Pakistan, through government approval route, and with prior RBI approval	n.a.
2013	Automatic route for LRS	US$75,000
	Automatic route	400% of net worth
	A resident individual may make outward direct investment in equity shares and preference shares of a JV or WOS outside India under the LRS	$125,000
	Eliminated ambiguity, whereby resident Indians were permitted to form a company outside India under LRS Notification No. 263/2013	n.a.

Sources: Khan 2012; Sauvant et al. 2014; World Bank data.
Note: JV= joint venture; LRS = Liberalized Remittance Scheme; n.a. = not applicable; OFDI = outward foreign direct investment; RBI = Reserve Bank of India; Rs = rupees; SAARC = South Asian Association for Regional Cooperation; WOS = wholly owned subsidiary.

The Export-Import Bank also provides advisory services at the pre-investment and post investment stages, including reports on overseas investment opportunities, partner identification, and feasibility studies. The scope of the program has widened to provide comprehensive support to small and medium enterprises. The Export Credit Guarantee Corporation of India offers political risk insurance. For a comparison of the different types of promotional policies used in extraregional economies and the institutional framework for OFDI, see box 3.5.

Bangladesh, Nepal, and Bhutan

Bangladesh, Nepal, and Bhutan have restrictive OFDI arrangements, and, in the latter two countries, the legislation stipulates that violation of such policies could result

BOX 3.5 Promotional Measures for Outward FDI in Selected Economies

Governments may promote outward foreign direct investment (OFDI) through information support, other networking support services, financial measures, and fiscal and insurance measures. Each of these types of assistance helps investors establish themselves abroad and provides them an advantage over other investors that do not receive such support. A government may provide information services on, for example, business opportunities and the economic and legal investment climate in host countries. It may offer advisory and consulting services and organize investment missions, matchmaking events, and training and educational services related to OFDI.

Home country actions can also involve concrete financial measures, such as grants for feasibility studies, other pre-investment work, and deferral of the costs of setting up foreign offices. Financial assistance may include loans, structured financing options, development financing, and equity participation. In addition, some home country governments have introduced fiscal measures to help their foreign investors. This assistance may include tax exemptions, deductions for certain expenditures, tax deferrals on income earned overseas, and tax credits for certain kinds of expenditures, as well as corporate tax relief. These measures are less common in developing economies. Governments have also provided political risk insurance that covers expropriation, damages from war and political violence, the conversion of local currency (or its transfer out of the host country), and the forced abandonment of assets. Investment treaties also provide certain guarantees to firms that invest abroad. Table B3.6.1 provides a broad

TABLE B3.5.1 OFDI Policy Measures in Selected Economies

	Information and network support		Financial		Fiscal	Insurance
	Information	Missions	Loans	Equity	Tax exemptions	Insurance
Advanced economies						
Belgium	x	x	x	x	x	x
Canada	x	x	x	—	x	x
France	x	x	—	—	x	x
Germany	x	x	x	x	x	x
Italy	x	x	x	x	x	x
Japan	x	x	x	x	x	x
Spain	x	x	x	x	x	x
Switzerland	x	x	x	—	x	—
United Kingdom	x	x	—	—	x	x
United States	x	x	x	x	—	x

(Table continues next page)

(Box continues next page)

BOX 3.5 **Promotional Measures for Outward FDI in Selected Economies** (*continued*)

TABLE B3.5.1 **OFDI Policy Measures in Selected Economies** (*continued*)

	Information and network support		Financial		Fiscal	Insurance
	Information	Missions	Loans	Equity	Tax exemptions	Insurance
Other economies						
Brazil	x	x	x	x	—	—
Chile	x	—	—	—	—	—
China	x	x	x	—	x	x
India	x	—	x	x	—	x
Malaysia	x	x	x	—	x	x
Mexico	x	x	—	—	—	—
Korea, Rep.	x	x	x	—	—	x
Philippines	x	x	—	—	—	—
Russian Federation	x	x	—	—	x	x
Singapore	x	x	x	—	x	x
Taipei, China	x	x	x	—	x	x
Thailand	x	x	x	—	—	x

Sources: Alcaraz and Zamilpa 2017; ESCAP 2020; Sauvant et al. 2014 for all advanced economies.
Note: — = not available; OFDI = outward foreign direct investment.

survey of the types of assistance provided by selected governments for their outward investing firms.

Compared with inward investment promotion, the promotion of OFDI appears less centralized, without a clear convergence in best institutional practices. Promotional services are provided by a wide range of institutions, including investment promotion agencies and trade promotion agencies, export credit agencies, development finance institutions, and ministries and other agencies. For example, the main player in India and in the Republic of Korea is each country's Export-Import Bank; in Spain it is the Instituto Español de Comercio Exterior under the Ministry of Commerce and the Ministry of Economic Affairs and Digital Transformation; the International Development Finance Corporation in the United States; and Enterprise Singapore in Singapore. Enterprise Singapore resulted from combining the overseas investment–focused International Enterprise Singapore with the local enterprise development and standards and conformance body, SPRING Singapore, in 2018.

Generally, inward investment promotion agencies do not engage in OFDI promotion, with a few exceptions, such as the China Investment Promotion Agency, which is charged with both "inviting in" foreign direct investment and the country's "going global"

(Box continues next page)

BOX 3.5 **Promotional Measures for Outward FDI in Selected Economies** *(continued)*

(OFDI) policies. Similarly, the Thailand Board of Investment, which is responsible for inward FDI promotion, absorbed the lead coordinating role for OFDI with the establishment of the Thai Overseas Investment Promotion Division. Previously there had not been a clear delineation of responsibilities among government agencies. ProMexico is tasked with "the attraction of foreign direct investment and the export of goods and services, as well as the internationalization of Mexican companies" (SEGOB 2007). And ProChile, which was designed as an export promotion agency, moved its focal activities to transforming exporters into outward investors.

Sources: Alcaraz and Zamilpa 2017; ESCAP 2020; Sauvant et al. 2014.

in imprisonment. OFDI from Bangladesh was effectively restricted by the Bangladesh Bank until the September 2015 amendment to the Foreign Exchange Regulation Act, 1947. Coinciding with the country's graduation to lower-middle-income status, the amendment provides conditional provisions for opening up overseas investment. OFDI is strictly limited to investors that are in the export business and requires prior approval from Bangladesh Bank for all investments. This approach has led to the cautious approval of a few investments, as well as several rejections. In 2018, the government waived the earlier mandatory requirement for obtaining Bangladesh Bank's prior permission for opening a branch or liaison office, allowing for outward remittances of up to US$30,000 per year for opening and maintaining an office. A 2019 amendment clarified that this provision applied strictly to representative offices. Investors may use foreign exchange in their Export Retention Quota accounts (which allow a share of export earnings to be retained) to maintain these offices.[5]

Nepal's OFDI policy is governed by the Act Restricting Investment Abroad, 1964, which prohibits any outward investment. A clause does allow the government to grant an exemption from the restriction, but it has not been used. Instead, Nepali outward foreign investment has occurred through a couple of loopholes. First, the Income Tax Act 2002 provision for nonresident Nepalis, defined as persons living outside Nepal at least 183 days in a year, allows investment abroad. Second, the Foreign Exchange (Regulation) Act, 1962, allows Nepalese citizens to accept free shares of foreign companies in return for work. The introduction of the Foreign Investment Policy, 2015, mentioned a future review of the policy on investing abroad, and draft legislation of the Foreign Exchange (Regulation) Act, 2019, identified sectors for liberalization. The Foreign Exchange (Regulation) Act, 2019, clause 4A, allows nonresident Nepalis to retain investments while earning money abroad. However, clause 4B requires payments for sales of goods and provision of services to be in a convertible currency, which seems to eliminate the second loophole of being paid by shares of companies. Nepal also introduced legislation to facilitate the repatriation of capital from abroad.

Bhutan's OFDI policy is governed by a 1993 regulation that requires permission from the Royal Monetary Authority (the central bank) to hold any foreign securities and permission of the Ministry of Finance to hold immovable property. The Ministry of Finance and the Ministry of Trade and Industry (now the Ministry of Economic Affairs) regulate the establishment of business ventures, subsidiaries, offices, and representations abroad. Exporters with large turnover may apply for approval to open offices abroad through the Ministry of Economic Affairs. Again, implementation of this policy has been restrictive. However, the government's Economic Development Policy, issued in December 2016, included a statement that it would review OFDI policies. Like Nepal, Bhutan is keen to repatriate the capital of domestic residents from abroad and introduced legislation to this effect.

Afghanistan and Maldives

There is no explicit mention of residents or resident parent firms investing abroad in Afghanistan's Private and Foreign Investment Law of 2005 or in Maldives' Law on Foreign Investments (1979, amended 1989). Nevertheless, there are several Afghan firms in the United Arab Emirates and Maldivian real estate investments in Sri Lanka. The governments of Afghanistan and Maldives do not promote or provide incentives for outward investment. However, the lack of transparency creates additional costs for firms that seek to invest abroad.

IFDI POLICIES IN SOUTH ASIA

IFDI policies refer to the investment incentives given to foreign investors and the regulatory environment in which they operate. Some economies, such as Maldives and Sri Lanka, provide equal incentives to national and foreign capital; the incentives are based on criteria such as expected employment generation, size of initial capital expenditures, and investment in a priority sector or geographic region. Others also offer special incentives for primarily export-oriented investments relative to those serving the domestic market. The global context for IFDI policies has been one of general investment liberalization, as seen in figure 3.6, and South Asia has tended to follow a similar, if not stronger, trend, from a lower base of liberalization. Most global investment measures since 2003 have been liberalizing in nature, although the share of restrictive measures increased between 2003 and 2018. The uptick in investment protection during the 2007–09 global recession resurfaced in 2018.

Most of the new restrictive measures focused on host countries', mostly advanced economies', national security concerns and introduce, widen, or deepen screening mechanisms for FDI with respect to strategic industries and infrastructure. Other restrictive policies included local content requirement laws (mostly in Sub-Saharan Africa) and further restrictions on land ownership. On the liberalizing front, about one-third of the measures were investment facilitation and promotion initiatives led by Asian economies. Some governments also simplified procedures and expanded their work permit programs, and others continued to expand the scope of their fiscal incentives for attracting foreign investors.

FIGURE 3.6 **Global Trends in Inward FDI Policies, 2003–18**

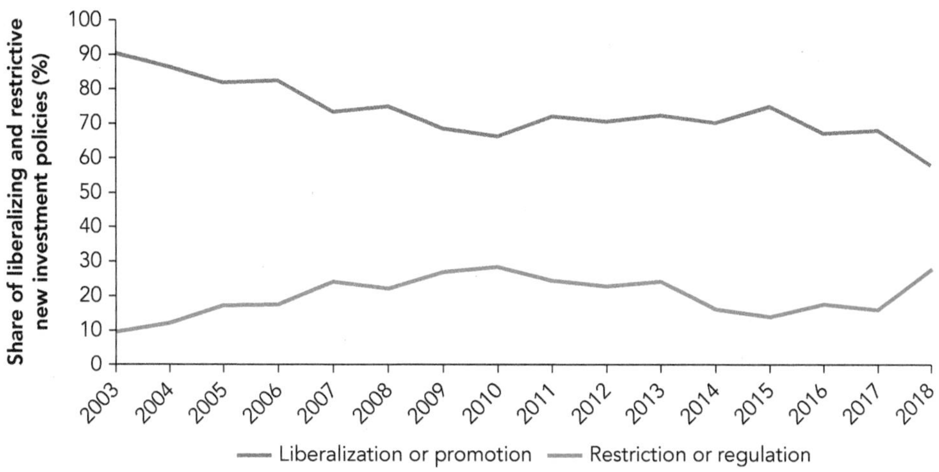

Source: UNCTAD, Investment Policy Hub, 2019 (https://investmentpolicy.unctad.org/).
Note: The sum of liberalizing and restrictive measures does not add up to 100 because the figure does not include neutral or indeterminate measures. FDI = foreign direct investment.

It is difficult to objectively benchmark the current openness of the FDI regulatory arrangements in South Asia relative to other regions because of the lack of data. In South Asia, foreign investment liberalization started in the late 1980s and early 1990s for most countries, with Sri Lanka having an earlier start (1978) and India gradually liberalizing in the early 1980s.[6] Since then, South Asian economies have taken a generally cautious investment liberalizing path, involving increasing foreign equity caps (above 49–50 percent, and subsequently eliminating caps), increasing the coverage of sectors open to FDI, establishing special economic zones, and facilitating investment through single-window approval processes or even automatic approvals. However, relative to other countries, the region does not compare highly in FDI liberalization. The only comparative measure recently reported that includes all South Asian economies is the 2021 investment freedom subindex of the Heritage Foundations' Index of Economic Freedom, which places all South Asian economies in the bottom half of the 184-country sample. The index incorporates security aspects of investing, and so is not a strict indicator of policy measures.[7]

The OECD's FDI Regulatory Restrictiveness Index is based solely on policies such as discriminatory screening or approval mechanisms, restrictions on foreign personnel and operations, and foreign equity restrictions. However, data collection is limited to 69 countries and, for South Asia, includes only India. The 2019 index measures India's FDI arrangements as being about three times as restrictive as the OECD average.[8] A similar regulatory FDI index (excluding security issues) with wider developing economy coverage, with data collected over 2010–12, was the World Bank's Investing

Across Borders index for 87 countries (and expanded to 103 countries in 2012) (IFC, MIGA, and World Bank 2010). South Asia (as represented by its six largest economies) placed below average in the ease of starting a foreign business, accessing industrial land, and arbitrating industrial disputes—substantially so in the latter two cases. The region's score was similar to the average for investing across sectors, based on equity ownership caps in different sectors, driven by liberalization in the telecom and electricity sectors (see figure A.3 in appendix A).

The index and its 2012 update provide some information on regulatory variation within the region across the six larger nations, including regulations on currency conversion and transfer of foreign currency and the ease of hiring foreign personnel. The region does poorly on conversion and transfer of foreign currency, with Bangladesh and Nepal receiving particularly low scores with respect to capital outflows. Delays in conflict resolution continued to be a problem, with length of time for arbitration and enforcement being particularly long in India and Pakistan. Nepal was a restrictive outlier in the number of days to open a foreign subsidiary, as was Afghanistan for its lack of information on land ownership. Foreigners are not allowed to own land in Afghanistan, but they are able to lease land for up to 50 years.

On the positive side, the region scored above average on obtaining temporary work permits, with India performing best. Afghanistan performed well in currency conversion and transfer and ease of opening a foreign subsidiary. The country allows 100 percent foreign ownership and has no sector restrictions for foreign investment, but all investments over US$3 million require the approval of the High Commission on Investment. These findings imply that the country's poor performances on the Heritage Foundation's investment freedom subindex and overall foreign investment outturn are largely driven by fragility and security issues.

South Asian economies have moved to improve their FDI arrangements since 2012, but, unfortunately, relative progress cannot be benchmarked globally because the Investing Across Borders index has not been updated. This discussion highlights some recent developments; for a more historical analysis of the liberalization of each FDI arrangement, see Sahoo (2006). This section also covers the FDI arrangements of Bhutan and Maldives, which were not captured in global data sets. Table 3.4 summarizes FDI legislation for the eight countries and provides links to their regulatory bodies and investment promotion agencies that provide the current incentive programs. The largest two economies have made significant strides in the overall investment climate, as reflected by their improved positions in the overall Ease of Doing Business rankings. India and Pakistan improved from the 130th and 138th positions in the Doing Business Report 2016 rankings to 63rd and 108th, respectively, in 2020 (World Bank 2020). The nations of the region have also paid increasing attention to the role of special economic zones in stimulating FDI. Table 3.5 summarizes the progress in establishing zones in South Asia relative to some East Asian economies.

India has shown renewed interest in accelerating FDI inflows since 2014, especially in the context of the government's "Make in India" campaign. The country

TABLE 3.4 Laws and Institutions Related to Inward Foreign Direct Investment

Country	Inward FDI laws	Inward FDI institutions
Afghanistan	Law on Domestic and Foreign Private Investment, 2005	Afghanistan Investment Support Agency; Ministry of Commerce and Industry; High Commission on Investment, http://investinafghanistan.af/en/
Bangladesh	• One-Stop Service Act, 2017 • Industrial Policy (2010) establishes 17 "controlled industries" • The Companies Act of 2013 • Industrial Policy Act of 2005 • Telecommunications Act of 2001 • Foreign Private Investment (Promotion and Protection) Act 1980 • Bangladesh Export Processing Zones Authority Act, 1980	Bangladesh Investment Development Authority; Bangladesh Economic Zones Authority; Bangladesh Export Processing Zones Authority; Board of Investment (regulator)
Bhutan	• Foreign Direct Investment Regulations, 2019 (amended 2020) • Foreign Direct Investment Policy, 2019 • Foreign Direct Investment Rules and Regulations, 2012 (amended 2014) • Foreign Direct Investment Policy, 2010 (amended 2014) • Foreign Investment Policy, 2002, implemented 2005	Ministry of Economic Affairs, Department of Industry
India	• Consolidated FDI Policy Circular of 2020 • Consolidated FDI Policy Circular of 2017 RBI/FED/2017-18/60 • FED Master Direction No. 11/2017-18 • Foreign Exchange Management Act, 1999 (FEMA) clause (b) sub-section 3 of section 6 and section 4; read with Foreign Exchange Management (Transfer or Issue of a Security by a Person resident outside India) Regulations, 2017, issued vide Notification No. FEMA 20(R)/2017-RB dated November 7, 2017, https://www.rbi.org.in/Scripts/BS_FemaNotifications.aspx?Id=175	National Investment Promotion and Facilitation Agency, https://www.investindia.gov.in; Foreign Investment Facilitation Portal, https://www.fifp.gov.in/; Department for Promotion of Industry and Internal Trade, https://dipp.gov.in/; Make in India, https://www.makeinindia.com/home

(Table continues next page)

TABLE 3.4 Laws and Institutions Related to Inward Foreign Direct Investment (continued)

Country	Inward FDI laws	Inward FDI institutions
	• FEM Regulations, 2000—FEMA20/2000-RB May 3, 2000 • RBI/2004-05/176 A.P. (DIR Series) Circular No. 11, September 13, 2004 • RBI/2007-2008/215 A.P. (DIR Series) Circular No. 22, December 2007 • DIPP (FC-I Section) Press Note No. 3 (2012 series) d/o IPP File No. 5/10/2011-FC.I dated August 1, 2012, https://www.rbi.org.in /scripts/ECMUserView .aspx?CatID=12&Id=21 FERA amended 1993	
Maldives	• Constitution (2008) change to Sections 2.7 and 4.5.2, foreign land ownership, 2015 • Special Economic Zones Act (Law No. 24/2014) and Presidential Decree No. 2017/1 (specifies the type of economic activities and the minimum capital in special economic zones) • The Business Registration Act (Law No. 18/2014) • Maldives Companies Act (Law No. 10/96) • Partnership Act (Law No. 13/2011) • Law on Foreign Investments, 1979, Law 25/79, amended 1989	Invest Maldives; Ministry of Economic Development, https://www.trade.gov.mv/
Nepal	• Foreign Investment and Technology Transfer Act, 2019 (amended in 2021) • Public-Private Partnership and Investment Act, 2019 • Special Economic Zone Act (First Amendment), 2019 • Foreign Exchange Regulation Act, 2019 • Foreign Investment Policy, 2015 • Foreign Investment and Technology Transfer Act, 1992 • Investment and Industrial Enterprise Act, 1987 • Foreign Investment and Technology Transfer Act, 1981	Investment Board Nepal Department of Industry, http://www.ibn.gov.np/about

(Table continues next page)

TABLE 3.4 Laws and Institutions Related to Inward Foreign Direct Investment *(continued)*

Country	Inward FDI laws	Inward FDI institutions
Pakistan	• Investment Policy, 2013 • Special Economic Zones Act, 2012 (amended 2016) • Protection of Economic Reforms Act, 1992 • Foreign Private Investment (Promotion and Protection) Act, 1976	Board of Investment, https://invest.gov.pk/
Sri Lanka	• Foreign Exchange Act No. 12, 2017 • The Inland Revenue Act No. 24, 2017—Enhanced Capital Allowances • Finance Act—Commercial Hub Regulation No. 1, 2013 • Board of Investment Act (BOI Law 4, 1978); amendments (1980, 1983, 2002, 2006, 2009, 2012)	Board of Investment of Sri Lanka, http://investsrilanka.com/

Sources: UNCTAD Investment Policy Hub (https://investmentpolicy.unctad.org/); investment laws; national sites listed.

TABLE 3.5 Special Economic Zones in South Asia and East Asia and Pacific, 2018

Country	Number of SEZs (established by law)	Number of SEZs under development	Number of SEZs in planning	Year the law was first promulgated	National SEZ law or other legal framework
Afghanistan	0	0	4	n.a.	n.a.
Bangladesh	39	24	60	1980	The Bangladesh Economic Zones Act, 2010
Bhutan	6	4	4	n.a.	n.a.
India	373	142	61	1965	Special Economic Zones Act, No. 28, 2005
Maldives	0	0	4	2014	Special Economic Zones Act, No. 24/2014
Nepal	2	1	12	2016	Special Economic Zone Act, 2073, 2016
Pakistan	7	—	39	1980	Special Economic Zones Act, No. XX, 2012

(Table continues next page)

TABLE 3.5 Special Economic Zones in South Asia and East Asia and Pacific, 2018 (continued)

Country	Number of SEZs (established by law)	Number of SEZs under development	Number of SEZs in planning	Year the law was first promulgated	National SEZ law or other legal framework
Sri Lanka	12	—	—	1978	Board of Investment of Sri Lanka Law, No. 4 of 1978 (amended in 2018)
Comparators, East Asia and Pacific					
Cambodia	31	13	10	2005	Anukret (Sub-Decree) on the Establishment and Management of the Special Economic Zone, No. 148
China	2,543	—	—	1984	Administrative Decree of the State Council
Indonesia	13	—	—	1973	Law on Special Economic Zones, No. 39, 2009
Malaysia	45	—	—	1971	Free Zones Act 1990, Act 438
Myanmar	3	2	2	2011	Myanmar Special Economic Zone Law, 2014
Philippines	528	143	220	1969	Special Economic Zone Act; 1995 Republic Act No. 7916
Singapore	10	—	—	1969	Free Trade Zones Act, Chapter 114 (revised edition 2014)
Thailand	74	10		1979	Industrial Estate Authority of Thailand Act, B.E. 2522 (1979)
Vietnam	19	—	3	1991	Decree No. 82/2018/ND-CP

Sources: UNCTAD 2019b; World Bank 2019.
Note: — = not available; n.a. = not applicable; SEZ = special economic zone.

had been gradually liberalizing its IFDI arrangements since 1991, particularly in the manufacturing sector, while maintaining restrictions in services. It partially liberalized the wholesale and retail sector in 2006, and by 2014 most of manufacturing, except pharmaceuticals, was open. The government gradually opened services to FDI, particularly in 2016. In 2017, 100 percent FDI was permitted via the automatic route for petroleum and natural gas, aviation, construction development, financial services, railway infrastructure, and most mining activity, among others. By 2017, the investment approval agency, the Foreign Investment Promotion Board, was made redundant, because about 95 percent of investment was entering through the automatic route. The institution was recast as the Foreign Investment Facilitation Portal. However, multibrand retail and e-commerce continue to be difficult sectors to liberalize, and India placed some restrictive measures on e-commerce in February 2019 to protect offline retailers. For the North Eastern Region of India (NER), the government provides special incentives for national and foreign investors under the North East Industrial Development Scheme, 2017.[9]

Among recent FDI policy initiatives, Nepal has pursued foreign investment through annual investment summits, and just before the March 2019 summit, Nepal introduced three new pieces of legislation intended to signal a friendlier climate for FDI. Two high-level institutional mechanisms facilitate foreign investment—the Investment Board Nepal, chaired by the prime minister, approves investments worth more than 6 billion Nepalese rupees; and the Industrial Promotion Board, chaired by the Minister of Industry, Commerce and Supplies, approves the rest. The 2019 legislation recognizes leases as foreign investment and enables one-stop-shop facilities and automatic approval for some services. Travel agency, trekking, and mountaineering are restricted sectors for FDI.

Pakistan has sought to attract investment through special economic zones (SEZs) (2012 Special Economic Zones Act, amended 2016), with nine SEZs planned specifically under the China-Pakistan Economic Corridor. "Investment Policy 2013" outlines the framework of incentives for foreign investors. The country even offered foreign business insurance coverage up to US$500,000 in 2013. Accelerated depreciation incentives are available for investments in rural and underdeveloped areas.

Bhutan has moved from being consciously isolated to cautiously liberalizing, to safeguard its culture and environment. The country's first foreign investment policy was issued in 2002 and implemented in 2005. It was amended in 2010 to expand the coverage of sectors and move to a negative list of sectors. In December 2014, FDI reforms eased profit repatriation rules and reduced minimum capital requirements. Continued reform will need to focus on broader liberalization of foreign currency restrictions on investment and profit repatriation, as well as on streamlining approval processes and facilitating issuance of business visas for investors and clarifying the rules on hiring foreign managers and workers (World Bank 2019).

Bangladesh FDI policy initiatives have included acceleration of the establishment of SEZs and increased incentives for SEZ developers and investors since 2016. A one-stop service for investors was set up in 2017. FDI is restricted in the high-growth sectors of apparel, pharmaceuticals, and telecommunications. A record inflow of FDI to the country, amounting to US$3.6 billion, was registered in 2018, but there is much scope for reform to accelerate investment inflows. A high share of IFDI is reinvested earnings (more than 50 percent until 2017), suggesting high confidence of existing investors but low new entry. Bangladesh would benefit from reforms of outdated frameworks and policies, such as arbitrary caps on technology transfer transactions, lack of incentives for research and development expenses, controls on expatriate skilled workers, approval prerequisites, and mandatory public listing upon entry in various sectors and products (World Bank 2018).

The Board of Investment of Sri Lanka has undertaken several initiatives to reduce the time necessary for the approval process and to resolve investor issues more efficiently through a joint committee approach, with potential additional clearances obtained from higher-level committees. Another investment facilitation measure is the establishment of a web portal to streamline and fast-track the investment approval process. With implementation of the Inland Revenue Act, No. 24 of 2017, in April 2018, the Sri Lankan government moved away from granting tax holidays to attract investments. Instead, investors are granted incentives by way of the accelerated depreciation allowance, based on investments made in depreciable assets.[10] (Bangladesh also offers accelerated depreciation allowances, but as an alternative choice to tax holidays of five to seven years.)

The foreign investment arrangements in Maldives remain liberal; 100 percent foreign ownership is permitted in all sectors except longline fisheries and retail trade. In 2014, each FDI application began to be reviewed on a case-by-case basis. In 2015, constitutional changes were made that opened land ownership to foreign investors. New investment incentives in SEZs, which are applicable to domestic and foreign investors, were provided in 2014, including permission to employ foreigners where suitably skilled Maldivians are not available. Through 2011, foreign investors faced a discriminatory royalty payment in Maldives' no-tax system. This royalty was equivalent to 7.5 percent of profits or 3 percent (1.5 percent if the foreign stake was less than 49 percent) of turnover, whichever was greater. After 2011, a business profit tax that applied to national and foreign firms was established, with exemptions for foreign investment in priority sectors promoted by the government, including public-private partnerships and renewable energy (World Trade Organization 2016).

INTERNATIONAL INVESTMENT AGREEMENTS IN SOUTH ASIA

International investment agreements and double taxation avoidance agreements are pursued to stimulate cross-border investment. They are both inward and outward FDI policies, given that they apply to situations in which the parent investor is a nonresident or a resident firm. International investment agreements provide standards for investor protections and treatment that typically include commitments to fair and equitable treatment, nondiscrimination, most-favored-nation treatment, the ability to repatriate proceeds, and protection from expropriation. They also allow for arbitration of alleged breaches of these protections directly between the investor and the host government (investor-state dispute settlement). They may be in the form of bilateral investment treaties (BITs), treaties with more than two countries such as the Comprehensive Investment Agreement of the Association of Southeast Asian Nations, or an investment chapter in a preferential trade agreement.

The current relevance of BITs to South Asia is related to India's strong stance toward addressing some of the downsides of traditional BITs. As of 2019, there were six double-taxation avoidance agreements and two BITs in force within South Asia (see table A.2 in appendix A). The BITs are between Pakistan and Sri Lanka (in force since 2000) and between Bangladesh and India (signed in 2011, with a Joint Interpretive Note issued in 2017). An India–Sri Lanka BIT (in force since 1998) is no longer valid. India's lukewarm stance reflects developing country governments' growing concerns about traditional BITs based on the fact that investors (mostly from advanced economies) have successfully challenged a wide array of sovereign regulatory measures, such as environmental policies, as being a potential breach of BITs and have been awarded substantial damages. With large payouts by developing economy governments, it has been argued that provisions such as the right of investors to initiate arbitration proceedings undermine the potential sustainable benefits of foreign investment. After losing a case in 2011 based on judicial delays and a subsequent rise in investor disputes on issues such as retroactive taxation, India reviewed its BITs, which numbered 84 signed and 73 in force in 2015.[11] India introduced a new model BIT with narrower provisions in 2015 and unilaterally withdrew from 61 BITs during 2017–18. The evidence on the impact of BITs on aggregate investment flows is inconclusive (especially given the FDI data issues related to investment hubs), but the evidence on costs is rising (Hallward-Driemeier 2013; Johnson et al. 2018; Pohl 2018; Ranjan et al. 2018). In addition to India, other developing nations, including Indonesia and South Africa, have withdrawn from many traditional BITs but have still managed to sustain rising levels of foreign investment.

REGIONAL BIAS OF INWARD AND OUTWARD FDI POLICIES

Policies that specifically restrict firms' ability to invest in and to invest from South Asian countries remain, although they have been gradually liberalized. This regional bias is inherent in Indian investment policy, and is reflected in the specific use of bans, the government approval route, and requirements for currency of transaction.

Specific Regional Aspects of OFDI Laws

Indian OFDI to Pakistan was liberalized in September 2012, but all investments are required to go through the approval route, which requires prior approval from the Reserve Bank of India. The investment limit was the same as for all countries at the time: 100 percent of net worth. Investments in Nepal are to be in Indian rupees only, whereas investments in Bhutan may be in Indian rupees and convertible foreign currencies.

The currency specification has a mixed effect. On the one hand, it may direct investment to Nepal and Bhutan when faced with foreign exchange shortages in India instead of other countries that require convertible foreign currency. On the other hand, it deprives Nepal and Bhutan of convertible foreign currency.[12]

Initially, India's OFDI laws reflected positive preferences for South Asia. In legislation that came into effect in 1995, the limit on the value of automatic-route OFDI was $37 million (denominated and transacted in Indian rupees) for Bhutan and Nepal and $30 million for other South Asian Association for Regional Cooperation (SAARC) countries and Myanmar; it was lower, $15 million, for the rest of the world. In 2003, again, higher than global limits were set for OFDI to Bhutan and Nepal (albeit denominated and transacted only in Indian rupees), Myanmar, and SAARC countries; but this time Pakistan was excluded.

Specific Regional Aspects of IFDI Laws

India liberalized inward investment from Sri Lanka in 2004, from Bangladesh in 2007, and from Pakistan in 2012.[13] In May 2000, a notification under the new Foreign Exchange Management Act 1999 allowed foreigners—except for citizens of Bangladesh, Pakistan, and Sri Lanka, and entities from Bangladesh and Pakistan—to buy shares in Indian firms.[14] Two other FDI-related notifications (on the acquisition of immovable property and the opening of branch offices) also required prior Reserve Bank of India approval for these three countries. The provisions applied to additional countries—Afghanistan, Bhutan, China, the Islamic Republic of Iran, and Nepal—for acquisition of immovable property, and Afghanistan, China, and the Islamic Republic of Iran for the opening of branch offices.[15]

Currently, all investments in India from a country that shares a land border with India, or where the owner of an investment into India is situated in or is a citizen of such a country, need to go the government route. In addition, a citizen of Pakistan or a company incorporated in Pakistan also needs to go the government route. Nepali and Bhutanese citizens, however, can invest in Indian companies if the payment is made in free foreign exchange through banking channels. For start-up companies, people resident outside India (other than those who are citizens of Bangladesh and Pakistan, or entities that are registered in Bangladesh or Pakistan) can invest in convertible notes.[16] Many of these exceptions are reiterated in the Consolidated FDI Policy 2020.

Scope of and Strategies for OFDI: Evidence from Firm Surveys and Case Studies

Just as with international trade, firm-level analysis is required to gain a clear understanding of cross-border investment flows. Concerns about the available aggregate bilateral data related to the complications posed by investment hubs for South Asia, and the lack of data for small and fragile economies, were key reasons for embarking on data collection for this study. Only India has adopted the practice of allowing public access to foreign investment approvals from the Department for Promotion of Industry and Internal Trade. Most of the precise work done on OFDI tends to use data about advanced economy multinationals. In the United States, for example, multinationals are required by law to respond to quarterly, annual, and five-year surveys conducted by the Bureau of Economic Analysis. Detailed firm data sets managed by private sector firms such as Bureau van Dijk's Orbis database are also very useful, but the coverage for South Asia is limited. The World Bank's Enterprise Survey, which covers developing economies, does not ask questions about outward investments, let alone questions related to information and knowledge connectivity.

Data collection was needed for many reasons. The main drivers were as follows:

- A commitment had been made to include firms from the entire region, including those in small and fragile economies.

- The survey sought responses on topics related to networks, trust, and information at the firm level that was not available in the existing data.

- The share of outward investment within the region is very small (2 percent by value), and preexisting data would likely miss many of the investing firms.

- Family firms that do not typically report data were identified as outward investors in a preliminary scoping exercise.

- Large firms also needed to be captured in the sample because they were important outward investors.

- It was important to capture small investments, such as the opening of representative offices (termed trade-supporting investments), which are neglected by some policy makers but are important in a dynamic sense. The role of these low-cost capital investments in stimulating other investments deserved investigation. For example, more than half of China's OFDI by number of investments is of the trade-supporting type, especially small representative offices and sales offices (China Council for the Promotion of International Trade 2010).

The data that were collected captured information relating to outward investors, family firms, large and medium firms, and firms from all countries in the region; it also captured rarely included variables such as knowledge connectivity and information frictions. In addition, it enabled consideration of the connectivity-challenged NER. The downside of the survey data is the limited sample size in some countries and the limited detail obtained (in some quantitative respects) in what is a voluntary survey, particularly from firms that typically do not share data. Thus, the results are not meant to deliver precise estimates along the lines of recent academic work on US and EU multinationals that had access to firm expenditures and revenues. The results are meant to point to interesting relationships, relative magnitudes, and unique features in the data. For details of the data and sampling technique used, see the Sampling and Summary Statistics section of appendix B.

VARIETY IN INVESTMENT TYPES, INVESTOR ORIGIN, AND DESTINATION

Four Types of Investment, Dominated by Trade-Supporting and Services Investments

The data-collection exercise delivered 1,274 South Asian firms. The survey identifies 860 investments (defined by investment type, investor, source, and destination) globally made by 399 South Asian firms.[17] The investments are of four types: production investments (agriculture and manufacturing), services operations investments, trade-supporting investments (representative offices for marketing and sourcing services, usually with fewer than five people), and turnkey investments with some equity finance. Turnkey investments include engineering, procurement, and construction projects as well as other forms of contracting common in the construction industry, public utilities provision, and some public asset management. Trade-supporting investments and services operations investments dominate, with 45 percent and 38 percent of all investments (by number), respectively (table 3.6). Goods production investors make up 14 percent, and turnkey investors constitute 3 percent of the data. This description underestimates the number of investments because the data do not capture the actual number of investments in a particular investment type–destination pair, but just the incidence of such an activity.[18]

Outward Investors Are Mainly Indian; More Than Half Are Non-Indian, with Few Women-Led Firms

India accounts for about 94 percent of the value of outward investment (on the basis of CDIS data, 2018). In the survey undertaken for this report, Indian outward investors accounted for 48 percent of investor firms, followed by Pakistan (22 percent), Afghanistan (16 percent), and Sri Lanka (8 percent). Nepal has no outward investors. All of Bhutan's investments are trade-supporting investments, consistent with its restrictions on OFDI. The 208 non-Indian firms made 400 outward investments. There were very few women-led firms in the sample, and the share of women-led outward investor firms was smaller than the share of women-led noninvestor firms (figure 3.7).

Investors Originate from a Wide Array of Sectors—Led by Manufacturing, Wholesale and Retail Trade, and Transportation

The sector breakdown illustrated in figure 3.8 shows the wide scope of activities represented in the sample. Manufacturers were the main segment that invested abroad, both in services investments to promote their products and in other manufacturing facilities. About 39 percent of the investors self-identified as manufacturers (figure 3.8), though only 20 percent of all investments were production investments. The next largest origin sectors were wholesale and retail trade and transportation and storage. About one-third of the firms are in the manufacturing sector. At a more disaggregated level, the largest sectors were (in order of size) retail, textiles and apparel manufacture, warehousing, food products manufacture, pharmaceuticals manufacture, and financial services. At the most disaggregated 4-digit level of the International Standard Industrial Classification code, the top 10 sectors, which made up 30 percent of the investments, were apparel manufacture, pharmaceuticals manufacture, travel agencies, logistics, commercial banks,

TABLE 3.6 **South Asian Outward Investments, by Investment Type and Investor Origin**

	Number of investors (bold rows)					
	Number of investment type–destination pairs (italics rows)					
Home	Services operations	Trade supporting	Turnkey with finance	Goods production	Total for all investment types	Unique total investors
Afghanistan	**18**	**46**	**0**	**10**	**74**	**62**
	27	*80*	*0*	*13*	*120*	*103*
Bangladesh	**7**	**5**	**0**	**1**	**13**	**9**
	9	*11*	*0*	*1*	*21*	*16*
Bhutan	**0**	**6**	**0**	**0**	**6**	**6**
	0	*8*	*0*	*0*	*8*	*8*
India	**105**	**97**	**14**	**39**	**255**	**191**
	178	*142*	*24*	*54*	*398*	*344*
Maldives	**13**	**4**	**1**	**1**	**19**	**14**
	13	*4*	*1*	*1*	*19*	*14*
Nepal	**0**	**0**	**0**	**0**	**0**	**0**
	0	*0*	*0*	*0*	*0*	*0*
Pakistan	**38**	**52**	**0**	**18**	**108**	**86**
	66	*114*	*0*	*29*	*209*	*178*
Sri Lanka	**17**	**9**	**0**	**11**	**37**	**31**
	37	*28*	*0*	*20*	*85*	*81*
Total South Asia	**198**	**219**	**15**	**80**	**512**	**399**
	330	*387*	*25*	*118*	*860*	*744*

Source: Compiled from the South Asian Regional Engagement and Value Chains Survey.
Note: Each bold number is the number of firms. Each italicized number is the number of firm–investment type–destination investments. This table should be read as follows: there are 18 Afghan firms making 27 services operations investments (first column). There are 860 investment type–destination pairs (each investment type is counted separately, but two goods factories in the same destination economy would count as one goods investment), potentially made by 512 firms. But these investments represent 399 unique investors, given that some firms make more than one type of investment. The 860 investments defined by investment type–destination pairs represent 744 unique firm–destination pairs that do not distinguish by investment type.

FIGURE 3.7 **Share of Female Chief Executive Officers in South Asia**

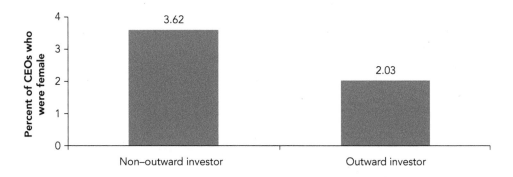

Source: South Asian Regional Engagement and Value Chains Survey.
Note: CEO = chief executive officer.

FIGURE 3.8 **Outward Investors from Various Sectors (Based on International Standard Industrial Classification of All Economic Activities)**

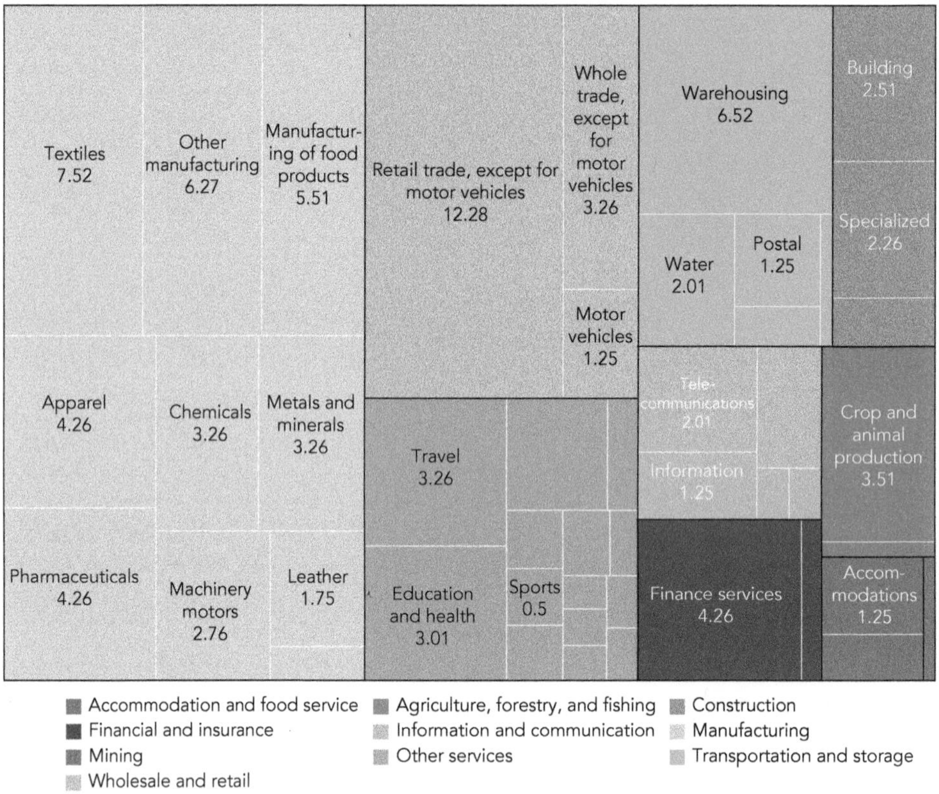

Source: World Bank data.
Note: Blank boxes represent investments with negligible shares.

manufacturers of tea and spices (other food products), carpets, construction, retail pharmaceuticals, and growers of beverage crops (for example, tea plantations).

Investment Destinations, Both within and outside the Region

In the sample of 399 investor firms, 167 firms (42 percent) invest in South Asia only, 105 firms (26 percent) invest only outside South Asia, and 127 firms (32 percent) invest both regionally and extraregionally. A more detailed description of the investor origin and destination is presented in table A.4 in appendix A.

Given the high logistical barriers that separate NER from the rest of India and that NER shares borders (in South Asia) with Bangladesh, Bhutan, and Nepal, NER was given special consideration as a separate destination in the data (see figure 1A.1, in annex 1A to chapter 1). A brief profile of the constituent states of the region and a figure to capture the state boundaries with its neighbors are presented in table A.3 and figure A.4 in appendix A. NER accounts for 8 percent of India's land area (and is about 1.75 times the size of Nepal and Bangladesh), 3.8 percent of the population, and 2.8 percent of GDP. The remoteness of the region has led to income per capita that is less than the national average for most of the states (Assam, Manipur, Meghalaya, Nagaland, and Tripura), and the region is a development priority for the government of India.[19]

Based on the survey, South Asia receives just about half of the number of outward investments from the region. Investments in NER make up the largest share. Excluding these investments in NER, the distribution of the number of investments in the sample is in line with the aggregate *value* from the bilateral data (CDIS), wherein Sri Lanka (42 percent) and Bangladesh (33 percent) are the largest destinations for South Asian investment, followed by Nepal (12 percent), Maldives (5 percent), India (3 percent), Afghanistan (2 percent), Bhutan (1.5 percent), and a negligible amount to Pakistan (table 3.7).

Non–South Asian destination investments are dominated by the investment hub and port city hubs of Hong Kong SAR, China; Mauritius; Singapore; and the United Arab Emirates, as seen in the bilateral data (figure 3.5). However, the survey upon which this report is based finds them to be less important relative to the aggregate bilateral investment data, perhaps better capturing the ultimate destination of the investment as opposed to the use of investment hubs to launch investments elsewhere (table 3.7). The importance of the European Union and the United Kingdom and of the United States and Canada is reinforced in the survey data. East Asia and Pacific (excluding Singapore) appears to be overrepresented in the sample, and Sub-Saharan Africa as a destination is underrepresented.

Comparing investor sector origin and destination region, investments in transportation and storage (logistics), construction, and travel agencies (under the International

TABLE 3.7 **Destination of South Asian Outward Investments**

Destination	Number of firms investing in destination	Share of firms (%) investing in destination	Number of investments in destination	Share (%) of investments in destination	OFDI value (US$, millions) 2017	Share of OFDI (%)
Afghanistan	29	3.9	34	4.0	56	0.05
Bangladesh	65	8.7	79	9.2	1,012	0.90
Bhutan	8	1.1	9	1.0	47	0.04
India_General	45	6.0	53	6.2		
India, North Eastern Region	81	10.9	99	11.5	87	0.08
Maldives	14	1.9	15	1.7	153	0.14
Nepal	26	3.5	29	3.4	385	0.34
Pakistan	28	3.8	31	3.6	7	0.01

(Table continues next page)

TABLE 3.7 **Destination of South Asian Outward Investments** (continued)

Destination	Number of firms investing in destination	Share of firms (%) investing in destination	Number of investments in destination	Share (%) of investments in destination	OFDI value (US$, millions) 2017	Share of OFDI (%)
Sri Lanka	56	7.5	72	8.4	1,274	1.13
Total South Asia	**352**	47.3	**421**	49.0	3,021	2.69
Total unique South Asia firms	**272**					
Australia and New Zealand	15	2.0	16	1.9	704	0.63
Hong Kong SAR, China; Mauritius; Singapore; United Arab Emirates	71	9.5	81	9.4	55,750	49.60
Europe and Central Asia	37	5.0	41	4.8	18,527	16.48
East Asia and Pacific	72	9.7	81	9.4	3,141	2.79
Japan	11	1.5	12	1.4	135	0.12
Latin America and the Caribbean	3	0.4	3	0.3	3,378	3.01
Middle East and North Africa	43	5.8	49	5.7	2,880	2.56
Sub-Saharan Africa	9	1.2	9	1.0	7,941	7.07
European Union and United Kingdom	71	9.5	77	9.0	2,943	2.62
United States and Canada	60	8.1	70	8.1	12,530	11.15
Total non–South Asia	**392**	52.7	**439**	51.0	109,370	97.31
Total unique non–South Asia firms	**232**					
Sum: total South Asia + total non–South Asia	504	67.7	n.a.	96.0	112,391	100
Sum: unique destinations per firm	**744**	100	**860**	100	n.a.	n.a.

Sources: South Asian Regional Engagement and Value Chains Survey; Coordinated Direct Investment Survey, International Monetary Fund.
Note: Investments are measured by firm–investment type–destination combinations. Total South Asia is obtained by summing individual country data, suggesting that there are 352 investing firms. However, there are actually 272 unique firms because some firms invest in more than one country. Summing South Asia and non–South Asia investors = 504, not 399 (from table 3.6), because 105 firms are investors into South Asia and non–South Asia. More unique firms (272) invest in the region than outside the region (232). The investment hubs and East Asia and Pacific were the dominant locations outside the region, followed closely by the European Union and the United Kingdom, and then by the United States and Canada. There are 860 firm–investment type–destination combinations. Given that one firm may have different types of investments in the same country, there are 744 unique investment destinations by firms (total number of investor-destination pairs). n.a. = not applicable; OFDI = outward foreign direct investment.

Standard Industrial Classification code for the administrative and support service category) are biased toward South Asia. Investments in information and communication, finance services, and manufacturing and wholesale and retail trade are tilted extraregionally (table 3.8). Finance services are likely meeting the needs of the migrant worker community in the Middle East.

TABLE 3.8 **Sector Origin Breakdown, by Investor and Noninvestor, and Destination Region**

Percent

Sector	Noninvestors	Investors	Destination: South Asia only	Destination: Both South Asia and non–South Asia	Destination: Non–South Asia only
A. Agriculture	4	4	5	0	4
B. Mining	1	..	0	1	0
C. Manufacturing	43	39	37	41	41
D. Electricity	..	..	0	0	1
E. Water supply	..	..	0	0	1
F. Construction	3	6	7	6	3
G. Wholesale and retail trade	22	17	14	17	20
H. Transportation and storage	5	11	12	13	6
I. Accommodation and food service	3	2	3	1	2
J. Information and communication	6	5	3	4	9
K. Financial and insurance	4	5	4	4	6
L. Real estate	..	0	0	0	0
M. Professional, scientific, and technical	3	3	2	6	1
N. Administrative and support services	3	5	6	5	3
P. Education	1	1	2	1	0
Q. Human health	1	3	4	1	2
S. Other services	..	1	1	0	1
T. Activities of households as employees	..	0	0	0	0
	100	100	100	100	100

Source: South Asian Regional Engagement and Value Chains Survey.
Note: .. = negligible. Number in each column represents the percentage of the number of investors in each sector.

REGIONAL PIONEERS: KEY DRIVERS OF OUTWARD INVESTMENT

This section presents the regional and extraregional motivations for OFDI from the survey data, with illustrative examples from the pioneer firm case studies. As listed in table 1.1 in chapter 1, the case studies covered four value chains: apparel, agri-food, the automotive industry, and the hotel industry. The investors came from Bangladesh, India, Nepal, Pakistan, and Sri Lanka. The host economies comprised Bangladesh, India, Nepal, and Sri Lanka. The wide array of motivations suggests multiple opportunities for outward investment. Even within one conglomerate, a variety of motivations for OFDI contribute to overall competitiveness (see box 3.7 on MAS Holdings of Sri Lanka).

Market sales development, connectivity, cost considerations, and value chain management and upgrading were the four primary motivations for investing in South Asia (figure 3.9). Firms set up retail and wholesale investments to expand market sales and capture wholesaler or retailer margins, get better control of their distribution, and acquire knowledge of continuously changing consumer preferences. Sri Lanka's Timex Garments' retail investments to sell their Avirate brand of women's fashionwear provides an example of these motivations.

Similarly, Bangladesh's Rahimafrooz Batteries set up a trade-supporting office and Sri Lanka's MAS Brands set up a distribution office to increase the efficiency of their distribution systems. Pakistan's denim manufacturer Soorty Enterprises made a trade-supporting investment in Bangladesh to facilitate sales of its denim textiles and

FIGURE 3.9 Motivations for Investing in South Asia and outside South Asia

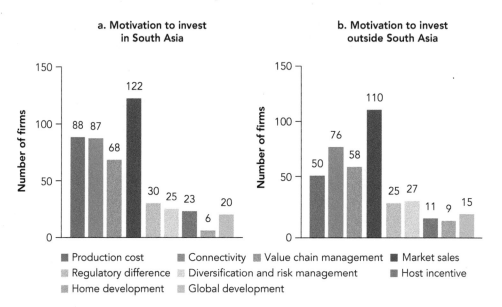

Source: Computations based on the South Asian Regional Engagement and Value Chains Survey.
Note: Firms could choose more than one option.

to increase connectivity with global buyers. For Pakistani firms facing buyers that are hesitant to come to the country for security reasons, trade-supporting outward investments in Dubai, United Arab Emirates, were vital for connecting with buyers from the European Union and the United States. Given that Dubai is also a global hub, it was also an experimental ground for apparel manufacturers to launch their brands globally. Overall, non-Indian investors were more motivated than Indian investors to engage in market sales development, as would be expected, given the asymmetric market size.

Migrants and the diaspora were also an important motivation for investment. When Nepal's Chaudhary saw migrants taking large packages of his Wai Wai instant noodles abroad, he was inspired to export. Dubai was his first market. Restaurants and food producers have made investments to cater to their migrant populations (diaspora as well as temporary workers). Many South Asian commercial banking investments in the Middle East were made to capture some of the rents associated with migrant workers' remittance transfers while reducing the transaction cost of these transfers. Some banks set up their own branches and in other situations entered into nonequity agreements with destination-based financial institutions, such as sending one or two of their officers to handle specific country transactions.

The same top four motivations applied to investments outside South Asia (figure 3.9, panel b). Although market sales development was clearly the dominant motivation, the relative weights of some other motivations were different. Connectivity is more important, and production cost less important, in non–South Asian investments compared with investments in South Asia. Value chain management was also more important than production cost. As part of market sales development, trade-supporting investments provide an opportunity to build relationships with clients and suppliers as well as to learn about markets and industry innovations. The trade-supporting offices are important for economies with security issues, but also for those seeking diverse connections in commercial hubs such as Singapore and Dubai. As part of managing the value chain, frontier firms have used OFDI to invest in foreign start-ups or buy foreign firms with better technology and established brands to improve competitiveness and to achieve the higher margins associated with research and design.

At a more detailed level (figure 3.10), the single most important factor for investing in South Asia was access to global networks, with the next two factors, labor cost considerations and market potential, also being important. Apart from global networks, the other key connectivity issue was access to infrastructure; other cost issues included increasing the scale of production, accessing support services, and availability of land. Other market-related factors that were important were being an experimental platform for global sales; pursuing untapped markets with less competition, which provides a first-mover advantage; and producing for buyback by the home market. Delivery of certain services involved a physical presence through FDI and is captured under the "nature of contract" category. An example involves Sri Lankan apparel manufacturers investing in distribution and retail in the mid-2000s, tapping an underserved market in India: women with increasing purchasing power. Similarly, other manufacturers are

FIGURE 3.10 **Detailed Motivations for Investing in South Asia**

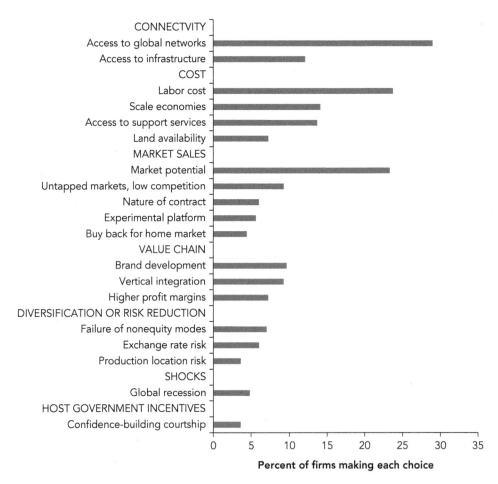

Source: Computation based on the South Asian Regional Engagement and Value Chains Survey.
Note: Firms, *N*, could make more than one choice. *N* = 267.

now investing in retail services to take advantage of the changing consumption basket of Bangladeshis with rising incomes.

The importance of cost—especially labor cost—in vertical and complex FDI runs counter to the traditional perception that factor endowments are similar in all South Asian countries. The traditional perception is that all countries are producing similar products, with little to offer by way of collaboration or specialization. Among the South Asian firms driven by production costs was India's tire manufacturer CEAT, which invested in tire plants in rubber-producing Sri Lanka. Sri Lanka's Brandix invested in a large apparel park in Andhra Pradesh, India, where land was cheaper. Another example of a vertical investment is Dabur India's investment in nurseries in Nepal to develop herbal plants.

Outward investment also facilitates the development of a value chain or upgrading along the chain (see box 3.6 for a summary of OFDI benefits from a value chain perspective). OFDI was motivated by brand development, vertical integration, and the pursuit of higher profit margins (figure 3.10), consistent with the importance of cost considerations and encouraging for the potential to develop a regional value chain. Sri Lankan apparel manufacturers, which developed their own brands in India, were able to move into higher profit margin segments; similarly, Indian and Sri Lankan hoteliers improved their profitability by investing in the high-end Maldivian hotel resort industry.

Among the less important factors are those related to exploiting regulatory and policy differences across countries (not shown in figure 3.10), diversification and risk reduction, government incentives, global shocks, and home shocks. Still, some investments were motivated by such factors, including fruit juice manufacturing investments in Nepal, geared for reexport back to India. In addition, Indian firms invested in Sri Lanka to take advantage of the low import tariffs in Sri Lanka on crude palm oil (the principal input for manufacturing vanaspati [hydrogenated vegetable oil]) and the preferential exports of vanaspati into the Indian market based on the India–Sri Lanka Free Trade Agreement. Once India reduced its own tariffs on crude palm oil, such investments

---

BOX 3.6 Summary of Outward Foreign Direct Investment Benefits from a Value Chain Perspective

- Capturing high–profit margin or high–valued added segments of the value chain when these activities are performed across the national border

- Allowing firms to develop scale and scope of production to meet requirements of global buyers

- Learning about markets and processes and building relationships with clients and suppliers

- Purchasing foreign intellectual property—from technology to brands—when development at home faces capability and time constraints

- Reducing markups on value chain inputs and activities provided by monopolistic suppliers

- Compensating for inefficient cross-border contractual partnerships

- Achieving bargaining power through ownership in difficult contracting environments

- Securing stable access to foreign raw materials and other essential inputs

- Diversifying locations to reduce exposure to country-specific shocks

- Reducing costs by undertaking chain activities in the location where they are undertaken most efficiently

- Overcoming international trade frictions, either by producing in the location of the consumer or the location with the best market access to third countries

BOX 3.7 How OFDI Helped MAS Holdings (Sri Lanka) Upgrade along the Apparel Value Chain

Value creation along the different activities that make up a global value chain (GVC) is distributed unevenly. So are the profit margins; Stan Shih's "smile curve" (Shih 1996) illustrates this phenomenon. In the apparel sector, the highest margins go to retailers and brand owners and to research and development and design activities. The lowest margins are associated with apparel manufacturing, where most of South Asian GVC participation is located.

In the face of the global liberalization of apparel quotas in 2005, many small economies and manufacturing firms situated within them felt vulnerable. Figure B3.7.1 illustrates part of the strategy adopted by MAS Holdings of Sri Lanka, a family-owned firm that, during the late 1980s and 1990s, had developed into a contract manufacturing partner of L Brands (the brand owner of Victoria's Secret) and Nike. In the context of rising wages in Sri Lanka and the lead-up to 2005, adjustments included specializing in one of the most complex of garments—the brassiere, which can have up to 50 components—and investing in becoming a full-package supplier to the buyer. This endeavor involved backward integration into textiles and some accessory manufacturing to reduce lead times and

FIGURE B3.7.1 How OFDI Helped MAS Holdings Upgrade along the Apparel Smile Curve

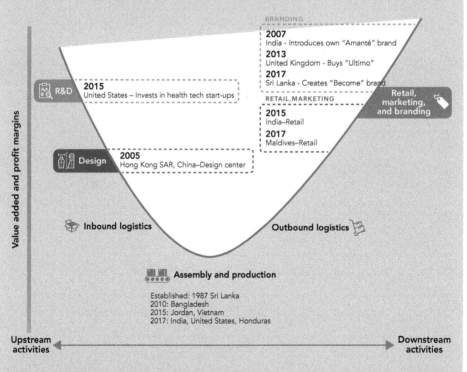

Source: Yatawara 2019.
Note: R&D = research and development.

(Box continues next page)

BOX 3.7 How OFDI Helped MAS Holdings (Sri Lanka) Upgrade along the Apparel Value Chain *(continued)*

developing close relationships with MAS's lead buyers. Inward foreign direct investment was important because backward integration was achieved with foreign partnerships. Today MAS Holdings is a major producer of intimate apparel and performance sportswear.

Outward foreign direct investment (OFDI) to develop design skills. The design center in Hong Kong SAR, China, was part of MAS's effort to become a full-package supplier for global buyers. It also served as a source of skills for designing products for its own brand.

Developing a brand in India and distribution investment: Amanté. MAS contemplated reducing its vulnerability by developing its own brand. The target market was India. Not only were incomes increasing rapidly for a youthful population, but Indian women were also acquiring more direct purchasing power by entering the workforce. Identifying a long-neglected market, MAS undertook countrywide market research in India to design a bra that would be suitable for the South Asian woman's body characteristics, the climate, and the culture. By 2007, the brand Amanté was launched in India with a high-quality product in the middle-upper segment of the market. Believing that it did not have a sufficient variety of product lines to warrant a retailing exercise, the firm sold its products in department stores (large format stores in Indian parlance). The products were made in the factories of related firms within the business group in Sri Lanka. MAS then invested in a distribution office and warehouse in Bengaluru. Within a couple of years, Amanté would capture 25 percent of its target market segment.

Retail investment. After five years in India, the product was launched in the firm's home turf of Colombo, Sri Lanka. The firm experimented with retailing In Colombo, given that rents were significantly cheaper than in Mumbai or Bengaluru. After the learning experience in Colombo and the development of a variety of product lines, the firm launched its own retail store in India in 2015. It continues to sell in department stores as well as in its own exclusive brand outlets. In 2017, a retail investment was made in Maldives. The firm entered Pakistan through a franchise agreement in 2018.

Buying a brand. While developing retail experience, the firm also found itself in a position to invest in the well-known United Kingdom bra brand Ultimo in 2013. Gaining ownership of a well-known brand in a competitive market such as the United Kingdom provided deeper experience in branding and the higher margins that come with time for well-established brands.

Investing in research and development (R&D) and health tech and femtech start-ups. MAS has invested in health start-ups in the United States related to women's health (menstruation, incontinence, and menopause). Using moisture-wicking, absorbent textiles, the products are manufactured in its factories. At the same time, MAS invested in technology to develop material that could monitor health and facilitate rapid muscle healing, financing start-ups in Pennsylvania. The firm was able to benefit from the higher value added and higher margins associated with R&D. MAS Holdings received approval from the Central Bank of Sri Lanka for these investments because there was no automatic approval of any kind. Technology partnerships are critical to MAS Holdings' success.

Volume and scope of products. As global buyers sought to consolidate their supply chains in the 2000s, OFDI allowed MAS, an innovative firm from a small country, to survive and thrive by facilitating higher volumes of production. Although not an aspect of moving up

(Box continues next page)

> **BOX 3.7 How OFDI Helped MAS Holdings (Sri Lanka) Upgrade along the Apparel Value Chain** *(continued)*
>
> the smile curve, higher production volumes have been a critical part of MAS Holdings' manufacturing business. MAS Holdings was able to deliver on volume and scope of products through increased production in Bangladesh, India, Jordan, and Vietnam.
>
> *Reshoring and near-shoring.* As lead times and quick response have become important in some segments for buyers, the 2017 purchase of a denim manufacturing company in North Carolina and its Honduran affiliate provided another channel through which MAS Holdings was able to accommodate buyers.
>
> With a turnover of about US$1.8 billion and 95,000 employees, MAS Holdings continues to grow, based on a culture of innovation, women's empowerment, and social responsibility.

were no longer profitable. As illustrated in box 3.3, Indian OFDI in the 1960s and 1970s was motivated by restrictive regulatory policies at home and tight control of the private sector.

Somewhat paradoxically, an uneven playing field at home could motivate firms to become global relatively quickly. Reminiscent of India's regulatory restrictiveness at home, the private Chinese auto firm Geely had to contend with preferential government treatment for state-owned automakers. After its establishment in 1997, it bought Swedish-based Volvo in 2010, seeking competitiveness through the brand value and high-tech automotive design knowledge base that came with the purchase.

At the lower end of the top 20 detailed motivations for investing in South Asia (figure 3.10) were investing in equity (once nonequity modes had failed), mitigating exchange risk and location risk, the impact of the global recession on traditional markets, and the confidence-building courtship of government officials. On the latter point, Nepal's Chaudhary cited the importance of the incentives offered by states in NER and the courtship and encouragement by the chief ministers that helped Chaudhary finally decide to invest in that region of India.

The region has also been a platform for escaping crises at home. For example, Nepal's CG Foods invested in factories in NER, India, when it was facing an insurgency at home, and Sri Lankan retailers invested in Bangladesh in the face of policy uncertainty in their homeland. These examples are in line with work showing that a domestic slump is found to encourage exporting (Almunia et al. 2018), and that policy uncertainty, as reflected by political disagreement on trade and related policies, reduces FDI inflows (Azzimonti 2019). However, regional investors tend to be less risk averse compared with global investors, such as when Nepal's CG Hospitality invested in Taj Hotels in Sri Lanka at the height of the civil war in 2008. Similarly, having dealt with insurgency at home in Nepal, CG Foods was equipped to handle civil disturbances in Assam in India's NER.

REGIONAL PIONEERS: MANY PATHS OF ENGAGEMENT

Use of the value chain framework from chapter 2 (see figure B2.1.1 in box 2.1) provides an intuitive illustration of the modes of engagement of the pioneer firms. The value chain is broken down into four activities: headquarters services, intermediates production, assembly, and distribution. In figures 3.11 through 3.18, the circle around the activity icon reflects ownership by the home country; a circle around an activity in the second or third frame indicates outward direct investment by home investors. From the viewpoint of the home country, a triangle represents national ownership in foreign country 1; while in foreign country 2, national ownership is represented by a square. This depiction captures the relationship between trade and investment. It is also very useful in illustrating the complex nature of international engagements, which do not fit easily into analytical constructs such as "horizontal vs. vertical" investments, or "market-seeking vs. efficiency-seeking" investments.

Distribution Investment Abroad

Pioneer firms' most common strategy was investing in distribution activity in India, as represented by the circle around the distribution activity icon in the third frame (figure 3.11).

This scenario may be used to explain the investment activity of four pioneers. The Bangladeshi firm Rahimafrooz Batteries has a distribution office in New Delhi and offices in Kolkata that distribute replacement auto batteries, among other batteries, in

FIGURE 3.11 **Distribution Investment Abroad**

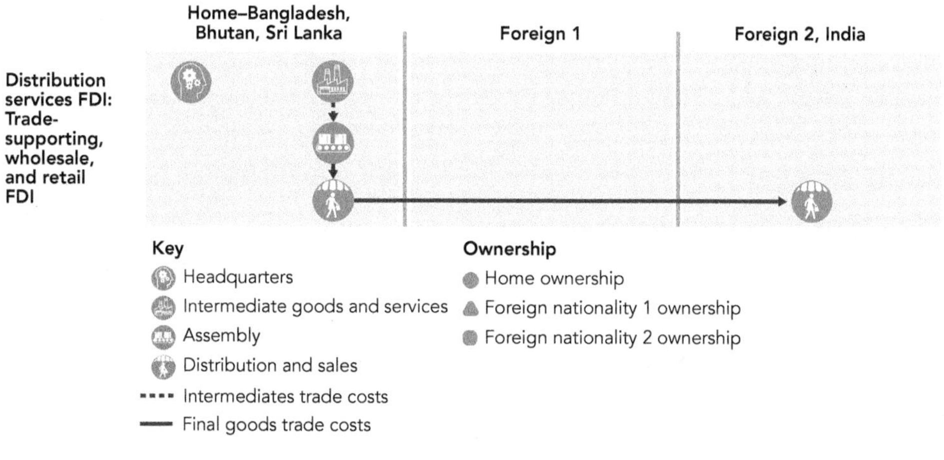

Source: World Bank.
Note: Input transfers from headquarters to all other activities at home and abroad are not illustrated to avoid clutter. ● in Foreign 1 and 2 represented OFDI by home country. FDI = foreign direct investment; OFDI = outward foreign direct investment.

the Indian market. Batteries are made in Bangladesh in a factory in the Ishwardi Export Processing Zone, close to the major land border post Benapole. The line that joins the distribution icon (at home, Bangladesh) to distribution in foreign 2 (India) represents exports. The circle around the distribution icon in India in the third frame indicates that Rahimafrooz owns that distribution office. Similarly, Bhutan Ferroalloys Ltd. exports ferrosilicon produced in Bhutan to India through its group distribution firm in Kolkata. This is not strictly owned by Bhutan Ferroalloys Ltd., but it is a related firm (Mehta and Yatawara 2018).

The same figure may be used to illustrate two different approaches by Sri Lankan firms to serve the Indian market. MAS Holdings is a major contract manufacturer for Victoria's Secret and Triumph brands. Within the conglomerate, MAS Brands sells under its own Amanté brand through Indian department stores (see box 3.7). The products are exported from Sri Lanka to a trading office in Bengaluru, which, by law, was initially a joint venture office. The Sri Lankan firm Timex Garments Pvt. Ltd. sells its Avirate brand of women's "western wear" by investing in retail stores in India.[20] Evening wear, professional attire, and casual wear are made in Sri Lanka and exported to Chennai Port in southern India. The circled distribution activity in India represents Timex's ownership of the retail stores—a strategy of retailing that separates it from simply branding.

Export Platform Investment Plus

The Sri Lankan firm Brandix Lanka Limited invests in Andhra Pradesh, India, to manufacture textiles and wearing apparel and export them to the United States. Its main products are weft fabric and brassieres, underwear, and yoga pants. Brandix owns the textile and apparel factories in India (second frame in figure 3.12) but does not own the distribution center in the United States. Exports from Sri Lanka and India go to the distribution office of the owners of the Victoria's Secret brand, L Brands Pvt. Ltd. The intermediates production in India represents the weft fabric factory. The Brandix story goes beyond its own factories: it also constructed a very large apparel park in the same location (designated a special economic zone) that houses firms that produce intermediate goods and services for the apparel value chain. The firm acts as apparel park manager and resident textile and apparel manufacturer.

Dynamic Story: From Distribution Investment to Export Platform Investment

The Pakistan pioneer firm Soorty Enterprises Pvt. Ltd. initially invested in a marketing office (a trade-supporting investment) in Dhaka, Bangladesh. Soorty Enterprises manufactures denim cloth as well as denim apparel. The investment in Dhaka was meant to market the denim fabric to Bangladeshi apparel manufacturers. The secondary motivation was to establish connectivity to global buyers, given that the security situation caused some buyers to be reluctant to go to Pakistan for a factory visit. The marketing office was eventually expanded to become a distribution office. After about three years in Dhaka, Soorty invested in an apparel manufacturing facility in the Comilla Export

FIGURE 3.12 **Export Platform Investment**

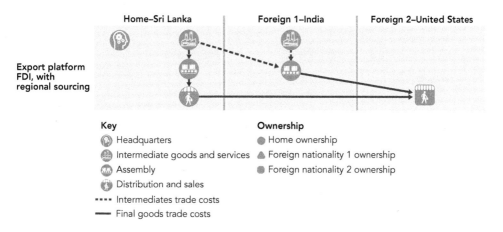

Source: World Bank.
Note: Input transfers from headquarters to all other activities at home and abroad are not illustrated to avoid clutter. • in Foreign 1 and Foreign 2 represented OFDI by home country. FDI = foreign direct investment; OFDI = outward foreign direct investment.

FIGURE 3.13 **Dynamic Story: From Distribution to Export Platform Investment**

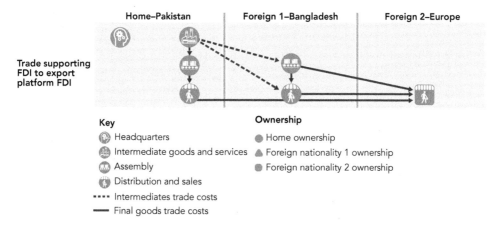

Source: World Bank.
Note: Input transfers from headquarters to all other activities at home and abroad are not illustrated to avoid clutter. • in Foreign 1 and Foreign 2 represented OFDI by home country. FDI = foreign direct investment; OFDI = outward foreign direct investment.

Processing Zone. The apparel products manufactured in Bangladesh include denim and cotton pants and differ from the products manufactured in Pakistan. Hence, fabric is exported to the Pakistan-owned distribution office as well as to the manufacturing facility in Bangladesh. The destination market for both the Bangladesh and the Pakistan facilities is Europe, as seen in the third frame of figure 3.13.

FIGURE 3.14 **Complex Investment with Horizontal, Vertical, and Export Platform Features**

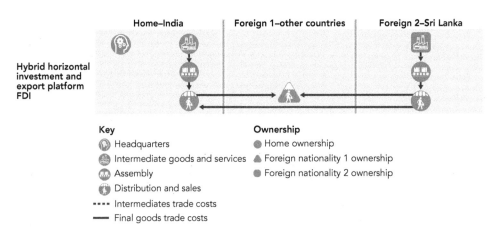

Source: World Bank.
Note: Input transfers from headquarters to all other activities at home and abroad are not illustrated to avoid clutter. ● in Foreign 1 and Foreign 2 represented OFDI by home country. FDI = foreign direct investment; OFDI = outward foreign direct investment.

Complex Investment with Horizontal, Vertical, and Export Platform Features

A horizontal investment is based on replicating production in the destination market of the final consumer. Figure 3.14 illustrates the case of the Indian tire manufacturing firm CEAT, which invested in a tire factory in rubber-producing Sri Lanka. The square for intermediates activity in frame 3 represents Sri Lankan ownership of rubber and the related inputs needed for assembly. CEAT has invested in a factory and a distribution office in Sri Lanka. This complex FDI serves the host market (like a traditional horizontal investment) and the investor home market (India), and exports to third countries directly.

Hybrid Horizontal Investment

The Indian firm Dabur India Limited invests in a production facility for fruit juices in Nepal. It uses local inputs (intermediates icon in a square in frame 3 in figure 3.15) and imported inputs from unrelated parties in countries such as Brazil (intermediates icon in a triangle in frame 2). It does not undertake its own distribution in Nepal. It also exports a substantial share of its products back to India.

Horizontal Investment with a Twist

The Nepalese firm CG Foods Pvt. Ltd. invests in factories in Assam in NER to make Wai Wai instant noodles. It relies on local inputs and produces for the Indian market. The company began with production for the markets in NER and eventually progressed to

FIGURE 3.15 **Hybrid Horizontal Investment**

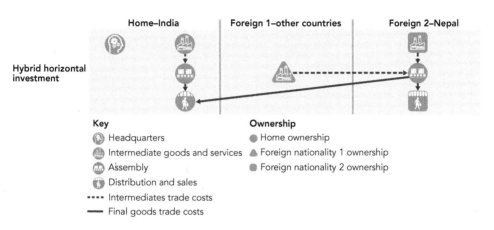

Source: World Bank.
Note: Input transfers from headquarters to all other activities at home and abroad are not illustrated to avoid clutter.
• in Foreign 1 and Foreign 2 represented OFDI by home country. OFDI = outward foreign direct investment.

FIGURE 3.16 **Horizontal Investment with a Twist**

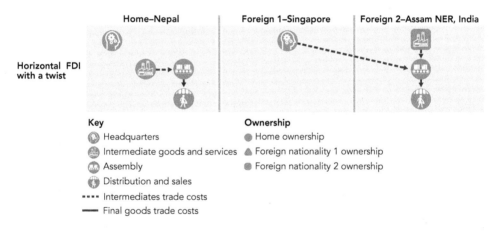

Source: World Bank.
Note: Input transfers from headquarters to all other activities at home and abroad are not illustrated to avoid
clutter. • in Foreign 1 and Foreign 2 represented OFDI by home country. FDI = foreign direct investment;
NER = North Eastern Region of India; OFDI = outward foreign direct investment.

Kolkata and beyond. It also has a distribution firm. The company had to find a loophole
in Nepal's laws to be able to invest abroad. Using foreign residency as a route, Binod
Chaudhary's sons moved to Singapore and Dubai and replicated headquarters services
in Singapore. The investment was made through this firm (figure 3.16) (Chaudhary
2016; Dhungana and Yatawara 2018).

FIGURE 3.17 **Franchise Option**

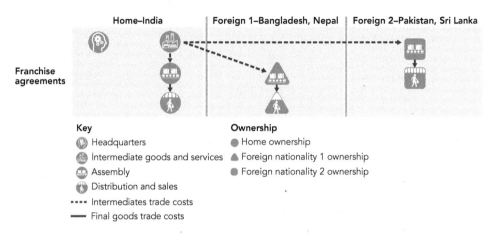

Source: World Bank.
Note: Input transfers from headquarters to all other activities at home and abroad are not illustrated to avoid clutter. Headquarters at Home provides technical and management services to assembly (stitching) and retail activities in Foreign 1 and Foreign 2. It also licenses the retail brand name. • in Foreign 1 and Foreign 2 represent OFDI by home country. NER = North Eastern Region of India; OFDI = outward foreign direct investment.

Franchise Option

Raymond Ltd. has the widest presence in South Asia among the regional pioneers. The firm is best known for its production of high-quality suiting material and custom suiting services, although the owner has expanded the company business into ready-made apparel manufacturing and retail. The broad expansion of its suiting business was achieved using franchise agreements to set up custom tailoring establishments (inter-mediates) throughout South Asia. Using the Raymond brand, locally owned franchisees set up retail stores (distribution) according to Raymond standards and import the suiting material from Raymond fabric factories in India (as represented by the dotted lines in figure 3.17). The flow of technical and management services, as well as intellectual property licensing exports of the brand name Raymond, are not depicted in the figure.

Management Contracts and Investment in Hotels

The pioneer Indian firm Taj Hotels has an equity investment in hotels in Sri Lanka and a management contract to run these hotels under the Taj brand. The firm first entered Sri Lanka in 1983 through the construction of its own hotel, the Taj Samudra in the capital, Colombo. A second hotel, Taj Exotica, was built at the beach, again owned and managed by Taj Hotels. By 2008, the firm was suffering from low occupancy rates as fighting intensified in Sri Lanka's civil war. A Nepali firm, CG Hospitality, provided a capital injection and gained joint ownership of the hotels in 2008. Large hotel brands today are increasingly moving toward an "asset-light" model, in which they do not own the hotel property. Brand licensing and hotel management services are the main sources

FIGURE 3.18 **Management Contracts and Investment in Hotels**

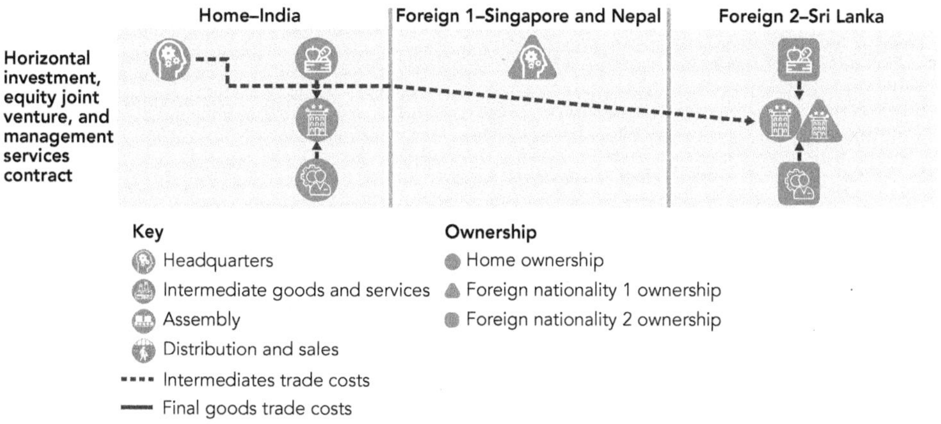

Source: World Bank.
Note: The framework was adjusted slightly to accommodate services industries. Intermediates include foods and beverages and recreational activity. Input transfers from headquarters to all other activities at home are not illustrated to avoid clutter. • in Foreign 1 and Foreign 2 represent OFDI by home country. OFDI = outward foreign direct investment.

of expansion and profit making. By separating the property ownership business from the management business, hotel brands are growing through the asset-light model.

This report's framework must be adjusted slightly to accommodate a services industry. Here, intermediates refer to inputs for hospitality services, such as food and beverages and recreational activities. Further, assembly activity is replaced by "operations," which represent hotel property development and management, and distribution refers to promotion and sales of hospitality services to clients. In figure 3.18, the Taj Samudra Hotel uses local inputs from Sri Lanka and local travel agencies to promote its hotel. The dotted line represents the management services and Taj Hotels brand intellectual property exports that are sold to the Taj Samudra Hotel in Sri Lanka from the Taj headquarters in India. The circle and triangle of operations in frame 3 represent the joint ownership (India and Nepal) of the hotel property. CG Hospitality headquarters (frame 2) does not provide any management services.

Concluding Remarks

This chapter provides a wide-ranging overview of outward investments in South Asia and the policy environments in which they operate. The region exhibits low levels of outward investment and intraregional investment relative to other developing regions. Although small, South Asia has a growing, varied, and rich investment landscape, as illustrated by the types of investment, sectors of origin, motivations, and modes of engagement. Outward investment motivations include labor cost considerations, countering the stereotype of the similarity of endowments among South Asian countries. The wide variety of investments pursued with varying start-up costs shows how OFDI participation is quite inclusive.

Some important policy implications result from this analysis. First, by incorporating an outward investment lens in the context of a firm choosing from among alternative engagement modes, the analysis brings attention to the stark distortions resulting from the OFDI policies of most countries in the region. Most OFDI arrangements are restrictive, discretionary, and lack transparency, with the exception of India and to a lesser extent Sri Lanka. Second, the diverse motivations of regional pioneers highlight new benefits of OFDI specific to emerging market multinationals, heightening the need for policy action on OFDI, even for small economies and those with balance of payments concerns. Third, region-specific IFDI and OFDI policies remain in place, distorting investment flows in the region.

The chapter also highlights the important role of investment hubs for the region. Estimates of ultimate investors suggest that intraregional investment is only marginally higher compared with unadjusted figures, but roundtripping is likely a larger issue. A study of South Asian firms, particularly in Dubai and Singapore, will likely produce a refined set of constraints that South Asian regulatory arrangements are imposing on actual and potential outward investors. Dubai and Singapore are not only global commercial port hubs but also demonstrate a strong presence of the diaspora and expatriate populations of many nations of South Asia.

The next chapter identifies the determinants of investment entry and the characteristics of firms and investors that succeed and the constraints they face. The econometric estimation relies on the framework for international engagement developed in chapter 2. Chapter 4 first establishes the low levels of, and high variance in, knowledge connectivity, networks, and trust across 56 bilateral pairs of countries and proceeds to estimate the importance of knowledge connectivity, among other factors, for South Asian investors.

Annex 3A: Investment Hubs: The India-Mauritius Connection and How Singapore Fits In

Mauritius plays a role that is much larger than expected in India's foreign investment landscape. Data on inward foreign direct investment (FDI) stocks show Mauritius as the largest source of FDI to India, with US$87 billion at the end of 2017. Similarly, for outward FDI from India, Mauritius shows up prominently (a close third place destination, after Singapore and the Netherlands, as measured by FDI stocks). How could this country, which is 200 times smaller than India in gross domestic product (GDP) (but five times richer in GDP per capita), become India's largest source of capital? What is driving this phenomenon? The foundation for this outcome is the Double Taxation Avoidance Agreement (DTAA), which India signed with Mauritius in 1982, when

Mauritius had just become the first African nation to undergo a change of government in a democratic process. As a leader in the nonaligned movement, India supported democracy in Mauritius with the DTAA, which was set up to boost trade and investment between the two countries.

At the core of the DTAA is a clause that allows investors from Mauritius to invest in the Indian stock market and pay capital gains tax in Mauritius—a "residence-based" tax principle, in which taxation occurs in the jurisdiction where the company is based. The alternative is a "source-based" structure, in which the tax is levied where the money is made. Mauritius does not and has not taxed the capital gains of any investor registered in Mauritius and investing offshore. Mauritius also had a low (5 percent) withholding tax on dividends (now zero) and a low corporate tax rate that could be effectively 3 percent (for exporters; 15 percent otherwise). Given the relatively low tax rates compared with India, the result was that Mauritius became a platform from which to invest in India for many countries, including the United States and the United Kingdom. One Cathedral Square on Jules Koenig Street in the country's capital city of Port Louis became the famous address of investment firms. These addresses were mostly mailboxes, which was initially sufficient to get the stamp of Mauritian residency.

Tracing investments back to their origin, Jaiswal (2017) finds that 97 percent of FDI flows from Mauritius to India during 2004–14 were routed flows—that is, the investor's headquarters is in a country other than Mauritius. Similarly, high shares of routed flows are found for inflows from the hubs in Cyprus, Singapore, and the Netherlands. By contrast, all Japanese investment inflows into India come directly from Japan-based firms (figure 3A.1). The loss of capital gains tax revenue to India was clear. In addition, there were potentially other tax losses from the profit-shifting behavior of multinational firms using transfer pricing. Transfer pricing happens when firms and their subsidiaries overinvoice or underinvoice to shift profits to a low-taxation territory. For example, an Indian firm that set up a subsidiary in Mauritius could export to Europe through the subsidiary. Through appropriate pricing, the profit accrues only to the firm in Mauritius, which pays a corporate tax of 3 percent compared with India's 15 percent. Then the profits could be remitted back to India as inward FDI from Mauritius.

Further, because Mauritius is also one of the largest destinations for Indian outward investment, these Indian outflows could possibly reflect some amount of roundtripping. Roundtripping is the concept of an Indian investor setting up a shell company in Mauritius (Indian OFDI) to invest back in India to avoid paying higher Indian corporate income taxes. The investor also would have been able to receive investment incentives for foreign investors.

During the early postliberalization period, the government of India was cautious about this issue because it needed foreign funds to flow into its stock market in the form of foreign portfolio investment, given that there were restrictions on FDI through the 1990s and early 2000s. Announcements by public officials of greater scrutiny of investment from Mauritius would lead to large drops in the stock market index and rescinding of initial intentions.

FIGURE 3A.1 **Indirectly Routed Inflows from India's Top Foreign Direct Investment Sources**

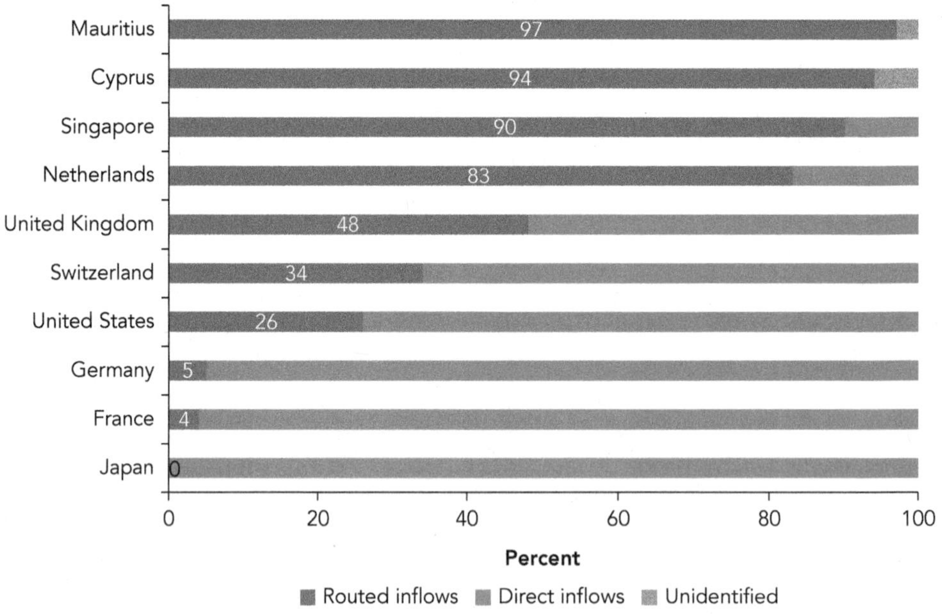

Source: Jaiswal 2017.

As the Indian government liberalized FDI, it also proactively curbed its potentially large loss of revenues. It responded initially by demanding more evidence of Mauritian residency for an investor to get tax breaks. Investors in Mauritius responded by setting up legitimate offices and hiring local staff. The government of India's next approach was to reduce the capital gains tax for all investors, thereby reducing incentives to invest from Mauritius. In 1997, the government of India eliminated the withholding tax on dividends. These policy moves entailed revenue losses, the opposite of the ultimate objective.

The Singapore Solution. In 2005, the Indian government updated the 1994 DTAA with Singapore in the context of the Comprehensive Economic Cooperation Agreement. It offered capital gains tax concessions similar to those in the India-Mauritius DTAA. It allowed residency-based taxation—that is, a Singapore-based firm that had capital gains on investments in the Indian stock market could pay Singapore's capital gains tax (zero). However, this provision applied only to genuine investors from Singapore and included a "Limitation on Benefits" clause intended to prevent roundtripping; it also established a financial floor (expenditures on operations for a 12-month period) for an investor to qualify for the tax exemption. Additionally, the 2005 amendment reduced the withholding tax on certain royalty payments and fees for technical services from

15 percent to 10 percent, so that all royalties paid to a Singapore resident company would be taxed at 10 percent. Importantly, the India-Singapore treaty included a coterminous clause with the India-Mauritius treaty. The capital tax preferences existed only if they existed for Mauritius. Given Singapore's more sophisticated financial sector, more effective dispute resolution system, and greater transparency of tax exemption eligibility, there was a flight of offices from Mauritius. Singapore's investments in India increased dramatically.

The Mauritius authorities requested a similar Limitation on Benefits clause, which India agreed to if the original capital gains clause could be reworded. The Limitation on Benefits for Mauritius included a financial floor of about US$40,000 for a firm to be considered eligible for tax concessions, less than half the US dollar equivalent of the S$200,000 requirement in the treaty with Singapore. This marked a shift from residence-based taxation to a source-based principle of taxation, where now India levied the tax.

The June 2016 amendment to the India-Mauritius DTAA grandfathered in all companies that had invested before April 2017 to be exempt from the capital gains tax. Firms that invested on or after April 1, 2017, and sold before April 2019, were taxable in India at 50 percent of the 15 percent tax rate (that is, 7.5 percent). Shares acquired on or after April 1, 2017, but sold on or after April 1, 2019, were subject to the full tax rate of 15 percent. Given the clause regarding Mauritius in the India-Singapore DTAA, the treaty with Singapore was also amended, shifting taxing rights on capital gains to India.

The overall result has been a shift in the importance of investment relations with Singapore. Although Mauritius remains the largest source of inward FDI using FDI stock data, FDI *inflows* dropped in 2018 to one-third of their 2017 levels. Meanwhile, FDI inflows from Singapore doubled and exceeded those from Mauritius (Chowdhary 2019). Singapore has also become the largest destination for Indian outward FDI. It has become an investment platform for Indian companies to the Association of Southeast Asian Nations economies and plays a key role in India's Act East Policy. However, with the elimination of the transition period for tax exemptions, total foreign investment inflows into India for fiscal year 2018/19, ending in March, dropped for the first time in many years. Beginning April 1, 2019, capital gains are taxed by India at the full rate of 15 percent.

Relevance of capital gains tax issues for FDI. Although the reform to the capital gains tax on selling shares should only affect foreign portfolio investment, impacts on FDI come through two avenues. First is definitional issues of FDI: Global FDI data flows are recorded based on the 10 percent of ownership principle, and because it was possible for institutional investors from Mauritius to buy more than 10 percent of an Indian firm, these technical portfolio investments would be classified as FDI. Thus, activity shifts from Mauritius to Singapore could be recorded as FDI changes. Second, the Indian data did not strictly follow global guidelines on recording FDI. India has included reinvested earnings in the definition of FDI only since 2001. The 10 percent threshold for FDI was adopted in 2017, but it only applies to firms listed on the stock exchange; inflows to other firms are considered FDI.

Notes

1. Because "Southern" is not explicitly defined, this report does not use this term further.

2. The United Nations classifies "Asia-Pacific" as including South Asia and East Asia and the Pacific.

3. An appreciation of a wider range of policies—including trade, investment climate, and macroeconomic policies—is vital, but it is beyond the scope of this study. For trade policy in South Asia, see Kathuria (2018).

4. The implication is that a capital account restriction on foreign investors repatriating capital is an IFDI policy restriction, whereas a capital account restriction on home firms investing abroad is an OFDI policy.

5. According to Foreign Exchange Circular No. 5, May 2015, from the Bangladesh Bank, exporters are allowed to retain 15 percent of earnings in foreign exchange or 60 percent if the exports are goods exports with high domestic content or are services exports.

6. A gradual shift in favor of FDI in India is noted in the Industrial Policy of 1980 and 1982 and the Technology Policy Statement of 1983.

7. The investment freedom subindex starts at the perfect score of 100 and deducts points (5–25 points) for restrictions on the investment arrangements based on national treatment of FDI, transparency of the foreign investment code, restrictions on land ownership, sectoral restrictions, expropriation with fair compensation, foreign exchange controls, capital controls, security issues, and lack of basic infrastructure. The 2021 index covered 184 countries (www.heritage.org/index/investment-freedom).

8. The OECD's restrictiveness index shows a total figure and nine component sectors, taking values between 0 for open and 1 for closed. Other factors, such as implementation issues, are not addressed.

9. See https://dipp.gov.in/sites/default/files/NEIDS_2017_16April2018.pdf. Incentives were previously provided under the North East Industrial Policy, 1997, and the North East Industrial and Investment Promotion Policy, 2007.

10. The straight-line depreciation method spreads the cost evenly over the life of an asset, whereas an accelerated depreciation method allows the deduction of higher expenses in the first years after purchase and lower expenses as the depreciated item ages.

11. The case was brought by White Industries of Australia using the Australia-India BIT of 1999. In a dispute with Coal India on the development of a coal mine in Bihar, White Industries received an award of A\$4.08 million through proceedings of the Indian Arbitration and Conciliation Act in 2002. Coal India commenced "set-aside" proceedings and White Industries commenced "enforcement" proceedings through the Indian courts, and it was this judicial delay that provided the justification for proceedings under the BIT. White Industries was awarded the amount of its original award plus interest. The tribunal found that the "effective means" standard (incorporated in the most-favored-nation provision) was violated (UNCTAD 2010).

12. Reserve Bank of India (https://rbi.org.in; see FAQs on "Overseas Direct Investments"). Note that India also prohibits OFDI to the OECD's Financial Action Task Force list of countries considered noncooperative in anti–money laundering and countering the financing of terrorism, under the "call for action" or blacklist category. In early 2020, the Democratic Republic of Korea and the Islamic Republic of Iran were on this list.

13. The following provide the liberalizing amendments concerning Sri Lanka, Bangladesh, and Pakistan, respectively: RBI/2004-05/176 A.P. (DIR Series) Circular No. 11, September 13, 2004; RBI/2007-2008/215 A.P. (DIR Series) Circular No. 22, December 2007; and DIPP (FC-I Section) Press Note No. 3 (2012 series), d/o IPP File No. 5/10/2011-FC.I, dated August 1, 2012.

14. Foreign Exchange Management (Transfer or issue of security by a person resident outside India) Regulations, 2000. Notification No. FEMA 20 /2000-RB, dated May 3, 2000; "5(1). A person resident outside India (other than a citizen of Bangladesh or Pakistan or Sri Lanka) or an entity outside India, whether incorporated or not (other than an entity in Bangladesh or Pakistan) may purchase shares or convertible debentures of an Indian company under Foreign Direct Investment Scheme, subject to the terms and conditions specified in Schedule 1" (https://m.rbi.org.in/scripts/FAQView.aspx?Id=26).

15. Foreign Exchange Management Regulations, 2000, (i) "Acquisition and transfer of immovable property in India," Notification No. FEMA 21/2000-RB; (ii) "Establishment in India of branch or office or other place of business," Notification No. FEMA 22 /2000-RB, both dated May 3, 2000.

16. See the consolidated FDI policy circular of October 2020 for more details: https://dipp .gov.in/sites/default/files/FDI-PolicyCircular-2020-29October2020_0.pdf. The land border restriction was somewhat broader than the more specific restrictions that existed before April 2020, which mostly excluded Bangladesh and Pakistan. According to the government circular of April 2020 (Press Note no. 3, 2020 Series), this was done to address concerns of "opportunistic takeovers and acquisitions of Indian companies due to the COVID-19 pandemic" (https://dipp.gov.in/sites/default/files/pn3_2020.pdf).

17. Summing up the number of investors by each type of investment overestimates the number of investors because one investor may be involved in more than one type of investment. For example, a firm may invest in both goods production and services operations.

18. For example, two factories built by Maldivian firm X in Nepal would be counted as a single incidence of production investment in Nepal.

19. See Kathuria and Mathur (2020) for details on the isolation of NER, how recent investments and agreements are improving its connectivity, and a take on development priorities for the region.

20. Terminology used in the Indian apparel retail sector to refer to dresses, skirts, blouses, shirts, and pants.

References

Aizenman, Joshua, Y. Jinjaarak, and H. Zheng. 2017. "Chinese Outwards Mercantilism: The Art and Practice of Bundling." NBER Working Paper 21089, National Bureau of Economic Research, Cambridge, MA.

Alcaraz, Jorge, and Johanan Zamilpa. 2017. "Latin American Governments in the Promotion of Outward FDI." *Transnational Corporations* 24 (2): 91–108.

Almunia, Miguel, Pol Antràs, David Lopez-Rodriguez, and Eduardo Morales. 2018. "Venting Out: Exports during a Domestic Slump." NBER Working Paper 25372, National Bureau of Economic Research, Cambridge, MA.

Azzimonti, Marina. 2019. "Does Partisan Conflict Deter FDI Inflows to the US?" *Journal of International Economics* 120 (C): 162–78.

Bimal, Samridhi. 2018. "Outward and Inward Investment Policies in South Asia." World Bank, Washington, DC.

Chaudhary, Binod. 2016. *Making It Big: The Inspiring Story of Nepal's First Billionaire in His Own Words.* India: Penguin Random House.

Casella, Bruno. 2019. "Looking through Conduit FDI in Search of Ultimate Investors—A Probabilistic Approach." *Transnational Corporations Journal* 26 (1): 109–46.

China Council for the Promotion of International Trade. 2010. "Survey on Current Conditions and Intention of Outbound Investment by Chinese Enterprises." April.

Chowdhary, Abdul Muheet. 2019. "Mauritius: India Cracks Down on a Major Tax Evasion Route." Tax Justice Network blog, May 24. https://www.taxjustice.net/2016/05/24/maurit ius-india-curbs-a-major-tax-evasion-route/.

Dhungana, Siromani, and Ravindra Yatawara. 2018. "Nepal's Noodles Go Global: CG Foods' Wai Wai Instant Noodles Steer the Way." Unpublished manuscript, World Bank, Washington, DC.

Dixit, Avinash. 2011. "International Trade, Foreign Direct Investment, and Security." *Annual Review of Economics* 3: 191–213.

ESCAP (United Nations Economic and Social Commission for Asia and the Pacific). 2020. *Outward Foreign Direct Investment and Home Country Sustainable Development.* Studies in Trade, Investment and Innovation No. 93. Bangkok: ESCAP.

Gomez-Mera, Laura, Thomas Kenyon, Yotam Margalit, Jose Guilherme Reis, and Gonzalo Varela. 2015. *New Voices in Investment: A Survey of Investors from Emerging Countries.* Washington, DC: World Bank.

Gravelle, Jane. 2015. "Tax Havens: International Tax Avoidance and Tax Evasion." Congressional Research Service, Washington, DC.

Hallward-Driemeier, Mary. 2003. "Do Bilateral Investment Treaties Attract FDI? Only a Bit… And It Might Bite." Policy Research Working Paper 3121, World Bank, Washington, DC.

Heritage Foundation. 2021. "Investment Freedom." 2021 Index of Economic Freedom. https://www.heritage.org/index/investment-freedom.

Hong, Qing, and Michael Smart. 2010. "In Praise of Tax Havens: International Tax Planning and Foreign Direct Investment." *European Economic Review* 54 (1): 82–95.

IFC (International Finance Corporation), MIGA (Multilateral Investment Guarantee Agency), and World Bank. 2010. *Investing across Borders 2010: Indicators of Foreign Direct Investment Regulation in 87 Economies.* Washington, DC: World Bank.

International Monetary Fund. 2013. *Sixth Edition of the IMF's Balance of Payments and International Investment Position Manual (BPM6).* Washington, DC: IMF.

International Monetary Fund. 2018. *Annual Report on Exchange Arrangements and Exchange Restrictions.* Washington, DC: IMF.

Jaiswal, Suraj. 2017. "Foreign Direct Investment in India and the Role of Tax Havens." Center for Budget and Governance, and Institute for Studies in Industrial Development, New Delhi.

Johnson, Lise, Lisa Sachs, Brooke Guven, and Jesse Coleman. 2018. "Costs and Benefits of Investment Treaties: Practical Considerations for States." Columbia Center on Sustainable Investment, Columbia University, New York.

Kathuria, Sanjay, ed. 2018. *A Glass Half Full: The Promise of Regional Trade in South Asia.* South Asia Development Forum. Washington, DC: World Bank.

Kathuria, Sanjay, and Priya Mathur, eds. 2020. *Playing to Strengths: A Policy Framework for Mainstreaming Northeast India.* International Development in Focus. Washington, DC: World Bank.

Kelegama, Saman. 2014. "Why Does Indian Investment Shy Away from South Asia?" East Asia Forum, September 12. https://www.eastasiaforum.org/2014/09/12/why-is-indian-fdi-shying-away-from-south-asia/.

Khan, H. R. 2012. "Outward Indian FDI—Recent Trends and Emerging Issues." Address at the Bombay Chamber of Commerce & Industry, Mumbai, March 2.

Markovits, Claude. 2008. *Merchants, Traders, Entrepreneurs: Indian Business in the Colonial Era.* London: Palgrave Macmillan.

Mehta, Sanjeev, and Ravindra Yatawara. 2018. "Bhutan Ferro Alloys Limited: Linking into India's Steel Value Chain." Unpublished manuscript, World Bank, Washington, DC.

Nepal Rastra Bank. 2018. "A Survey Report on Foreign Direct Investment in Nepal." Research Department. June.

OECD (Organisation for Economic Co-operation and Development). "FDI Regulatory Restrictiveness Index." https://data.oecd.org/fdi/fdi-restrictiveness.htm.

Panagariya, Arvind. 2008. *India: The Emerging Giant.* New York: Oxford University Press.

Perea, Jose Ramon, and Matthew Stephenson. 2018. "Outward FDI from Developing Countries." In *Foreign Investor Perspectives and Policy Implications, Global Investment Competitiveness Report 2017/2018*, 101–34. Washington, DC: World Bank.

Pohl, Joachim. 2018. "Societal Benefits and Costs of International Investment Agreements: A Critical Review of Aspects and Available Empirical Evidence." OECD Working Papers on International Investment 2018/01, Organization for Economic Co-operation and Development, Paris.

Ranjan, Prabhash, Harsha Vardhana Singh, Kevin James, and Ramandeep Singh. 2018. "India's Model Bilateral Investment Treaty: Is India Too Risk Averse?" Brookings India IMPACT Series No. 082018, Brookings Institution, Washington, DC.

Rao, Chalapati K. S., and Biswajit Dhar. 2018. "India's Recent Inward Foreign Direct Investment: An Assessment." Institute for Studies in Industrial Development, New Delhi.

Reserve Bank of India. 2019. "Master Direction on Direct Investment by Residents in Joint Venture and Wholly Owned Subsidiary Abroad, Updated September 18, 2019." RBI/FED/2015-16/10, FED Master Direction No. 15/2015-16. https://rbidocs.rbi.org.in/rdocs/notification/PDFs/10 MD06102016E550559916C346E0BC93720658286729.PDF.

Sahoo, Pravakar. 2006. "Foreign Direct Investment in South Asia: Policy, Trends, Impact and Determinants." ADB Institute Working Paper 56, Asian Development Bank, Mandaluyong, Philippines.

Sauvant, K. P., P. Economou, K. Gal, S. Lim, and W. P. Wilinski. 2014. "Trends in FDI, Home Country Measures and Competitive Neutrality." In *Yearbook on International Investment Law & Policy 2012–2013*, edited by A. K. Bjorklund, 3–108. Oxford: Oxford University Press.

SEGOB. 2007. *Decreto por el que se ordena la constitución del fideicomiso público considerado entidad paraestatal denominado ProMéxico.* Diario Oficial de la Federación, Mexico City.

Shih, S. 1996. *Me-Too Is Not My Style: Challenge Difficulties, Break through Bottlenecks, Create Values.* Chinese Taipei: Acer Foundation.

Tumbe, Chinmay. 2017. "Transnational Indian Business in the Twentieth Century." *Business History Review* 91 (4): 651–79.

UNCTAD (United Nations Conference on Trade and Development). 2010. "White Industries v. India." Investment Dispute Settlement Navigator, UNCTAD, Geneva. https://investmentpolicy .unctad.org/investment-dispute-settlement/cases/378/white-industries-v-india.

UNCTAD (United Nations Conference on Trade and Development). 2015. *World Investment Report 2015: Reforming International Investment Governance.* Geneva: UNCTAD.

UNCTAD (United Nations Conference on Trade and Development). 2019a. "Investment Policy Hub." https://investmentpolicy.unctad.org/.

UNCTAD (United Nations Conference on Trade and Development). 2019b. *World Investment Report 2019: Special Economic Zones.* Geneva: UNCTAD.

World Bank. 2018. "Bangladesh Policy Note: Enhancing FDI through Investment Policy Reform." World Bank, Washington, DC.

World Bank. 2019. "Bhutan's Business Infrastructure Policy and Industrial Parks." World Bank, Washington, DC.

World Bank. 2020. *Doing Business 2020.* Washington, DC: World Bank.

World Trade Organization. 2016. "Trade Policy Review Report by Maldives." World Trade Organization, Geneva.

Yatawara, Ravindra. 2019. "Navigating a Turbulent Global Economy: What's a Small Economy to Do?" World Bank, Washington, DC.

CHAPTER 4

Knowledge Connectivity in South Asia and Its Impact on Outward Foreign Direct Investment

Introduction

Making decisions about engaging in international trading or undertaking international investments is difficult. Entrepreneurs need information about markets and potential partners in unfamiliar locations to take calculated risks. In developing economies, frictions in the flow of information and knowledge could be even more important obstacles to trade and investment than traditional trade frictions (Atkin and Khandelwal 2019). These knowledge frictions reflect the high costs of search and matching across borders and the high costs of market failures in the provision of channels or technologies with which to alleviate these frictions. Acknowledging the important role of knowledge connectivity, separate from other forms of traditional connectivity, is important because policies that reduce information frictions differ substantially from policies that reduce traditional trade costs.

The research presented in this report builds on the nascent understanding of the role of information for trade, with an application to the foreign investment decision. Although the importance of information barriers has been recognized (Anderson and van Wincoop 2004), international economists are just beginning to quantify the power of information (see Dickstein and Morales [2018] on exporters). For example, it is accepted that information about a prevailing price in a distant market acts as a demand signal for certain products (Allen 2014; Steinwender 2018);[1] and information frictions lead to knowledge spilling over from foreign affiliates of multinational enterprises only to domestic input suppliers (Javorcik 2004). Further, knowledge intermediaries may not exist, even though experiments show that firms benefit from their presence. For example, intermediaries that connect producers to foreign buyers or those that provide productivity-enhancing management practices improve productivity and profits, yet wholesalers take expensive international flights in search of innovative products, even with an established supplier abroad (Atkin, Khandelwal, and Osman 2017; Bloom et al. 2013; Pietrobelli and Staritz 2018).

This analysis relates to information and knowledge flows, which have been studied extensively in international business management. It includes interfirm information sharing; knowledge flows within a multinational enterprise between headquarters, foreign affiliates, and domestic affiliates; and knowledge flows among partners along a value chain (Szulanksi 2003).[2]

Information and knowledge connectivity are also related to trust, and it is this combination that could overcome contracting frictions in weak regulatory environments abroad. The importance of trust in trading and investment relationships has been documented (Arrow 1973; Da Rin, Di Giacomo, and Sembenelli 2018; Guiso, Sapienza, and Zingales 2009). Further, networks that reduce both matching and contracting costs increase bilateral trade flows, as documented for Chinese ethnic networks (Rauch and Trindade 2002).[3] Thus, a lack of information and trust could lead to a dearth of the kinds of networks and relationship building that are needed for cross-border engagement. This concept also has implications for the development of cross-border value chains that rely on relational contracting and trust.

The case study research on regional pioneers provides unique insights into how entrepreneurs make investment decisions and the types of information important for them in forming expectations of profits to be earned in a foreign destination. These insights are used in this chapter to investigate the foreign investment participation decision.

Understanding the foreign direct investment (FDI) entry decision is vital because it is likely to drive much of the variation in investment volumes for most economies. FDI has relatively high fixed entry costs, which makes it less reversible and therefore a more stable form of foreign engagement compared with trade and portfolio investment.[4] Thus, to predict how investment flows will change as a result of policy reform and changes in the investment climate, understanding the firm's decision of whether to invest abroad is important.

This chapter presents the results of an econometric estimation of the outward investor entry decision, keeping in mind the simple framework on investment entry among heterogeneous firms outlined in chapter 2, the nature of South Asian investments, the investment policy landscape discussed in chapter 3, and the importance of information and networks distilled from case studies of investment pioneers. The collection of original data specifically for this report allowed the compilation of information and network-related variables that are not typically available in a standard data set. As in the simple framework for investment entry, information, networks, and trust are analytically separated from traditional trade costs related to trade policy, trade facilitation, and transportation infrastructure. Information and networks are analyzed as primarily affecting the firm's fixed entry costs of investing in a particular destination.

The chapter offers five findings on knowledge connectivity and learning as well as results on other factors important for outward investment by South Asian firms:

- Having knowledge connectivity, in the form of networks abroad, is important for investment entry.

- For services firms, knowledge connectivity may be more important than improving productivity.

- Investors were previous exporters, suggesting that exporting offers informational gains that reduce uncertainty and the fixed cost of investment entry.

- Information flows from related firms in business groups are also likely to induce investment by follower firms.

- Unrelated follower firms may face "sticky knowledge" or frictions in learning from knowledge spillovers from competitor pioneer firms.

Other results show that outward investment pioneers are large, high-productivity firms with surplus investible funds. They tend to invest closer to their home base, as reflected by the negative influence of trade costs on entry. Although the relationship between trade costs and investment is theoretically ambiguous, the results suggest that reduced trade costs would directly increase the probability of investing, and would also indirectly, through increased exporting, increase the probability of investing. This confirms the importance of both physical connectivity and digital connectivity. Investing firms tend to have founders or chief executives with high risk appetites. National policy factors, including a restrictive outward FDI (OFDI) policy and investment climate, are embedded in the fixed effects of the model.

The rest of the chapter is organized as follows: The next section uses the data on information and social capital collected from the South Asian Regional Engagement and Value Chains Survey to explore variation in average knowledge connectivity, networks, and trust across 56 bilateral pairs of countries in South Asia. Having established the existence of a knowledge connectivity problem and sufficient variation across bilateral pairs, the subsequent core section presents the results of an empirical estimation of the determinants of investment entry that incorporates information-related variables. Separate estimations are performed for three types of investments: trade-supporting services (such as representative offices), services operations, and goods production. A dynamic analysis of postentry behavior follows the key results. The penultimate section examines the key channels of awareness for the private sector, with a view to providing an understanding of the most appropriate way to contend with information barriers. The last section concludes.

Knowledge Connectivity, Networks, and Bilateral Trust in South Asia

Knowledge connectivity, networks, and bilateral trust indicators were compiled, on a scale of 1 (low) to 4 (high), based on survey responses from entrepreneurs about how well informed they were about the various South Asian economies, how well connected they were in each of these economies, and how much they trusted individuals from these economies. Firm-destination values are averaged across respondents by home country and destination to create origin-destination measures. They are represented in figure 4.1 by the height of the bars. In addition, "surplus" (green) and "deficit" (orange) bilateral pairs are identified. The surplus pairs indicate that the home country's bilateral knowledge, networks, and trust are significantly above the home country average for the region. The deficits, in contrast, indicate bilateral relationships for which the values are significantly lower than the home country average for all destinations. Individual country scores are reported in table 4A.1 in the annex to this chapter.

LOW AND POLARIZED KNOWLEDGE CONNECTIVITY

South Asia is characterized by low and polarized knowledge connectivity. Figure 4.1 presents a measure of bilateral knowledge connectivity across the 56 country pairs in the region. The measure is based on responses to questions on how well-informed South Asian entrepreneurs were of opportunities in regional economies (ranging from a minimum score of 1 for "not at all" to a score of 4 for "very well-informed"). An average bilateral score of 1.9 (between "not at all" and "not very well" informed) indicates low overall knowledge connectivity. The results are presented from the destination economy perspective in the nine panels of figure 4.1. The same results are presented in figure 1.4 from the home perspective. India was the most well known, whereas Afghanistan, Bhutan, Maldives, and Nepal were least well known.

The polarization of knowledge is better seen by identifying bilateral pairs with substantial knowledge surplus (green) or knowledge deficit (orange) relationships. The bilateral scores were compared with the mean score for the home country relative to the dispersion from the mean (Z-scores). Cutoffs regarding a substantial relative knowledge surplus or deficit were set as greater or less than 1 standard deviation from the mean, respectively. For example, in the Bhutan panel, Sri Lanka shows a sharp lack of knowledge on Bhutan, relative to Sri Lanka's knowledge levels of other countries. Note that even though Afghanistan has a lower absolute score (smaller Afghanistan bar in the Bhutan frame), it is not marked orange (deficit) because Afghanistan's low score for Bhutan is not much different from the low scores reported by Afghan managers for other countries.[5]

There is a geographical bias to information flows. Entrepreneurs are familiar with India and one or two countries near to them, but know little about the rest of the region. Neighbors Bangladesh and Bhutan have a knowledge surplus on opportunities

FIGURE 4.1 **Bilateral Knowledge Connectivity Scores, by Destination: Identification of Knowledge Surplus and Deficit Pairs**

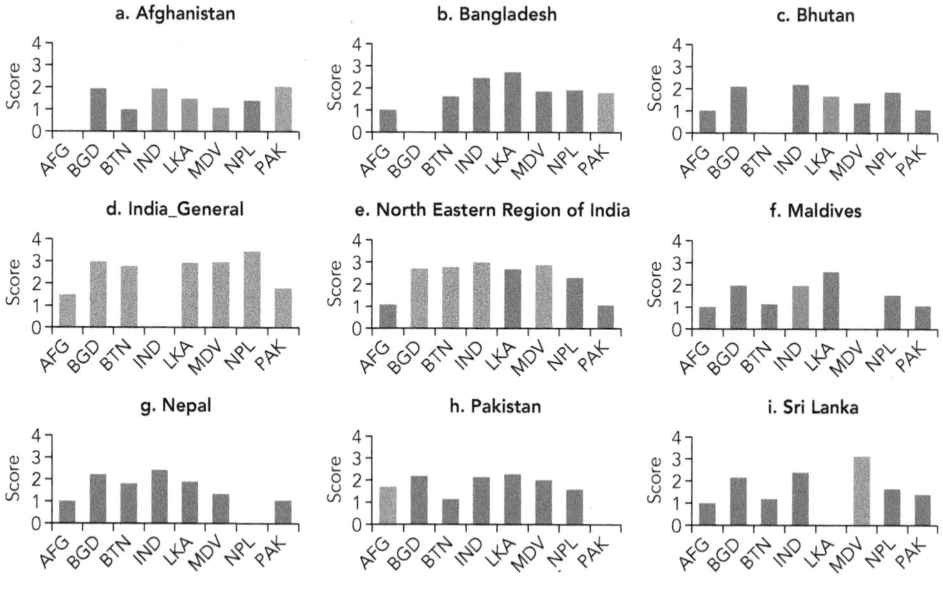

How well informed do you feel about the opportunities abroad?

Source: South Asian Regional Engagement and Value Chains Survey.
Note: Scores range from 1 (low) to 4 (high). Colored bars represent countries whose scores are 1 standard deviation above (green) or below (orange) the home country mean. As an example, the Afghanistan frame presents each of the other South Asian economies' perceptions of how well informed they are about investment opportunities in Afghanistan. Scores are for bilateral pairs of countries with 30 or more observations. AFG = Afghanistan; BGD = Bangladesh; BTN = Bhutan; IND = India_General (India without North Eastern Region); LKA = Sri Lanka; MDV = Maldives; NPL = Nepal; PAK = Pakistan.

in the North Eastern Region of India (NER), Pakistan on Afghanistan opportunities, Afghanistan on Pakistan opportunities, and Maldives on Sri Lanka opportunities. As indicated by the orange bars in figure 4.1, India, Sri Lanka, and Maldives all suffer a relative knowledge deficit about Afghanistan.[6] The India panel makes the point that countries know significantly more about India than other countries, as reflected by the knowledge-surplus green bars. This result reflects India's large and central position in South Asia. In contrast, most Indians have balanced knowledge about their neighbors, which could reflect India's shared borders with, or proximity to, most countries.[7] For a graphical representation of all the Z-scores, see figure 4A.1 in the annex to this chapter.

Lack of knowledge of opportunities in the region extends to both markets and firms. Over the past 20 years, many firms in South Asia have attained global competitiveness. However, their focus on advanced economy markets and East Asian suppliers may be contributing to low intraregional knowledge. Recently maturing South Asian firms are also not likely to have wide visibility in the region, owing to status quo bias and even reputational bias of low quality that may persist from decades earlier. Business culture could also play a part in limiting information flows, for example, if the South Asian business community tended to be relatively more modest during times of success and more secretive during downturns. Similarly, the large presence of family firms and unlisted firms, for which the public release of information is not required, could lead to a cautious attitude toward information sharing. Also, the presence of large, diversified business groups may create incentives to keep information flows within the affiliates.

SMALL BILATERAL NETWORKS AND FEW RELATIONSHIPS

Figure 4.2 reports the results of survey questions that asked whether managers felt sufficiently well connected in each of the countries to readily pursue emerging business opportunities. The results were similar to those relating to knowledge connectivity, with an average score of 1.85 (between "not at all" and "not very well" connected).

FIGURE 4.2 Bilateral Network Connection Scores, by Destination

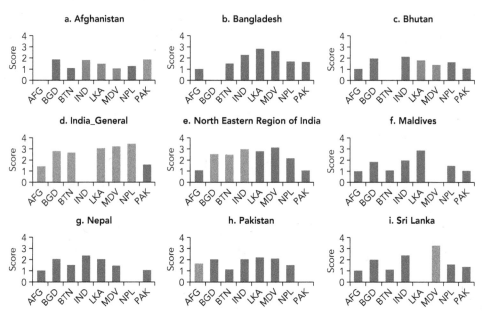

How well informed do you feel with social and business network contacts to pursue transactions abroad?

Source: South Asian Regional Engagement and Value Chains Survey.
Note: Scores range from 1 (low) to 4 (high). Colored bars represent countries whose score is 1 standard deviation above (green) or below (orange) the home country mean. As an example, the Afghanistan frame presents each of the other South Asian economies' perceptions of how well connected it is in Afghanistan. Scores are for bilateral pairs of countries with 30 or more observations. AFG = Afghanistan; BGD = Bangladesh; BTN = Bhutan; IND = India_General (India without North Eastern Region); LKA = Sri Lanka; MDV = Maldives; NPL = Nepal; PAK = Pakistan.

Based on the height of the bars, countries felt most connected to India. Again, most countries had a network surplus with India. India's largest network surplus was with its own NER. South Asian entrepreneurs felt least networked in Afghanistan, Pakistan, Bhutan, and Nepal. From the home country perspective, entrepreneurs from Afghanistan and Pakistan felt least connected to the region (table 4A.1). Interestingly, although Pakistan had a knowledge surplus with India (figure 4.1), it did not feel especially networked.

LACK OF BILATERAL TRUST

When entrepreneurs were asked how much trust they have in people from various South Asian countries on a scale of 1 to 4 (highest), the average bilateral score was 2.58 (between having "not that much" and "some" trust). The bilateral trust scores show the variation across pairs. Despite the earlier discussion on potential mistrust based on asymmetric size, the survey responses indicate that India is the most trusted (highest average score by destination), followed closely by Sri Lanka, India's NER, and Bangladesh. Meanwhile, Bhutan is the most trusting country (highest score by home), followed by India, Sri Lanka, and Bangladesh (table 4A.1).

Applying the previous methodology, figure 4.3 presents the bilateral trust scores, along with trust surplus (green) and trust deficit (orange) relationships. These scores are somewhat similar to those for knowledge connectivity, but also show the trust surplus of Bangladesh with Nepal and Sri Lanka, and Pakistan's trust surplus with Sri Lanka. In figure 4.3, two of the six trust deficit relationships—Bhutan's score for Bangladesh and Sri Lanka's score for Pakistan—are not likely to be a concern because they are driven by very close scores for countries (low standard deviation); thus, a trust deficit is signaled even though the absolute trust score is above the sample mean for the destination.

Trust is important for business because it lowers transaction costs by reducing search costs for trustworthy partners and the need for intensive contracting. "Personalized" trust is based on repeated interactions that reveal information about one another to the concerned parties. It is the basis for the relational contracting (informal self-enforcing agreements) that dominates many global value chain (GVC) relationships. By contrast, "generalized" trust reflects a stereotypical view of others that matters before personal interactions unfold. In the context of FDI, entrepreneurs' trust of a foreign country's institutions also matters.

The measure of trust in this report is closer to an indicator of "generalized trust." The trust question used was exactly the same that was specified in the European Commission's version of the World Values Survey, which asked the question for European Union members.[8] The South Asian score, though low, is not much lower than the score of 2.84 reported by Europeans (EU-15) (Guiso, Sapienza, and Zingales 2009). (However, the EU-15 score was recorded for a random sample of the general public, as opposed to members of the business community, as in South Asia.) Another way to interpret these similar scores could be to say that bilateral mistrust among the South Asian private sector business community is not as low as is generally believed.

FIGURE 4.3 Bilateral Trust Scores, by Destination

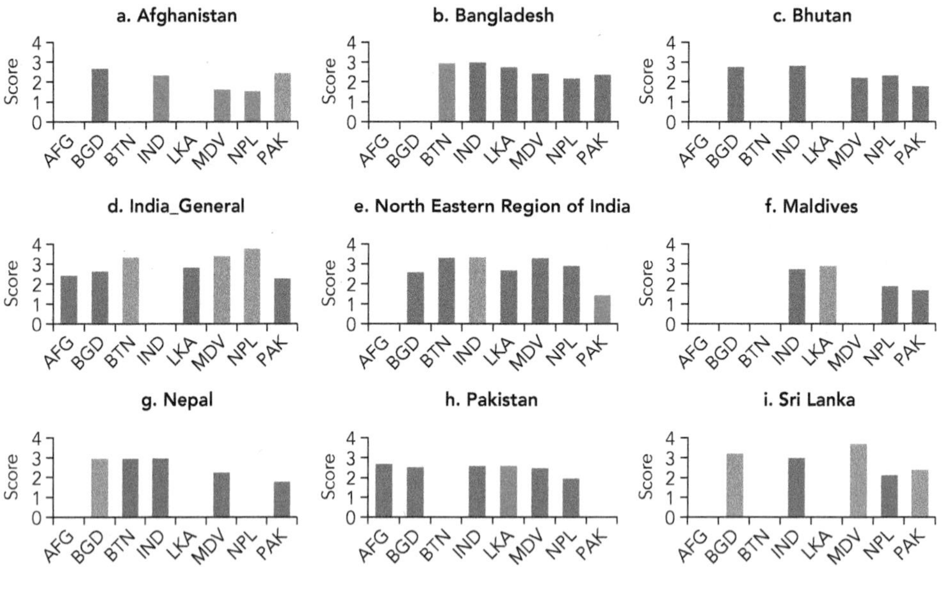

Source: South Asian Regional Engagement and Value Chains Survey.
Note: Scores range from 1 (low) to 4 (high). Colored bars represent countries whose scores are 1 standard deviation above (green) or below (orange) the home country mean. As an example, the Afghanistan frame presents each of the other South Asian economies' bilateral trust in citizens from Afghanistan. Scores are for bilateral pairs of countries with 30 or more observations. AFG = Afghanistan; BGD = Bangladesh; BTN = Bhutan; IND = India_General (India without North Eastern Region); LKA = Sri Lanka; MDV = Maldives; NPL = Nepal; PAK = Pakistan.

ASSOCIATION BETWEEN BILATERAL TRUST AND KNOWLEDGE CONNECTIVITY

Plotting average bilateral knowledge connectivity against bilateral trust, figure 4.4 points to a positive correlation, perhaps suggesting that the bilateral trust deficits are driven by a lack of knowledge connectivity. Thus, activities that enhance knowledge connectivity are likely to build trust and create the relationships needed for cross-border engagement. In turn, bilateral trust also increases the perceived quality of information received, making entrepreneurs feel more well informed about opportunities in an economy.

Key Results on Investor Decision-Making in South Asia

Given the suggestive evidence that knowledge connectivity is a problem in South Asia, and that bilateral pairs exhibit noticeable variation, this section estimates an empirical model of the determinants of a firm's investment decision abroad using indicators

FIGURE 4.4 **The Knowledge-Trust Nexus: To Know Me Is to Trust Me?**

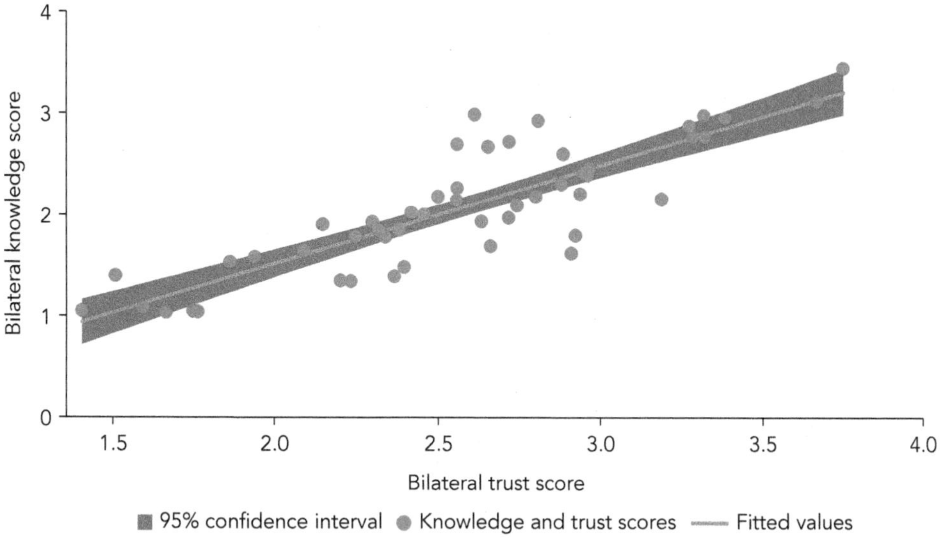

Source: World Bank calculations based on data from the South Asian Regional Engagement and Value Chains Survey.
Note: Scores range from 1 (low) to 4 (high). Each dot represents the average for a bilateral pair of countries. Scores are for bilateral pairs of countries with 30 or more observations.

of information and learning. Using data collected specifically for this exercise from 1,274 South Asian firms, the empirical strategy is guided by the framework outlined in chapter 2. Differences across firms in bilateral knowledge are modeled as variations in the bilateral entry costs to a particular market destination. South Asian investors' outward investing decisions for each destination are explored separately by the type of investment: goods production (agriculture and manufacturing), services operations, and trade-supporting investments. Details of the data, sampling strategy, and empirical strategy are in provided in appendix B (see box 4.1 for a brief description of the esti-mated equation).

Investigating the determinants of entry for goods production investments, services operations investments, and trade-supporting investments, the key results are listed in tables B.6 through B.13 in appendix B. The data that were collected capture rare out-ward investors, family firms, large and medium firms, and firms from all countries in the region. The downside of the survey data is the limited sample size in each country and the limited detail obtained (in some quantitative respects such as expenditures and revenue) in what is a voluntary survey, particularly from firms that typically do not share data. Thus, the estimation results are not meant to deliver precise estimates along the lines of recent academic research on US and EU multinationals for which detailed firm data were available. The results point to interesting relationships and relative

---

BOX 4.1 Estimated Equation for the Determinants of Outward Investment

To assess the determinants of firms' decisions to invest abroad, the analysis considers the following empirical specification:

$$Y_{isd} = \alpha + \beta_1 productivity_i + \beta_2 type_i + \beta_3 finance_i + \beta_4 network_{id} +$$
$$\beta_5 export_{id} + \beta_6 enti + \gamma Z_{sd} + \lambda_s + \lambda_d + \varepsilon_{isd},$$ (B4.1.1)

in which Y_{isd} is an outcome of interest, such as the binary decision of firm i from source country s to invest in goods production, services operations, and trade-supporting services in destination country d. For each investment, $productivity_i$ is firm productivity; $type_i$ is firm type, including state-owned enterprise, foreign owned, and family owned; $finance_i$ is firm source of financing, including internal funds, business group, home and host commercial banks, and international banks; $network_{id}$ is the firm's network in country d; $export_{id}$ is the firm's export experience in country d; ent_i is a characteristic (i.e., risk appetite) of the entrepreneur; Z_{sd} is a vector of source-destination country characteristics, such as distance, contiguity, and common language; λ_s and λ_d are vectors of source and destination country dummies to control for all country-specific factors; and ε_{isd} is the error term, which is clustered at the industry level to account for potential correlations in the error term across firms in the same industry.

---

magnitudes, and they capture factors that are not typically quantified, yet are important for investment entry.

The estimation results are presented first with standard variables, and information-related indicators are subsequently included. National policy (which chapter 3 has shown to be important) and other individual country characteristics are captured in the country fixed effects.

INVESTORS ARE NEIGHBORS: SEEKING HIGH-CONNECTIVITY LOCATIONS

The "standard" specification starts with table B.6 in appendix B, which does not include data on being well informed or on knowledge. The results show that trade costs matter, as reflected in the negative and statistically significant impact of distance on investment and the positive impact of contiguity. The impact of distance on services operations and trade-supporting investments, as reflected in the respective coefficients, is more than double that on goods production investments. This outcome is consistent with studies that find that cross-border services delivery requires greater communications with customers and a greater sensitivity to cultural aspects, and involves more complex information (Oldenski 2012). Thus, multinational enterprises from neighboring economies are more likely to be successful in cross-border investments, especially in services operations and trade-supporting investments, than in distant nations.

Theoretically, the impact of trade costs on FDI is ambiguous and depends on the nature of the investment. For example, high tariffs may induce foreign investors to produce near their consumers to circumvent trade restrictions—a horizontal invest-ment, "tariff-jumping FDI," or "quid pro quo FDI" (Bhagwati 1987). However, high trade costs may deter firms that engage in vertical investments (in which they produce inputs abroad for assembly activities at home and anticipate frequent border crossings). Similarly, they would reduce trade-supporting FDI and distribution FDI (as reflected in chapter 2).

This result validates the importance of the trade and transportation infrastructure and trade-facilitation initiatives that national governments and partners have sup-ported to reduce trade costs. These investments increase trade but also support FDI.

The case study evidence also validates the importance of proximity for entry strate-gies. Nepal's CG Foods first invested in the nearby NER; Bangladesh's Rahimafrooz first set up a distribution office in nearby Kolkata, West Bengal; and Sri Lankans began by investing in southern India (Timex's first retail store was in Bengaluru and Brandix's apparel park is in Visakhapatnam, Andhra Pradesh).

PIONEERING INVESTORS ARE HIGH-PRODUCTIVITY FIRMS WITH INVESTIBLE SURPLUS FUNDS

High-productivity, large firms are the ones that invest abroad (table B.6 in appendix B), consistent with the framework given in chapter 2. Large, productive firms have production volumes that provide them with sufficient funds to incur the sunk costs of entry. This construct applies to all types of investments. The higher the sunk costs, the higher the level of firm productivity needed to cover the sunk costs (thereby restricting the activity to fewer firms). Increases in productivity increase the likelihood of investing for all goods production, services operations, and trade-supporting invest-ments. As expected, a given increase in productivity will have a larger impact on trade-supporting investments because they have the lowest sunk costs. Services operations investments seem to have smaller sunk costs compared with goods production, judging by the larger relative magnitude of the impact of productivity on services investments.

Because the data set includes agriculture, manufacturing, and services firms, there is no standard measurement of productivity that applies to all firms. Firm productivity is measured by the firm's position in its industry productivity distribution in the home country. Thus, a firm with the highest productivity would be placed in the 99th percen-tile of the industry productivity distribution. Firm size was similarly measured, that is, relative to the size of other firms in its industry.

Higher-productivity firms participate in all three forms of investment. The median investor is in the 75th percentile of the productivity distribution compared with the median noninvestor, who is at the 50th percentile. Replacing the productivity variable with a turnover measure provides similar results, in that larger firms (those with higher turnover) tend to be the ones that invest. This outcome is to be expected, given the cor-relation of 0.9 between turnover and productivity (table B.5 in appendix B). Accordingly, the turnover results are not reported.

Financing matters, and the results indicate that internal funds are crucial for all types of investments (table B.6 in appendix B). Internal funds are much more important for trade-supporting and services operations investments. Intraconglomerate financing appears to matter for goods production and trade-supporting investments. Therefore, smaller firms with insufficient internal funds that do not belong to a conglomerate will be constrained. Home commercial banks are important for goods production investments.

NETWORKED FIRMS ARE MORE LIKELY TO INVEST, MAKING INVESTING MORE INCLUSIVE

The regional pioneers have information networks, and these networks make investing abroad more inclusive. Firms with founders or chief executive officers with ethnic or visible social networks abroad tend to have an increased likelihood of investing (table B.7 in appendix B). Firm-level indicators of knowledge connectivity, networks, and bilateral trust could not be used in the regressions, given that they represented knowledge, relationships, and trust today that could be outcomes of investments as opposed to the determinant of investments. Instead, networks were measured by the ethnic or visible social network (for example, marriage) of the founder or chief executive officer. Networks allow for variation in sunk entry costs across firms. The ethnic network variable is statistically significant for all types of investment, but stronger and larger in magnitude for services operations and trade-supporting investments, which is consistent with other studies that find that cultural factors are more important in services industries. The network provides the investor with extra information and an uncertainty-reducing property that drives down the entry costs for the networked investor compared with other investors or potential investors.

For services investments, networks appear to have a larger effect on investment decisions than does productivity. The effect of the ethnic network exceeds the effect of moving up eight rungs in the productivity distribution.[9] However, for the same increase in productivity, this same relationship does not hold for goods production and trade-supporting investments. This is an important result, because when entrepreneurs are asked to rank important factors in decision-making, they always tend to rank networks low. As with distance, this effect of ethnic networks may signal the importance of cultural sensitivity in delivering many types of services, such as hospitality, retail, education, and medical services. This result is in line with research that finds that cultural distance is more relevant for mergers and acquisitions in services (Barattieri, Borchert, and Mattoo 2016).

Networks make the investing activity more inclusive—smaller, lower-productivity firms that are networked may also invest abroad, thereby widening the pool of potential investors. The higher the sunk entry costs of an activity, the higher the required level of firm productivity to be a potential investor, implying that fewer firms qualify to be in the pool. Thus, networked firms with medium productivity may also invest in regional markets and, to enter, do not have to be as large and productive as firms without networks.

The data show that, on average, networked investors are 3 percentage points lower on the productivity distribution.

An illustrative scenario is presented in figure 4.5. Starting from the benchmark scenario without networks set up in chapter 2, figure 2.2, a medium-productivity firm exports and a high-productivity firm serves foreign markets by investing abroad (marked by stars in figure 2.2). Networks reduce the fixed entry costs of exporting and investing. If only the medium-productivity firm has networks abroad, the new equilibrium results in both firms investing abroad, and the profits for the medium-productivity firm are marked by an X. Allowing for networks, the illustration highlights some important implications. First, it is possible to have a large, high-productivity (unnetworked) firm and a networked medium-productivity firm both entering through FDI. Second, a similar medium-productivity firm without networks would remain an exporter and receive lower profits compared with the networked investor or a networked exporter. Third, larger networks lead to greater multinational activity through a lower FDI survival productivity cutoff, $\phi^*_{FDI\_Net}$ (due to lower fixed entry costs). Fourth, larger networks lead to greater profit. Fifth, larger neworks also encourage more exporting as the respective export survival productivity cutoffs drop (not illustrated in figure 4.5).

FIGURE 4.5 Networks Reduce the Fixed Entry Costs of Investing and Lead to More Investors with Greater Variability in Productivity

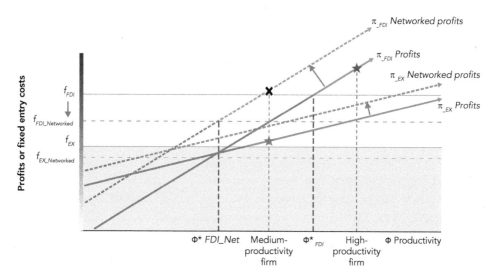

Source: World Bank. This is a highly stylized version of the Helpman, Melitz, and Yeaple (2004) framework.
Note: The colored lines represent positive profits above respective fixed entry costs and identify the range of firms, by productivity, that could engage in exporting or investing. The survival productivity cutoffs ϕ^* are obtained at the points at the x-axis where the profit line changes color from gray. See figure 2.2 in chapter 2 for more details. Without networks, the medium-productivity firm exports and the high-productivity firm serves foreign markets by investing (marked by stars). Networks reduce the fixed entry costs of exporting and investing. If only the medium-productivity firm has networks abroad, the new equilibrium shows both firms investing abroad, with profits for the medium-productivity firm marked by an **X**. Networks reduce fixed entry costs (to $f_{FDI\_Networked}$), shifting the profit function to the left, resulting in a lower survival productivity cutoff $\phi^*_{FDI\_Net}$. The pool of potential investors expands relative to the benchmark scenario of no networks.

South Asians have large potential networks abroad because they have the largest regional diaspora, at 38.6 million migrants, accounting for 15 percent of the world's migrants. India is the global leader, with 16.7 million migrants, and Bangladesh and Pakistan also make the top 10 (with 7.5 million and 6 million, respectively). These numbers do not include the population movements brought about by the partition in 1947 and the founding of Bangladesh in 1971. Singapore and the United Arab Emirates are large commercial hubs, but also the location of large South Asian diaspora communities. The main sources of Indian migrant traders are the states of Gujarat and Tamil Nadu, followed by Sind, the Punjab region, and Kerala.

Migrant networks may stimulate investment through information flows, access to other relevant contacts abroad, trust-inducing relationships that reduce international transaction costs, and better contract enforcement. Research on migrants and refugees finds a positive impact on outward FDI from the United States to the countries of origin (Javorcik, Ozdenc, and Spatareanu 2011), and that the effect is mainly driven by a reduction in information frictions, not by better contract enforcement or similarity in tastes (Burchardi, Chaney, and Hassan 2018). Most research on migrants and FDI analyzes the role of migrants' investing in their homeland, as opposed to investment from the homeland, reflecting perhaps larger flows toward the country of origin. Investment by nonresident Indians and the diaspora, for example, has been important for the growth of the information and communication technology industry in India.

REGIONAL PIONEERS TEND TO BE HIGH-PRODUCTIVITY FIRMS WITH ETHNIC NETWORKS

The regional pioneers tend to be high-productivity, networked firms with internal funds for investment. Almost all the non-Indian pioneers among the regional pioneers interviewed for the case studies had ethnic networks in India. They all very much identify with their current nationality, but ethnic, social, marriage, and education ties to India seemed to have a positive effect. The grandparents of the pioneers were migrants from India in many cases. Nepal's Chaudhary family's lineage is from Rajasthan; the Sri Lankan apparel pioneers Amalean, Omar, and Sattar have their ancestral origins in Gujarat; and Bangladesh's Rahim family had roots in Kolkata. The late Dasho Ugen Dorji, founder of the Tashi Group, was a regular at the Royal Calcutta Golf Club, which was a vibrant source of business contacts. His son, Dasho Topgyal Dorji, who leads Bhutan's largest ferrosilicon firm, obtained his secondary education in India.

When accounting for other factors, the importance of networks remains for services investments and trade-supporting investments. However, the effect on goods production investment becomes statistically insignificant (table B.7 in appendix B). Focusing on goods production investment, the impact of ethnic networks may be reestablished by using bilateral data on trust and knowledge (how well informed the respondents are). To compensate for the potential endogeneity associated with using firm-level bilateral trust and knowledge connectivity data, country average data are used and interacted with the ethnic networks variable. The results indicate that, for goods production investments (table B.9 in appendix B) and trade-supporting investments (table B.10), ethnic networks have a larger effect in countries with low bilateral trust. The importance of networks is greater in low-knowledge environments for trade-supporting investments (table B.11). For all types of investments, bilateral trust and knowledge connectivity were statistically important, with the effect being largest for trade-supporting investments (tables B.10 and B.11).

As discussed earlier in this chapter, "personalized" trust is the basis for the relational contracting that is typically found within GVCs. The implications of this type of trust suggest a nonlinear relationship between trust and OFDI. At low levels of trust, as trust increases, the likelihood of investment entry increases. However, when trust in foreign partners is very high, firms may opt for nonequity (asset-light) engagement strategies.

EXPORTERS BECOME INVESTORS THROUGH DYNAMIC LEARNING EFFECTS

Having a history of exporting increases the likelihood of all types of investment (table B.8 in appendix B). The magnitudes of the effects are the largest of any of the determinants modeled. The magnitude of the export history effect is highest for trade-supporting investments, which is intuitive, given that the investment itself is geared toward further export development. This result remains strong for all types of investments under different models and estimation techniques.

This result is consistent with a dynamic setting in which the existence of uncertainty about foreign market profitability can only be resolved by actively entering the market. A firm would maximize two-period profits by entering the foreign market through a low-fixed-entry-cost mode of entry (exporting) in the first period to ascertain information about the market. Given that the information resolves uncertainty, the firm would undertake FDI, remain in exporting, or exit based on the profits calculated for the second period after the information uncertainty had been resolved. A formal extension of the framework in chapter 2 involves added complexity and a loss of tractability such that most researchers have opted for simpler frameworks with which to discuss firm dynamics with demand-side uncertainty (Albornoz et al. 2012; Conconi, Sapir, and Zanardi 2016). Nevertheless, the framework still provides useful intuition.

Under uncertainty and capital scarcity, firms may enter foreign markets through modes with low sunk entry costs and, through the resulting experiential learning, will be inclined to engage in riskier, higher-capital activities. The uncertainty discussed is about the demand side of foreign markets, but for emerging market multinationals, it may also reflect their more recent entry into the business of cross-border ownership and management. The experience of the initial low-entry-cost engagement (say, of exporting) reduces the sunk entry cost associated with the other risky activities in the next period because the firm has gained greater insider market knowledge and connectivity with host-based firms and the host government. Such connections also make investing more inclusive because, again, it is not only the largest firms that can afford to incur sunk entry costs of investment. Smaller firms with experience in exporting would also be able to do so, given that the entry costs of investment facing them are lower.

Consider the case illustrated in figure 4.6 of how exporters may eventually serve the foreign market through investment in plants abroad. The fixed entry costs of investing are higher than the fixed entry costs of exporting: $f_{EX} < f_{FDI}$. After one period of exporting, the fixed entry cost of investing drops to f_{FDI_EX}. Assume that there are common entry costs involved in exporting and investing, such as the costs of developing a marketing strategy, f_{MS}. Thus, at a minimum, an exporter's sunk entry cost of investing becomes $f_{FDI} - f_{MS} = f_{FDI\_EX}$, which is less than the sunk entry cost that another potential investor with no experience in the market would face. The ordering of fixed entry costs $f_{EX} < f_{FDI\_EX} < f_{FDI}$ is supported by research on the internationalization process of firms, such as that by Conconi, Sapir, and Zanardi (2016), who find that exporting precedes investment and attest to the complementarity of

FIGURE 4.6 Exporters Become Investors

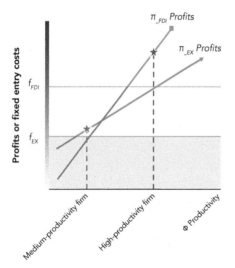

a. Period 1: The medium-productivity firm only exports in the first period because it cannot cover the high fixed costs of investing

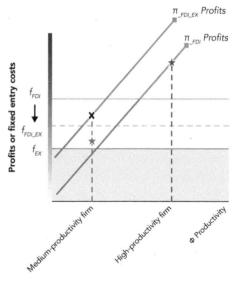

b. Period 2: The experience of exporting last period reduces the medium-productivity firm's fixed entry costs of investing. It is now profitable to incur the (now lower) entry costs of investing

Source: World Bank. This is a highly stylized version of the Helpman, Melitz, and Yeaple (2004) framework.
Note: The colored lines represent positive profits above respective fixed entry costs and identify the range of firms, by productivity, that could engage in exporting or investing. See figure 2.2 in chapter 2 for more details. Under a benchmark equilibrium scenario represented as "Period 1," the medium-productivity firm exports and the high-productivity firm serves foreign markets by investing (marked by stars). The survival productivity cutoff for investment, ϕ^*_{FDI} (not shown) is obtained at the point at the x-axis where the profit line turns green. Period 2 considers a medium-productivity firm with previous export experience compared with a high-productivity firm that has not previously participated in serving foreign markets. The case for the high-productivity firm is the same as in Period 1. Export experience reduces the fixed entry costs of investing for the medium-productivity firm (to f_{FDI_EX}), which shifts the profit function to the left and results in a lower survival productivity cutoff $\phi^*_{FDI\_EX}$ (not shown to avoid clutter). In the new equilibrium, both firms are investing abroad, and the profits for the medium-productivity firm are marked by an **X**. The pool of potential investors expands relative to the benchmark scenario of no exporting experience.

trade and investment. The information value of entry is confirmed by a study of Japanese multinationals, whose sales forecasts tend to suggest the presence of imperfect information and the benefits of entry—the forecast errors decline as experience in the destination market increases (Chen et al. 2020).

As seen in figure 4.6, the medium-productivity firm that becomes an exporter incurring the requisite fixed entry cost of exporting, f_{EX}, in period 1 faces lower sunk entry costs of investment in period 2, f_{FDI_EX}, which is much lower than what a potential investor who had no previous market knowledge would have to pay, f_{FDI}.[10] As a result, the medium-productivity firm would become an investor in period 2. Thus, investors include high-productivity firms and medium-productivity firms with exporter experience. New firms with similar or higher productivity, but below the survival productivity cutoff ϕ^*_{FDI} (not shown in the figure), would export.

GRADUALIST APPROACH TO INVESTING UNDER UNCERTAINTY THROUGH LEARNING

> ### Start small, learn big.
>
> —Ajay Amalean, managing director of MAS Brands, on one of the key principles that guided him when entering the Indian market

Export experience leading to investment is consistent with the international business literature on the dynamics of firm internationalization and has wider implications. The Uppsala model explains internationalization as a gradual process of incremental engagement, which starts with some ad hoc exporting by firms (Johanson and Vahlne 1977, 2009). The uncertainty of foreign markets leads firms to commit only a small amount of capital to ventures abroad initially, and investment flows slowly increase through a gradual process of learning and network development. Similarly, Freund and Pierola (2010) document small export orders that reflect a trial-and-error approach to exporting.

This intuition applies to the experience of firms that want to enter using any strategy that has low entry costs for the purposes of learning. The quote from the managing director of MAS Brands (Sri Lanka) on his guiding principles when entering a market, "start small, learn big," encapsulates the concept. He continued that it was okay to lose money ("but not too much!"), perhaps an indication of the value of the information acquisition that accompanies initial entry. MAS Brands started with sales of its Amanté brand of high-quality brassieres in department stores, and it was only after eight years in the Indian market that it opened its own retail shops in India, moving from being a brand owner to a brand retailer.

Similarly, Sri Lankan hoteliers initially entered Maldives through management contracts. Only after years of working under this arrangement did they pursue outward equity investment by leasing land and building their own hotels. The management contract strategy allowed them not only to learn about the market but also to learn how to navigate the complex land leasing laws of the time. In attempts to capture some of the market for remittances transactions from migrant workers, some commercial banks initially developed partnerships with banks in the Middle East, then sent two or three personnel to handle the foreign remittances business in a bank-within-a bank business model, and finally opened their own bank branches abroad.

Additionally, Soorty Enterprises of Pakistan initially opened a marketing office to promote its denim cloth to local manufacturers in Bangladesh. As the business developed, a larger distribution office was set up. The company has since set up an apparel manufacturing plant in the Comilla Export Processing Zone. The opening of a trade-supporting office with low fixed entry costs, $f_{FDI\_TRAD\_SUPP}$, compared with the entry costs of setting up a factory f_{FDI_PROD} (with $f_{FDI\_TRAD\_SUPP} < f_{FDI\_PROD}$), provided a period of information acquisition that reduced uncertainty and led to a production investment in which the fixed entry costs, $f_{FDI\_PROD\_TRAD\_SUPP}$, were lower than for a potential investor that had no previous engagement with the Bangladesh economy ($f_{FDI\_PROD\_TRAD\_SUPP} < f_{FDI\_PROD}$).

In the survey sample, trade-supporting investments are the most common form of investment. They also lead to the largest amount of similar investments. The time span of the collected data on investment is not sufficiently large to estimate the impact of an initial investment of the trade-supporting type on investment in services operations and goods production.

The framework on uncertainty and gradualism would also suggest that firms are initially more likely to enter through a joint venture than through a wholly owned subsidiary, and more likely to enter through a greenfield investment than to purchase an existing firm in the host country. Joint ventures offer the advantage of requiring a smaller initial capital investment compared with going it alone, and the ability to reduce endogenous uncertainty through the use of the knowledge, networks, and influence of the usually host-based partner company. Greenfield investments may also be preferred because they allow sequential investment based on information acquisition and profit realization, whereas purchasing a locally based firm of optimal size involves the full disbursement of money at the time the transaction is settled.

Finally, a common strategy used by multinational enterprises to deal with uncertainty is imitation. Whenever there is uncertainty inherent in the potential destination country, companies tend to follow the choices of other home-country firms (Henisz and Delios 2001) and imitate their market entry strategies (Li and Yao 2010). These strategies are related to notions of learning from pioneer behavior.

INVESTORS ARE FOLLOWERS OF PIONEERS IN THEIR CONGLOMERATES OR BUSINESS GROUPS

In addition to learning from their own experience, firms can learn from others that have invested, given that learning from pioneer firms may reduce the entry costs of follower firms in the industry. Pioneering activities thus provide an information diffusion effect from a pioneer firm to the home industry. Will regional pioneers automatically create a cascade or herd effect with a diffusion of regional transactions? Will these pioneers be the spark that ignites regional engagement? The understanding of the pioneer-diffusion framework here is informed by research on export discoveries (Hausmann and Rodrik 2003), export pioneers in Latin America (Sabel et al. 2012), Chinese export pioneers (Wei, Wei, and Xu 2017), and export catalysts (Rhee and Belot 1990).

The pioneer-diffusion framework is built on an information externality from a single pioneering firm that has entered foreign markets to the rest of the industry at home. Thus, the action of the first investor in a new market has a public good nature to it because it may reduce the fixed costs of entry into the same market for follower firms. The implication is that there could be a suboptimal number of pioneers, and governments should support the development of pioneers. This information externality applies to any entry mode and its impact on the likelihood of other home producers pursuing a similar mode of entry into the same market.

Some suggestive evidence of the pioneer-follower herd effect is the emergence of OFDI by pioneer-related firms (in the same conglomerate or business group) in different sectors or in different segments of the value chain. For example, OFDI in hotels has led to investments in travel agencies and logistics firms within the business group. Dabur India's investment in fruit juice manufacturing in Nepal is maintained along with an investment in a nursery for plants with high health benefits, which it uses in its division for herbal medicinal products in India. A Sri Lankan furniture retail investment in India has expanded to include a tourism business. Tashi Group's entry into processed food distribution in India in the 1980s facilitated the distribution of ferrosilicon a decade later. These examples suggest that pioneer firms are willing to share contacts, referrals, networks, and knowledge about markets with the other member firms within their own groups. This information flow is typically smooth and involves minimal frictions.

CONGLOMERATES AS KNOWLEDGE PROVIDERS

The introduction of a conglomerate dummy in the econometric exercises is important for services operations and goods production investments, which have greater capital requirements than trade-supporting investments (table B.12 in appendix B). The conglomerate's role as a financier was borne out in the responses to the South Asian Regional Engagement and Value Chains Survey, in which the conglomerate's financing role was considered its most important. The second most important role, according to managers, is as a source of information. The other relevant roles are listed in figure 4.7. This finding suggests that the business group is not only valuable as an internal capital market but also as an organizational structure that allows the sharing of cross-border knowledge within the group.

Thus, these results support and add to the business group literature (Colpan and Hikino 2010; Khanna and Yafeh 2007) that argues that the development of business groups is a response to "institutional voids" or market failures or frictions, particularly

FIGURE 4.7 **The Role of Conglomerates and Business Groups in South Asia**

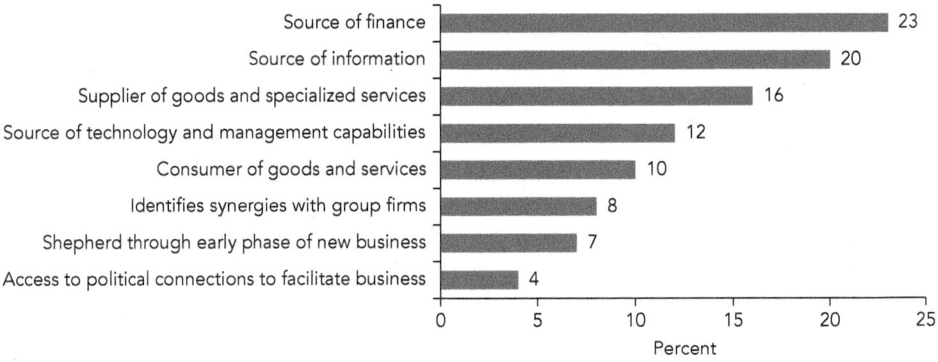

Source: South Asian Regional Engagement and Value Chains Survey.
Note: Figure shows the percentage of respondents (*N* = 313) who chose each category in the question "How is your business group most important in facilitating trade and investment, and conducting business abroad?"

in capital markets, talent markets, and contracting. Although conglomerates tend to be regarded as less important in advanced economies, there is some evidence that they are equally or more profitable than firms unaffiliated with a business group. The results here suggest that business groups also act as a means of capturing the spillovers of knowledge generated outside the source firm by passing the knowledge to other firms in the group or even incubating new firms that could use the generated knowledge.[11] Most of the pioneers in the case studies belonged to conglomerates. Only Timex Garments of Sri Lanka and Soorty Enterprises of Pakistan are not parts of conglomerates.

UNRELATED FOLLOWER FIRMS ARE LESS LIKELY TO SUCCEED BECAUSE OF "STICKY KNOWLEDGE"

The limited number of investors in the survey sample makes an econometric analysis with national follower firms in the same industry difficult. Although there certainly have been pioneering activities, the cascade effect or the herd effect has not been visible for investments. The closest evidence of an industrial cluster of national firms abroad in South Asia is the presence of some Indian, Pakistani, and Sri Lankan apparel manufacturers that have invested in Bangladesh. Both of Sri Lanka's top apparel conglomerates have also invested in apparel manufacturing in India, albeit a decade apart. The success of CG Foods' Wai Wai noodles has fostered a vibrant instant noodle industry in Nepal, with some firms exporting. Other than CG Foods' investments in the NER, not many Nepali firms have invested outside the country. Similarly, although the growth of Bhutan Ferro Alloys Ltd. in Bhutan has led to the development of other ferrosilicon exporters, no exporters have engaged in trade-supporting investments. On the other hand, Bhutan Ferro Alloys' growth has induced inward foreign investment from India.

Note, however, that the lack of an investment response from firms in Nepal and Bhutan reflects these countries' restrictive OFDI policies, which restrain the private sector.

The missing herd effect may also point to information frictions in South Asia, that is, the transfer of knowledge gained from the experience of the pioneer firm to the cohort firms in the same industry at home is incomplete—"sticky knowledge."[12] This sticky knowledge is driven by motivational factors and information barriers. The South Asian Regional Engagement and Value Chains Survey data point to the fact that the incidence of national competitors abroad creates a sense of general awareness, but it seems that it does not provide sufficient information with which to make business decisions. In business, private information has significant value, and it may not be in the interests of the pioneer firm to share information (a motivational barrier) because the firm may be achieving high profits through a first-mover advantage. Further, some firms, such as family firms and unlisted firms that do not publicly release data, may be more cautious about sharing information. However, there may be benefits to having a national cluster abroad (for negotiation purposes, for example), which would suggest that such knowledge may eventually be diffused among nationally competing firms or at least among firms along a particular value chain.

LEARNING AND INFORMATION FRICTIONS

In the face of uncertainty and capital scarcity, firms may prefer not to be pioneers. Instead, they may prefer to learn from the experiences of pioneers and imitate them. Figure 4.8 captures the pioneer-follower diffusion effect in the framework of chapter 2. It presents a scenario in which, first, learning from the experience of pioneers reduces follower firms' fixed entry costs of investing. The expected profit function shifts up and to the left, resulting in lower survival productivity cutoffs and expanding the range of potential investor firms. Follower firms related to the pioneer have lower fixed entry costs and higher expected profits compared with unrelated follower firms. Taking the specific case of a medium-productivity investor, figure 4.8 shows how learning from a competitor pioneer (gray to red profit line) may not lead to a change in participation mode, whereas learning from a related firm within a conglomerate does. This is explained by "sticky knowledge," or greater information diffusion imperfections in learning from competing pioneers.

Figure 4.9 summarizes the connections between learning, information frictions, and the reduction of the sunk entry costs of investing through different types of learning. First, a potential investor firm could learn from its own experience through alternative engagements with lower fixed entry costs, such as exporting, management contracts (for example, by hotels), or franchising. Second, in addition to learning from their own experience, firms can learn from competitors' experiences: the learning from unrelated pioneer firms reduces the entry costs of follower firms in the industry. Third, firms may learn from the experience of related firms within their conglomerate or business group

FIGURE 4.8 Learning from Pioneers Induces Entry of Follower Firms by Reducing Follower Entry Costs

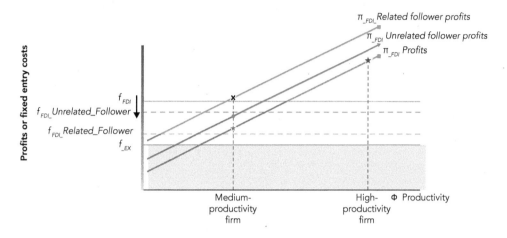

Source: World Bank.
Note: This figure illustrates the pioneer-follower diffusion framework with sticky knowledge. Follower firms have lower entry costs and higher expected profits than pioneers. Related-to-pioneer follower firms have lower fixed entry costs and higher expected profits compared with unrelated follower firms. The profit functions for three firm types are represented—a standard pioneer investor; a potential follower investor with an unrelated pioneer investor in the same industry that is already abroad; a potential follower investor with a related pioneer firm within the conglomerate or business group that is already abroad (within the same value chain or in a completely different industry). Learning from the experience of pioneers reduces the fixed entry costs of investing, f_{FDI}, of follower firms. Entry costs drop more with related pioneers because of fewer information frictions within a business group compared with learning from competing unrelated pioneers. The profit functions for followers shift up and to the left. Thus, pioneers expand the set of potential investors. The survival productivity cutoffs for investment, ϕ^* (not shown in figure), are obtained at the points at the x-axis where the profit line changes color from gray, with the following relation: $\phi^*_{FDI\_Related\ follower} < \phi^*_{FDI\_Unrelated\ follower} < \phi^*_{FDI}$. The drop in the survival probability cutoff from ϕ^*_{FDI} to $\phi^*_{FDI\_Unrelated\ follower}$ represents the pioneer-diffusion framework.

Under a standard scenario, a medium-productivity firm serves foreign markets through exports whereas a high-productivity firm invests abroad (marked by stars). In the illustrated case for the medium-productivity firm, the presence of an industry pioneer does not lead to a change in entry mode because information imperfections ("sticky knowledge") lead to a scenario in which profits (red dot) do not cover the new relevant fixed entry costs of investing, $f_{FDI\_Unrelated\ follower}$. However, learning from a related firm reduces entry costs to such an extent that it moves the medium-productivity firm exporter into a new equilibrium (marked by **X**) as an investor with higher profits.

that may be involved in other activities along the value chain or in activities completely outside their industry.

These three types of learning, however, involve varying levels of information frictions that hinder learning and the ability to reduce the fixed costs of investing. Sticky knowledge—the highest information frictions—is most prevalent when trying to learn from the experience of unrelated parties. Learning from firms within one's business group (a related firm) causes less loss of information, whereas learning from one's own experience in the destination market through an entry strategy with lower initial start-up costs (such as exporting) provides the greatest flow of information.

FIGURE 4.9 Varying Reduction of Fixed Entry Costs of Investing Based on Level of Information Frictions

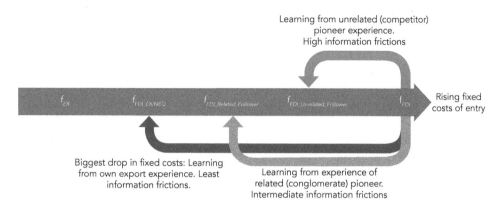

Source: World Bank.
Note: The main arrow marks fixed entry costs in increasing order from lowest (f_{EX}) to highest (f_{FDI})
f_{EX} = sunk entry costs of exporting
$f_{FDI\_EX/NEQ}$ = sunk entry costs of investing, given own prior exporting or other nonequity engagement
$f_{FDI\_Related\_Follower}$ = sunk entry costs of investing, given prior entry of a related firm in the firm's business group or conglomerate
$f_{FDI\_Unrelated\_Follower}$ = sunk entry costs of investing, given prior entry of an unrelated pioneer in the same industry
f_{FDI} = sunk entry costs of investing
This figure illustrates that a follower firm faces high information frictions when learning from a competitor firm's experience of entry in the previous period, as reflected by a small drop in fixed entry costs ($f_{FDI} - f_{FDI\_Unrelated\_Follower}$). The largest drop in fixed entry costs of investing is achieved from the firm's own learning experience in exporting ($f_{FDI} - f_{FDI\_EX/NEQ}$).

ENTREPRENEURS WITH HIGH RISK APPETITE ARE MORE LIKELY TO INVEST ABROAD

It is important to take into consideration the characteristics of the entrepreneur in understanding firm behavior (Cusolito and Maloney 2018), as has been backed up by research on management quality and culture and the psychological traits of successful entrepreneurs (Bloom et al. 2013). The characteristics of the entrepreneur are also related to behavioral economics and issues such as why people may not use the information they have (Handel and Schwartzstein 2018; Kremer, Villamor, and Aguinis 2019). Entrepreneurship in the region before the 1990s was subdued, which sociologists have attributed to a British education system geared toward producing graduates with a high preference for service and the episodes of socialism that involved large public sectors and tight control of the private sector. Analysts have also discussed the "attitude" of some state bureaucracies toward entrepreneurs and the role of this attitude in reform (see Panagariya [2005] for a discussion of different views). In addition, society was risk averse and individuals placed a high value on employment stability (Jagannathan et al. 2017).

Thus, certain personal characteristics are needed to overcome obstacles, pursue innovative paths, or even use available information. Risk appetite can be proxied by whether the founder or chief operating officer is a member of a business community or a traditionally well-known business family. Most South Asian countries have important family-owned business groups (or collections of subgroups that have developed after the founder's passing). The results indicate a positive relationship between investment and being part of a business community or family (table B.13 in appendix B). A person raised in a household in which family businesses routinely succeed and fail is likely to be more open to taking risks. This variable may also be related to ethnic networks, in the case of cross-border business communities working together, and so was not initially introduced in the model. In the lead-up to partition and before, many families in business communities migrated.

The results presented here do not capture the fact that recent technology-driven entrepreneurial success in India suggests a break from the past when family business background mattered or the family business acted as an incubator. For example, entrepreneurship cells in engineering colleges have encouraged entrepreneurship among students from nonbusiness communities, and partnerships are forged through university experiences as opposed to community allegiances.

In India, business communities are identified through a mix of religion, caste, culture, and region. The main business communities include the Marwari, Parsi (of Persian origin), and Gujarati communities (Gujarat-Kathiawar-Kutch area), as well as the Punjabis, Chettiars (of southern India), and Maharashtrians (Patankar and Mehta 2018). In colonial times, the business communities were not identical to the trading communities because for some orthodox Hindu communities, foreign travel was taboo (Gupta et al. 2020). The Marwaris, which originate from Rajasthan state, are characterized by wealth and risk appetite. The top 10 Marwari-owned companies at one point accounted for 6 percent of the Bombay Stock Exchange's market capitalization (Khaitan 2014). India is home to the largest family businesses in the Asia Pacific region, including the Tata Group (Tata family), Reliance Industries (Ambani family), and Aditya Birla Group (Birla family).

In Pakistan, prominent business communities include Gujarat Muslim Khojas, Memons, and Bohras; the Punjabi commercial communities of the Khatris, Pirachas, Shamsis, and Chinioti Sheikhs; and the Ismailis–Aga Khanis. More specifically, 22 families were identified as dominating business during the 1950s and 1960s, until a wave of nationalizations in the early 1970s (Ghani, Haroon, and Ashraf 2011; Javaid, Shamsi, and Hyder, forthcoming). In Sri Lanka, the Bohras, Sindhis, and Memons have a strong business presence, the first in diverse sectors and the latter two primarily in the apparel industry. Moors also have a strong presence in business activities.

In Nepal, the Newars are the traditional business community, whereas the Marwaris are more dominant in large-scale enterprises. The Thakalis and Sherpas are more recent entrepreneurs in trading, carpet manufacturing, and the tourism industry. Communities living in the Terai of Nepal along the border with India are naturally involved in cross-border trading, often with connections to India. They are diverse communities of different religions, though sometimes they are collectively grouped as Madheshis. Family businesses are also prevalent in Bangladesh. Many of the families that owned large businesses in East Pakistan (but had their main assets in West Pakistan) left after Bangladesh became independent in 1971 and businesses were immediately nationalized. However, by 1982 the government had divested many of its acquisitions, and Bengali Muslim family businesses dominated the private sector landscape (Kochanek 1996).

All the regional pioneers in the case studies come from business families. Three of the regional pioneers (Chaudhary of Nepal, and Singhania and Goenka of India) are Marwari. The three Sri Lankan apparel pioneers all have parents born in Gujarat, and two of them are from the Memon community. The Burman family leading CEAT is Punjabi, and the founder of Taj Hotels is Jamsetji Tata, the Parsi founder of the Tata Group.

OTHER FACTORS

Other firm characteristics tested for their influence on OFDI decisions were related to their being family firms, state-owned firms, and foreign-owned firms. There were no consistent results for these explanatory variables. In some cases, the state-owned dummy variable was negative, implying that, unlike Chinese state-owned enterprises, South Asian ones were less likely to invest abroad. An exception is the Indian public sector investment in Bhutan's hydropower sector, which has led to new private sector investment by Tata Power Ltd. on a public-private partnership basis with the Bhutan-government-owned Druk Green Power Corporation.

A positive coefficient, especially for goods production, was expected for family firms because they can take a longer-term perspective on investment. The argument is that family firms are more inclined to take risks when the return could be backloaded because they are not motivated by shareholders to maximize share value on an annual basis. The impact of family firms was small but negative, and only for services operations investments. However, the coefficient loses statistical significance when only South Asian destinations are considered. The impact of foreign ownership on investment was statistically not different from zero, suggesting that South Asian–based affiliates were not a channel through which foreign parent companies invested in other economies. In contrast, Singapore has become a platform from which foreign firms enter other Association of Southeast Asian Nations countries and the broader East Asia and Pacific region.

ROBUSTNESS CHECKS

The results of the estimation stood up to robustness checks of the analysis and the estimation techniques. First, investors that were not investing in the South Asia Region were removed from the data set, but variation across the noninvestors was sufficient to generate similar results. The relative importance of networks compared with productivity is higher for the South Asian destinations compared with the results obtained using the entire sample of global destinations. Second, an assessment was made of whether, despite its remoteness, the NER may be driving the results, given that it could be very familiar to Indian investors. Thus, a model was estimated without NER as a destination. Finally, a logit model was estimated and provided similar results (tables B.14–B.16 in appendix B).

Beyond Entry: Evolution of Investment Destinations

This section explores sequential investing and the potential for a neighboring region to act as an experiential platform for global activity. The intuition for the evolution of investment is similar to that of the gradualist learning path in the preceding section. In a dynamic setting, investment in a first destination leads to a learning experience that reduces the sunk cost of entering a second market in the following period. It also justifies incurring initially high sunk costs. A regional dimension arises if the sunk entry cost in a regional market is lower than that in an extraregional market, making the region the likely first destination. Evidence of sequential exporting has been found (Albornoz et al. 2012; Yatawara 2013), and recent research on US manufacturing affiliates finds that the sunk entry costs are higher for first affiliates compared with subsequent affiliates (Garetto, Oldenski, and Ramondo 2019).

About two-thirds of the investor firms in the survey provided data on the first as well as subsequent investment destinations by investment type (table 4.1). Two important results are obtained. First, South Asia is the dominant first destination for South Asian investors.[13] About 65 percent of all first outward investments were in South Asia, which confirms the results from the econometric research on distance. This share is substantially higher than earlier estimates (28 percent) for South Asia as a first destination for exports (Yatawara 2013). There is not much variation across the different types of investments. Trade-supporting services investments showed the greatest share of investors whose first entry was outside the region, with just the United States, Canada, the European Union, and the United Kingdom accounting for 22.5 percent of first investment destinations. For services operations investments, the most important locations, in order, after South Asia for first investments were the investment hubs of Hong Kong SAR, China; Mauritius; Singapore; and the United Arab Emirates.

Second, the data provide suggestive evidence of the region being used as an experiential investment platform from which to launch into global markets. Sequential investing was recorded by 34 percent of the firms (table 4.1). On average, 28 percent of the firms that first invested in a South Asian country went on to invest outside the region. An additional 6 percent moved on to invest in another country in South Asia, different from their original country of investment. Thus, the first destination helps reduce the entry costs of the subsequent investment destinations, but South Asia being the dominant first investment destination does not seem to confine the next investment

TABLE 4.1 Evolution of Investment Destinations: First Destination and Sequential Investing, by Investment Type

Destination	Goods production	Services operations	Trade-supporting services
First investment destination, by investment type (percent)			
Australia, New Zealand	0.0	0.8	0.0
Hong Kong SAR, China; Mauritius; Singapore; United Arab Emirates	6.7	11.1	5.6
Europe and Central Asia	0.0	1.6	3.4
East Asia and Pacific	6.7	6.4	4.5
Japan	2.2	0.0	0.0
Middle East and North Africa	4.4	2.4	1.1
South Asia	64.4	65.1	59.6
Sub-Saharan Africa	6.7	1.6	3.4
European Union and United Kingdom	4.4	6.4	9.0
Canada and United States	4.4	4.8	13.5
TOTAL (firms)	100 (45)	100 (126)	100 (89)
Destination evolution of investments with South Asia as first entry (percent)			
Original South Asia only, no further evolution	65.5	63.4	65.4
Other South Asia only	6.9	4.9	5.8
Other South Asia and non–South Asia	10.3	8.5	5.8
Outside South Asia only	17.2	19.5	23.1
Divest	n.a.	3.7	n.a.
TOTAL	100	100	100

Source: South Asian Regional Engagement and Value Chains Survey.
Note: The information in the table should be read as follows: 65.1 percent of services operations investments were first established in South Asia. Of these investing firms, 63.4 percent did not invest beyond their original destination. n.a. = not applicable.

to the region. This result is line with Garetto, Oldenski, and Ramondo (2019), who find that the location of a new affiliate does not depend on the location of a preexisting affiliate.[14] An example of sequential investing by a regional pioneer is MAS Brands' development of its Amanté brand in India and Sri Lanka, learning from which generated enough comfort for MAS to invest in the established Ultimo brand in the United Kingdom. Similarly, CG Hospitality's success in investing in the Taj Hotels in Sri Lanka led to more partnerships in Sri Lanka, such as investments in Sri Lanka's Jetwing Hotels led by Hiran Cooray. The Chaudharys have also developed hotels back in Nepal as well as in other locations.

Although data issues prevent a corresponding study from being undertaken of the evolution from the first investment type to other types of investment, case study evidence points to a gradual path.[15] In addition to the case of Soorty Enterprises's gradual path, discussed in chapter 3, MAS Brands originally started with a distribution investment in Bengaluru in 2007 to facilitate sales of its intimate wear in department stores, and eight years later it opened up its own retail store. However, as firms expand overseas, they may take different approaches to different markets. For example, MAS Brands expanded to Maldives with a direct retail investment, but it chose a franchise agreement for Pakistan.

Bridges of Knowledge: Key Channels of Awareness of Investment Opportunities

Having established the importance of knowledge connectivity for investment entry, understanding the key sources of information on which investors and potential investors rely is important, with a view to understanding the most appropriate way to address information barriers. These information sources should be targeted to enhance knowledge connectivity for potential investors. Three broad channels of information are identified in the survey: an investor demonstration effect, an informal network effect, and an institution-based effect. Giving a score of one to a broad channel if at least one of its component options was chosen by a firm, and zero otherwise, suggests that all broad channels are important, with the investor demonstration effect leading (accounting for 35 percent of all sources), just ahead of the network information effect (33 percent) and institution-based information flows (32 percent).

Business networks, the demonstration effect of national and global competitors, business travel, and matchmaking events are the main sources of awareness about investment opportunities (figure 4.10). Figure 4.10 also reveals the channels that are reported to be of low importance, including ethnic networks, South Asia Region trading relationships, and the activities of foreign investment promotion agencies and embassies in home countries. The result for ethnic networks is a typical response from entrepreneurs when asked directly about the importance of ethnic networks (as by Gomez-Mera et al. 2015). Perhaps psychological aspects, or their "bundling" of this issue with business networks, leads them to downplay this aspect.

Figure 4.11 presents differences in information channels between large country investors and other investors, and investors that are active outside the region and those that currently do not invest. For investors in South Asia, the top three factors in each broad channel of information are investor demonstration effects from a national competitor or global competitor, or business group entry demonstration effects; informal network effects from business contacts, business travel, and tourist travel; and institutional sources at matchmaking events, unpaid media reports, and industry meetings

FIGURE 4.10 **Awareness of South Asian Investment Opportunities: Actual Investors**

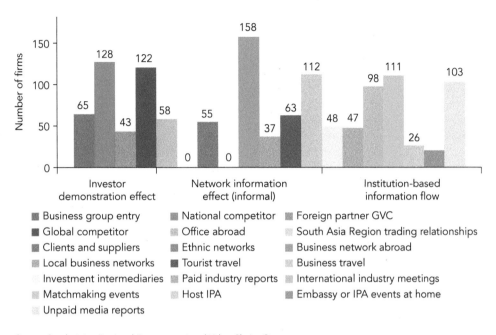

Source: South Asian Regional Engagement and Value Chains Survey.
Note: GVC = global value chain; IPA = investment promotion agency.

(figure 4.11, panel a). The importance of business group entry is consistent with the empirical findings in the previous section.

The key difference for non-Indian investors in South Asia is that they place greater importance on the demonstration effect of global competitors than on national competitors (figure 4.11, panel b). India is the only country that places higher importance on the demonstration effect of national competitors (cited by 65 firms) compared with global competitors (cited by 35 firms). This finding is consistent with India's size and the large OFDI activity of Indian firms. In India, national investors are the largest source of awareness, followed by business networks abroad. Compared with firms in other countries, Indian firms also have a greater tendency to obtain information from investment intermediaries.

Entrepreneurs investing outside South Asia rely more heavily on their GVC partners for information (from within the demonstration effect channel and the network information channel). The importance of international industry meetings also rises to first position in institution-based channels of awareness (figure 4.11, panel c).

Meanwhile, noninvestors rely primarily on unpaid media reports and online research for their information. Noninvestors do not cite business groups' entry demonstration effects but rely on GVC partners' demonstration effects. Noninvestors' reliance on business networks abroad for information is in third place overall, lower than all types of investors (figure 4.11, panel d).

An analysis of the data from the perspective of the investment destination yields broadly similar results. Some notable differences are that the national competitor demonstration effect is the most important source of awareness when investing in Nepal and the NER, likely reflecting the importance that Indian outward investors place on the demonstration effect of national competitors. Other differences include the primacy of matchmaking events for investment heading to Pakistan, a higher relative role

FIGURE 4.11 **Top Three Channels of Awareness of Investment Opportunities in South Asia and Outside South Asia, across Investors and Noninvestors**

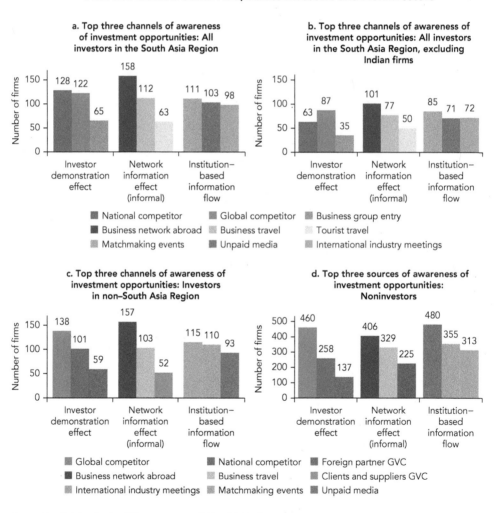

Source: South Asian Regional Engagement and Value Chains Survey.
Note: Sample sizes: panel a, 267; panel b, 110; panel c, 222; panel d, 675. GVC = global value chain.

for information from clients and suppliers in GVCs for investing in Sri Lanka, paid industry reports for investing in Bangladesh and the NER, and business group entry for investment destined for Maldives.

DOES SOUTH ASIA HAVE ENOUGH INVESTMENT INTERMEDIARIES?

Being informed and being able to investigate investment options relatively cheaply are vital for fostering investment. Investment intermediaries reduce the sunk fixed costs of investing. Globally, investment intermediaries play an important role in uncovering the most suitable options for firms. Intermediaries may be site location consultancy firms that reduce search costs and provide cross-cultural knowledge and expertise that would facilitate specification, negotiation, and enforcement of contracts. If there are no intermediaries, the work is done in house within large conglomerates that can afford to allocate workers to this task. It is important to have consultancy firms that can provide market research and perform due diligence at reasonable prices so that medium firms would also be able to afford them. The evidence from South Asia is sparse and uncertain. The clearest message is that most managers do not know. Asked to comment on the statement that there were competent intermediaries or consultancy firms to investigate opportunities in each of the South Asian economies, the blue bars in figure 4.12 dominate, reflecting lack of knowledge, followed by the orange bars, which reflect disagreement with the statement. It is not clear whether the issue is one of the actual existence of knowledge intermediaries (a missing market), lack of information about their existence, or a pricing structure that makes them accessible only to a few elite large firms. This issue deserves further exploration.

Concluding Remarks

This chapter documents the knowledge and networking frictions in South Asia and their variation across bilateral pairs of countries. It then estimates the importance of knowledge connectivity in the investment entry decision. From these results, the constraints facing potential outward investors may be discerned. First are investment policy constraints—outward investment policies at home, inward FDI policies abroad—and other factors, such as investment climate, that are captured in the fixed effects of the model. The main knowledge frictions are lack of information about markets, potential partner firms, and regulations; lack of networks; lack of trust; potential lack of knowledge intermediaries; low productivity; low number of exporters; high trade costs; high communication costs; low access to finance; and need for risk appetite among potential investors. The findings here have several policy implications that are addressed in the next chapter.

FIGURE 4.12 Due Diligence Intermediaries, by Destination

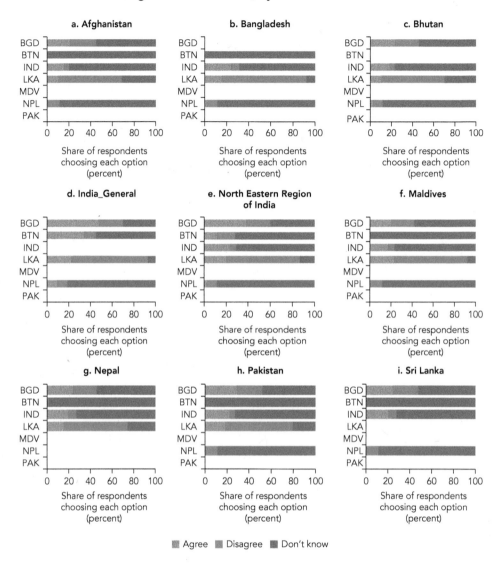

Source: South Asian Regional Engagement and Value Chains Survey.
Note: Scores are for bilateral pairs of countries with 30 or more observations. AFG = Afghanistan;
BGD = Bangladesh; BTN = Bhutan; IND = India_General (India without North Eastern Region); LKA = Sri Lanka;
MDV = Maldives; NPL = Nepal; PAK = Pakistan.

This research suggests there are many potential fruitful lines of investigation for South Asian investment and investors, including the following four issues. First, although this analysis focuses on the investor participation decision, the gradual nature of investing by emerging multinational enterprises suggests that explicitly understanding investment expansion decisions is also very important. This notion is reinforced by the importance of retained earnings of existing investors as a source of investment inflows, as in some countries such as Bangladesh. The experiences of pioneers with respect to the challenges in the region, the solutions used, and the results of the investment for the home country and the destination country are important. Second, although this report opts for inclusivity of country coverage and firm type coverage at the expense of the precision of estimated results, more research with available, detailed firm-level data is encouraged. Perhaps this need will encourage statistical agencies to develop procedures that allow the use of firm-level data, even if only on agencies' premises, as is sometimes the case in the United States.

Third, greater incorporation of structural features of the private sector and the culture of business and their implications for knowledge connectivity is likely to be important. For example, the large presence of diversified business groups and family firms and how they interact with small and medium enterprises deserves study. Further, documenting the existence and accessibility of knowledge intermediaries and consulting firms would be useful. Fourth, this report does not pursue the role of political connections for outward investment decisions, which could be relevant for many aspects of firm behavior. For example, countries with higher shares of politically connected firms are associated with capital controls (Faccio 2006), and politically connected firms tend to have lower-quality accounting information (Chaney, Faccio, and Parsley 2011).[16] In the context of discretion in OFDI approval, political connections could be important for overseas investments.

Annex 4A: Information, Networks, and Learning

TABLE 4A.1 **Rank of Most Trusting and Trusted Countries, Most Knowledgeable, Most Well-Known, and Most Connected**

Score from 1 (lowest) to 4 (highest), except as noted

(1) Rank	(2) Most trusting country		(3) Most trusted country		(4) Perception of trustworthiness of people (percent)		(5) Most knowledgeable country in the region		(6) Most well-known by the region		(7) Most well-connected to the region		(8) Most connected by the region	
1	Bhutan	3.11	India_General	2.93	Afghanistan	89	India_General	2.31	India_General	2.62	Sri Lanka	2.37	India_General	2.59
2	India_General	2.82	Sri Lanka	2.85	Bangladesh	24	Sri Lanka	2.28	NER	2.20	Maldives	2.27	NER	2.26
3	Sri Lanka	2.72	NER	2.77	Bhutan	27	Bangladesh	2.28	Bangladesh	1.9	India_General	2.23	Bangladesh	1.93
4	Bangladesh	2.71	Bangladesh	2.58	India_General	13	Maldives	2.07	Pakistan	1.86	Bangladesh	2.12	Sri Lanka	1.80
5	Maldives	2.65	Nepal	2.56	Maldives	81	Nepal	1.96	Sri Lanka	1.84	Nepal	1.83	Pakistan	1.79
6	Afghanistan	2.53	Pakistan	2.45	Nepal	19	Bhutan	1.68	Nepal	1.67	Bhutan	1.55	Nepal	1.63
7	Nepal	2.31	Bhutan	2.36	Pakistan	84	Pakistan	1.40	Maldives	1.61	Pakistan	1.32	Maldives	1.60
8	Pakistan	1.99	Maldives	2.32	Sri Lanka	11	Afghanistan	1.16	Bhutan	1.6	Afghanistan	1.14	Bhutan	1.56
9			Afghanistan	2.09					Afghanistan	1.55			Afghanistan	1.48

Source: South Asian Regional Engagement and Value Chains Survey.

Note: Columns 2 and 3: "I would like to ask you a question about how much trust you have in people from various countries. For each, please tell me whether you have a lot of trust, some trust, not very much trust, or no trust at all."

Column 4: "Generally speaking, would you say that most people can be trusted or that you need to be very careful in dealing with people?"

India_General = India without NER; NER = North Eastern Region of India.

FIGURE 4A.1 Bilateral Knowledge Connectivity, Network Connectivity, and Trust: Raw Z-Scores

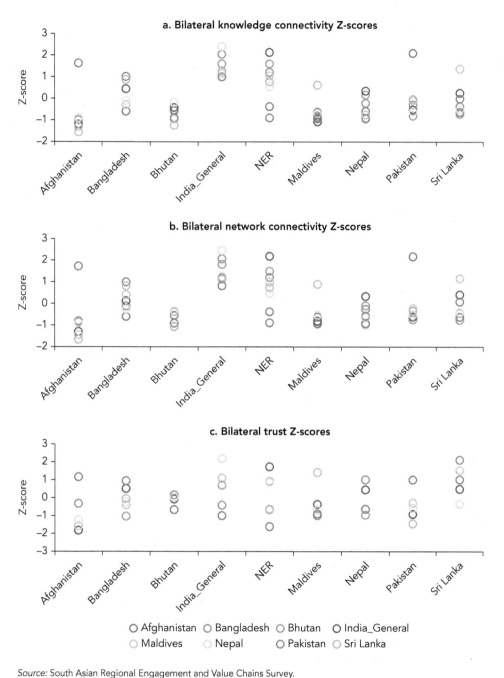

Source: South Asian Regional Engagement and Value Chains Survey.
Note: The Z-score is a measure of how many standard deviations below or above the population mean a data point is. A score greater than 1 standard deviation is considered a significant surplus, and below 1 a significant deficit. Scores are for bilateral pairs of countries with 30 or more observations. India_General = India without North Eastern Region; NER = North Eastern Region of India.

Notes

1. Price differences across geographic space over and above those related to transportation costs are thought to represent information costs. However, this approach works better for commodities without product or quality differentiation, a competitive environment (low markups), and low intranational trade costs.

2. In fact, the choice of foreign direct investment over an alternate engagement strategy may itself be driven by the risk of leakage of internal knowledge beyond firm boundaries.

3. Networks provide a kind of enforcement mechanism through sanctions, substituting for weak international enforcement of formal contracts.

4. The FDI entry decision is distinct from the FDI expansion decision (the extensive margin versus the intensive margin of FDI, respectively). In international trade, it has been shown that for the United States, it is the extensive margin—the entry and exit of exporter firms—that determines the variation in export volumes, as opposed to adjustments in export volumes by existing exporters, that is, the intensive margin (Bernard et al. 2010). No similar analysis has been applied to FDI entry and exit at the firm level, but a similar finding is assumed. In some countries, FDI in the form of retained earnings is important, which would imply that studying the investment expansion and retention question is also important.

5. The Z-score is calculated as $(x_d - \text{mean})/\text{standard deviation}$, where x_d is the bilateral home score with respect to destination d, mean is the average home score across all destinations, and standard deviation measures the dispersion of home's x_d scores. A greater-than–1 standard deviation Z-score indicates a surplus and less than 1 indicates a deficit. The designation is driven by the score relative to both the mean and the standard deviation. Thus, if a country has scores that are very close for all countries (low standard deviation), small score differences may generate a knowledge surplus or deficit. To counter these situations, an additional absolute threshold (say, the overall population mean) could also be used in the classification. This implies that a score of 2.2, which is initially marked as a knowledge deficit (orange) based on the Z-score, would not be marked as such because it exceeds the population mean of 1.89.

6. The relatively high score for NER may reflect a bias in that the NER destination option followed directly after India in the survey, and respondents may have chosen the same score for both.

7. Similar perspectives are observed when respondents were asked about how well informed they were about rules and regulations in South Asian countries. The scores (not reported here) tend to be lower than those for knowledge connectivity, and Afghanistan and Pakistan had a knowledge deficit (low score) on Indian regulations.

8. The question was, "I would like to ask you a question about how much trust you have in people from various countries. For each, please tell me whether you have a lot of trust, some trust, not very much trust, or no trust at all."

9. With eight categories of productivity, the impact of going from the bottom to the top is 3.2 (8 × 0.004) percent, compared with a 5 percent network effect for services investment.

10. Unfortunately, insufficient data on prior importing or the first year of importing from a country that has OFDI were collected to explore the role of importing in investment. In interviews, entrepreneurs were more familiar with their export market statistics than with

import-sourcing information. Importing is expected to have a similar pattern on investment as exporting. For instance, Indian ferrosilicon importers of Bhutanese ferrosilicon have invested in ferrosilicon factories in Bhutan.

11. Conglomerates are either multidivisional organizations or business groups. Business groups differ from a multidivision organization in that each company in a business group is a separate legal entity. Additionally, in business groups, ownership tends to be more involved in management. This report does not explore the difference between these diverse types of conglomerates.

12. This phrase was first coined in the management literature by Szulanski (2003) to refer to frictions in the transfer of best practices between affiliates and headquarters. He made the distinction between motivational barriers and information barriers. Motivational barriers are interdivisional jealousy, lack of incentives, resistance to change, and turf protection. Knowledge barriers are such factors as recipients' initial knowledge, ability to shed old practices, and preexisting social ties between the source and the recipient.

13. The finding is consistent with the aggregate data on FDI *values* that show much higher shares for extraregional investments.

14. These results differ from the "extended gravity" results of Morales, Sheu, and Zahler (2019) for exports. They find that new export destinations are affected by the geographic location of previous export destinations.

15. The response rate for the initial year of the first investment was more unstable than the response for the initial destination. Many managers responded to the first market rather than the first year of investment. Sometimes the year was given for only one type of investment, thus precluding an effective study of investment evolution by investment type.

16. Establishing political connections objectively at the firm level is a time-consuming task, usually connecting the firm's leadership to a politician using the annual reports of publicly listed firms. Some recent firm-level studies use state-owned enterprises as a proxy for politically connected firms.

References

Albornoz, F., H. F. Calvo Pardo, G. Corcos, and E. Ornelas. 2012. "Sequential Exporting." *Journal of International Economics* 88 (1): 17–31.

Allen, T. 2014. "Information Frictions in Trade." *Econometrica* 82 (6): 2041–83.

Anderson, J. E., and E. van Wincoop. 2004. "Trade Costs." *Journal of Economic Literature* 42 (3): 691–751.

Arrow, Kenneth. 1973. "The Theory of Discrimination." In *Discrimination in Labor Markets*, edited by Orley Ashenfelter and Albert Rees. Princeton, NJ: Princeton University Press.

Atkin, David, and Amit Khandelwal. 2019. "How Distortions Alter the Impacts of International Trade in Developing Economies." Working Paper 26230, National Bureau of Economic Research, Cambridge, MA.

Atkin, D., A. K. Khandelwal, and A. Osman. 2017. "Exporting and Firm Performance: Evidence from a Randomized Experiment." *Quarterly Journal of Economics* 132 (2): 551–615.

Barattieri, Alessandro, Ingo Borchert, and Aaditya Mattoo. 2016. "Cross-Border Mergers and Acquisitions in Services: The Role of Policy and Industrial Structure." *Canadian Journal of Economics* 49 (4): 147–501.

Bernard, Andrew B., J. Bradford Jensen, Stephen J. Redding, and Peter K. Schott. 2010. "The Margins of US Trade." *American Economic Review* 99 (2): 487–93.

Bhagwati, J. 1987. "VERs, Quid Pro Quo FDI and VIEs: Political-Economy-Theoretic Analyses." *International Economic Journal* 1 (1): 1–14.

Bloom, N., B. Eifert, A. Mahajan, D. McKenzie, and J. Roberts. 2013. "Does Management Matter? Evidence from India." *Quarterly Journal of Economics* 128 (1): 1–51.

Burchardi, K. B., T. Chaney, and T. A. Hassan. 2019. "Migrants, Ancestors, and Foreign Investments." *Review of Economic Studies* 86 (4): 1448–86.

Chaney, Paul K., Mara Faccio, and David Parsley. 2011. "The Quality of Accounting Information in Politically Connected Firms." *Journal of Accounting and Economics* 51 (1–2): 58–76.

Chen, Cheng, Senga Tatsuro, Sun Chang, and Zhang Hongyong. 2020. "Uncertainty, Imperfect Information, and Expectation Formation over the Firm's Life Cycle." CESifo Working Paper 8468, CESifo, Munich.

Colpan, Asli, and Takashi Hikino. 2010. "Foundations of Business Groups: Towards an Integrated Framework." In *The Oxford Handbook of Business Groups*, edited by Asli Colpan, Takashi Hikino, and James R. Lincoln, 15-66. Oxford: Oxford University Press.

Conconi, Paola, André Sapir, and Maurizio Zanardi. 2016. "The Internationalization Process of Firms: From Exports to FDI." *Journal of International Economics* 99 (C): 16–30.

Cusolito, Ana P., and William F. Maloney. 2018. "Productivity Revisited: Shifting Paradigms in Analysis and Policy." World Bank Group, Washington, DC.

Da Rin, Marco, Marina Di Giacomo, and Alessandro Sembenelli. 2019. "Trust and Foreign Ownership: Evidence from Intra-European Foreign Direct Investments." *Review of International Economics* 27 (1): 313–46.

Dickstein, Michael J., and Eduardo Morales. 2018. "What Do Exporters Know?" *Quarterly Journal of Economics* 133 (4): 1753–801.

Faccio, Mara. 2006. "Politically Connected Firms." *American Economic Review* 96 (1): 369–86.

Freund, Caroline, and Martha Denisse Pierola. 2010. "Export Entrepreneurs: Evidence from Peru." Policy Research Working Paper 5407, World Bank, Washington, DC.

Garetto, Stefania, Lindsay Oldenski, and Natalia Ramondo. 2019. "Multinational Expansion in Time and Space." Working Paper 25804, National Bureau of Economic Research, Cambridge, MA.

Ghani, Waqar I., Omair Haroon, and Junaid Ashraf. 2011. "Business Groups' Financial Performance: Evidence from Pakistan." *Global Journal of Business Research* 5 (2): 27–39.

Gomez-Mera, Laura, Thomas Kenyon, Yotam Margalit, Jose Guilherme Reis, and Gonzalo Varela. 2015. *New Voices in Investment: A Survey of Investors from Emerging Countries*. Washington, DC: World Bank.

Guiso, L., P. Sapienza, and L. Zingales. 2009. "Cultural Biases in Economic Exchange?" *Quarterly Journal of Economics* 124 (3): 1095–131.

Gupta, Bishnupriya, Dilip Mookherjee, Kaivan Munshi, and Mario Sanclemente. 2020. "Community Origins of Industrial Entrepreneurship in Pre-Independence India." Discussion Paper 14263, Centre for Economic Policy Research, London.

Handel, Benjamin, and Joshua Schwartzstein. 2018. "Frictions or Mental Gaps: What's Behind the Information We (Don't) Use and When Do We Care?" *Journal of Economic Perspectives* 32 (1): 155–78.

Hausmann, Ricardo, and Dani Rodrik. 2003. "Economic Development as Self-Discovery." *Journal of Development Economics* 72 (2): 603–33.

Helpman, E., M. Melitz, and S. Yeaple. 2004. "Export versus FDI with Heterogeneous Firms." *American Economic Review* 94 (1): 300–16.

Henisz, W., and A. Delios. 2001. "Uncertainty, Imitation, and Plant Location: Japanese Multinational Corporations, 1990–1996." *Administrative Science Quarterly* 46 (3): 443–75.

Jagannathan, R., M. J. Camasso, B. Das, J. Tosun, and S. Iyengar. 2017. "Family, Society and the Individual: Determinants of Entrepreneurial Attitudes among Youth in Chennai, South India." *Journal of Global Entrepreneurial Research* 7, article 14 .

Javaid, Omar, Aamir Shamsi, and Irfan Hyder. Forthcoming. "How Memon, Delhi Saudagaran and Chinioti Entrepreneurs Create New Ventures?" *Pakistan Business Review*.

Javorcik, B. S. 2004. "Does Foreign Direct Investment Increase the Productivity of Domestic Firms? In Search of Spillovers through Backward Linkages." *American Economic Review* 94 (3): 605–27.

Javorcik, B. S., C. Ozdenc, and M. Spatareanu. 2011. "Migrant Networks and Foreign Direct Investment." *Journal of Development Economics* 94 (2): 231–41.

Johanson, J., and J. E. Vahlne. 1977. "The Internationalization Process of the Firm: A Model of Knowledge Development and Increasing Foreign Market Commitments." *Journal of International Business Studies* 8 (1): 23–32.

Johanson, J., and J. E. Vahlne. 2009. "The Uppsala Internationalization Process Model Revisited: From Liability of Foreignness to Liability of Outsidership." *Journal of International Business Studies* 40 (9): 1411–31.

Khaitan, A. 2014. "The Power of the Marwari Business Community." *Forbes India*, March 17.

Khanna, Tarun, and Yishai Yafeh. "Business Groups in Emerging Markets: Paragons or Parasites?" *Journal of Economic Literature* 45 (2): 331–72.

Kochanek, Stanley A. 1996. "The Rise of Interest Politics in Bangladesh." *Asian Survey* 36 (7): 704–22.

Kremer, H., I. Villamor, and H. Aguinis. 2019. "Innovation Leadership: Best-Practice Recommendations for Promoting Employee Creativity, Voice, and Knowledge Sharing." *Business Horizons* 62 (1): 65–74.

Li, Jiatao, and Fiona Kun Yao. 2010. "The Role of Reference Groups in International Investment Decisions by Firms from Emerging Economies." *Journal of International Management* 16 (2): 143–53.

Morales, E., G. Sheu, and A. Zahler. 2019. "Extended Gravity." *Review of Economic Studies* 86 (6): 2668–712.

Oldenski, Lindsay. 2012. "The Task Composition of Offshoring by U.S. Multinationals." *International Economics* 131: 5–21.

Panagariya, Arvind. 2005. "India in the 1980s and 1990s: A Triumph of Reform." In *India's and China's Recent Experience with Reform and Growth*, edited by W. Tseng and D. Cowen, 170–200. London: Palgrave Macmillan.

Patankar, Vishnu A., and Nikhil K. Mehta. 2018. "Indian Entrepreneurial Communities: The People Who Set-up Their Businesses." *IOSR Journal of Business and Management* 20 (2): 41–49.

Pietrobelli, C., and C. Staritz. 2018. "Upgrading, Interactive Learning, and Innovation Systems in Value Chain Interventions." *European Journal of Development Research* 30 (3): 557–74.

Rauch, J. E., and V. Trindade. 2002. "Ethnic Chinese Networks in International Trade." *Review of Economics and Statistics* 84 (1): 116–30.

Rhee, Yung Whee, and Therese Belot. 1990. "Export Catalysts in Low-Income Countries: A Review of Eleven Success Stories." Discussion Paper 72, World Bank Group, Washington, DC.

Sabel, Charles, Eduardo Fernández-Arias, Ricardo Hausmann, Andrés Rodriguez-Clare, and Ernesto Stein, eds. 2012. *Export Pioneers in Latin America*. Washington, DC: Inter-American Development Bank.

Steinwender, C. 2018. "Information Frictions and the Law of One Price: When the States and the Kingdom Became United." *American Economic Review* 108 (3): 657–96.

Szulanski, Gabriel. 2003. "Sticky Knowledge: Barriers to Knowing in the Firm." *Knowledge and Process Management* 12 (2): 150–52.

Wei, Shang-Jin, Ziru Wei, and Jianhuan Xu. 2017. "Sizing Up Market Failures in Export Pioneering Activities." Working Paper 23893, National Bureau of Economic Research, Cambridge, MA.

Yatawara, Ravindra. 2013. "Boosting South Asian Export Performance through Regional Integration." Chief Economist's Office, South Asia Region, World Bank, Washington, DC.

CHAPTER 5

Policy and Operational Implications

Introduction

This report is framed within the same context as its predecessor, *A Glass Half Full: The Promise of Regional Trade in South Asia* (Kathuria 2018); that is, it explores the suboptimal level of engagement within South Asia. It focuses on investment, an important issue on which comprehensive regional research on South Asia has been scarce. The report highlights the emerging issue of knowledge connectivity and information barriers in the decision to trade and invest, which is particularly relevant to the region. Given trade-investment links, improving regional foreign direct investment (FDI) will also improve regional trade. Similarly, initiatives that promote trade, such as reducing trade costs, increase investment directly as well as indirectly through informational gains from trading. The report also highlights distortions in some countries' outward investment arrangements.

To investigate the relationship between investment and information barriers, this report embarked on an extensive data-collection exercise that provided detailed information on 1,274 firms and entrepreneurs across all eight countries in the region. This firm-level survey enabled rich diagnostic and econometric exercises to be undertaken, which were combined with aggregate national data analysis and distillation of case studies of regional pioneers.

The analysis was conducted through an outward investment lens and highlights outward investment from emerging economies and the importance of information in investment decision-making. South Asian firms face high and varying information barriers, as documented by limited and polarized bilateral knowledge connectivity within South Asia. The results show that firm-level information, network availability, and learning reduce fixed entry costs and lead to investment entry. Firms may learn from their own experience in different modes of engagement with lower start-up costs, from the pioneering activities of related firms in their business group or conglomerate, and from unrelated competitor firms. The results also indicate that knowledge connectivity is relatively more important than productivity improvements, especially for services firms. The finding on the importance of knowledge connectivity applies to trade as much as it does to investment, and thus offers an additional element with which to explain the shortfall of potential trade in South Asia.

Given the limited trust in the region, which is critical for value chains that rely a great deal on relational contracting, FDI (with its security of ownership) appears to be the best option for developing regional value chains in South Asia. Once investment occurs, the firm's presence in neighboring countries should lead to deeper trust through greater knowledge, networks, and people-to-people interactions. These regional value chains offer an increasingly important alternative mechanism for upgrading. Upgrading is important in an environment in which the growth of global value chains has slowed; global and regional lead firms are seeking or facing pressures to diversify and locate at home or nearer home, a trend accelerated by the pandemic; trade protection measures are on the rise; and COVID-19 (coronavirus) has led to an increase in trade costs arising from the need to accommodate global health security concerns, disruptions in shipping, and reductions in passenger travel (which affects air freight).

The findings of the report provide important new, actionable implications for policy interventions and investments. These recommendations are organized around enhancing knowledge connectivity, boosting physical and digital connectivity, addressing regulatory and promotional policies for outward FDI (OFDI), finessing inward FDI (IFDI) promotion strategies, incorporating emerging global business practices into both inward and outward investment policy making, identifying national policy reforms that may have regional implications, and spelling out the implications of the pandemic for policy prioritization and regional engagement. These policy recommendations have global relevance and are applied regionally to address frictions in regional engagement.

Information Frictions and Enhancing Knowledge Connectivity

Establishing a prominent role for knowledge connectivity, separate from other forms of traditional connectivity, is important because policies that reduce information frictions differ substantially from policies that reduce traditional trade costs. These information frictions reflect the high costs of search, matching, and contracting across borders and the high costs or market failures in the provision of channels or technologies to alleviate these frictions. The common determinants in the different modes of international engagement imply that addressing information barriers would support intraregional investment and trade alike.

Policy interventions for potential regional investors are warranted to tackle information and coordination failures. For example, some firms may suffer from being late entrants (and hence are unknown to the wider business community), arising from more recent maturity to global competitiveness. Other competitive regional firms that are already linked to global value chains may resist incurring the sunk costs and switching costs associated with new partnerships (a "status quo bias"). Structural features of the private sector, such as the prevalence of family firms and diversified business groups, may create an atmosphere in which information sharing is generally more circumscribed and restricted to a selected group.

Information dissemination and network development can democratize regional investment by reducing the fixed costs of entering new markets and new partnerships for a broader set of firms and entrepreneurs. Just as the inherent ethnic and social networks of some pioneers have enhanced the inclusivity of investing beyond the largest firms, knowledge connectivity–related interventions may further diffuse the opportunities of international engagement to a broader set of firms and entrepreneurs. The solutions for addressing information and networking frictions are not well established, but recent experience provides some guidance.

NETWORK DEVELOPMENT

Networks are important for a variety of reasons that include information provision, referrals, training, intermediate goods sourcing, finance, and other services. Business networks were deemed the single largest source of awareness about business opportunities abroad in the South Asia Regional Engagement and Value Chains Survey.

At first glance, network development may not seem to be a good target for policy interventions, with networks benefiting the more inherently connected and those most comfortable forming cross-border connections. Nonetheless, policy interventions have addressed the networking frictions that lead to suboptimal relationships. Studies have documented that business association formation at the national level has been found to have positive effects on firm performance through learning and partnering (Cai and Szeidl 2018; McKenzie and Woodruff 2014). However, managers may not initiate such associations to avoid "free rider" problems, such as high setup costs that fall unevenly onto the organizer, and because they underestimate the gains of network formation. Such issues may call for policy guidance that encourages such networking, albeit in a structured way designed to maximize participation and information exchange.

The survey results suggest that useful interventions could include support for regional and international business associations, industry meetings, matchmaking events, and travel missions abroad. Industry veterans could be a prime resource for guidance, one-on-one mentoring, and networking.

Cross-border women's networks may address the very low share of women entrepreneurs and the even lower share of women-led outward investments. Network formation targeted at women can help reduce their specific fixed entry costs of engagement.

A business and policy platform that is open to the diaspora would help businesses led by women develop cross-border activity and partnerships, and would help identify unique challenges to women's participation and advancement and collectively develop solutions. Diaspora women could enable access to capital and information, provide mentoring, and act as a bridge between their countries of origin and their current home markets. Such an intervention may be justified, given that some evidence suggests women are less likely to proactively network because of, among other things, different beliefs about appropriate networking norms. Additionally, individuals may be more at ease networking with others of the same gender (Howell and Nanda 2019).

Multilateral institutions could play a convening role to build networks nationally and across borders, support business development (capital access and capabilities development), and support policy initiatives and solutions with technical assistance (for example, to overcome regulatory barriers to women's participation).

INFORMATION SUPPORT

Low knowledge connectivity implies that firms have suboptimal knowledge about opportunities and potential partners abroad. This report endorses and deepens the arguments in favor of information-enhancing operations and technology-enabled platforms to promote trade and investment in developing countries. For example, established web portals could provide the foundation for dynamic activities to support information updating and exchange and network formation. Such portals could enable industry-specific curation with guidance from industry veterans and include all the relevant players in the pertinent value chain (such as logistics firms and consultancy firms). Portals and similar instruments need to be publicized to promote their wide use, and registration should be actively encouraged at home. At the same time, their existence should be publicized abroad (Ecorys 2014).

The most important type of OFDI-related information support requested by the survey respondents was about market opportunities abroad, followed by information on legal and management issues, conducting business abroad in South Asia, and experiences of previous investors (figure 5A.1 in the annex to this chapter). Information on regulations, procedures, and opening a representative office in South Asia and key commercial hubs was also deemed useful. This report attempts to fulfill the demand for knowledge of firm strategies that have worked. In this context, detailed expositions of pioneer firm experiences through case studies and interactive forums with entrepreneurs, focusing on solutions and outcomes of investments, would be valuable.

ENHANCING VISIBILITY AND COMPENSATING FOR RESTRICTED AVAILABILITY OF INFORMATION

Firms that are not listed on the stock exchange and do not make their annual reports public (for example, family firms and medium firms) have a harder time signaling their value as potential partners. In addition to setting up corporate websites, they may need to use external mechanisms to signal their value, such as globally recognized certifications for management quality standards and sustainability practices (for example, from the International Organization for Standardization). The costs of these certifications have been prohibitive for some firms. The visibility issue for medium firms may be one reason that primarily large firms get involved in regional or global partnerships. These concerns are equally relevant for both IFDI and OFDI.

HARNESSING THE POSSIBILITIES OF INVESTMENT PROMOTION AGENCIES AND EMBASSIES

The survey responses relating to channels of information on business opportunities abroad indicated only a minor role for destination countries' foreign investment promotion agencies and their embassies in the home country. This result could be interpreted to mean that such agencies will need appropriate focus and reorientation to possibly play a larger role. Further, embassies of home countries in investment destinations could provide information on markets, firms in relevant sectors, and steps toward opening a representative office.

AIR CONNECTIVITY FOR INFORMATION EXCHANGE AND RELATIONSHIP BUILDING

Investors and potential investors identified business travel and tourism as important sources of awareness about regional business opportunities. Thus, direct air connections would be a valuable source of connectivity. Direct air connections between India and Sri Lanka have played an important role in bilateral trade and investment. Nepal's regional pioneer confirmed that tourist travel in Sri Lanka and interaction with Sri Lankans induced him to invest in Sri Lankan hotels, which has led to his undertaking much bigger investments in the hospitality industry in Nepal and elsewhere. Recent research using data on travel from Germany to the United States (Hovhannisyan 2019) has also shown that business travel by air is associated with increased innovation. Air connectivity is especially important for trade by landlocked economies because it offers possibilities for market and product diversification and for building new relationships, within South Asia and beyond the region. After COVID-19, regional air travel is likely to become more important relative to global travel, at least in the near term, which will help regional networking and relationship building.

Policy interventions may build on the lessons from India–Sri Lanka air travel liberalization, including adopting an incremental approach to the freeing up of air services (see Kathuria [2018], chapter 4, for details). The bilateral relationship continues to deepen with the upgrading of Jaffna airport in northern Sri Lanka and its links to southern Indian cities, which could help revive this postconflict area of Sri Lanka. An air corridor program that subsidizes air freight may not be financially viable in the long term, but a limited catalytic intervention could help develop important relationships and networks in the short term that could lead to profitable trade and investment in the long term. Regional airport hubs that serve a cross-border clientele could also be feasible in some parts of the region: Varanasi in the Indian state of Uttar Pradesh, for example, could also serve parts of Nepal. Finally, trade-facilitation expenditures on technology and process simplification, and regional cooperation to ensure health security in the context of pandemics, would be important to reviving air travel. In this context, the issuance of business visas could be an important precursor to opening up tourist travel.

DEVELOPMENT OF LOCAL INVESTMENT INTERMEDIARIES

Entrepreneurs rarely have all the information they need to make investment decisions—but they should know where they can go to get such information. Investment intermediaries reduce entry costs by providing information at a lower cost than entrepreneurs trying to secure the knowledge on their own. The availability of these services, access to them at reasonable prices, and a wide awareness of their existence matter. However, there appear to be failures in the market for knowledge in South Asia. The survey indicates that most of the respondents were unaware of whether intermediaries such as consultancy firms that can provide due diligence on regional markets and implementation support existed. India has local affiliates of both international and national consultancy firms. However, pricing is an issue. The Sri Lankan pioneer Brandix, which invested in the development of an apparel special economic zone in India, was forced to do its due diligence in house for what turned out to be one-third of the price quoted by the Indian affiliate of a prominent global consulting firm. This revelation suggests that there is a profitable space for the private sector to provide high-quality consultancy services that specialize in cross-border issues. Existing consulting firms should be publicized in the national trade and investment facilitation portals. The absence of competitive consulting service providers may be related to a desire for secrecy, trust-related issues, or other behavioral concerns of medium firms. Further work is needed to assess the actual landscape of investment consulting services, and knowledge-providing intermediaries more broadly, in each country.

Physical and Digital Connectivity

It costs more to trade within South Asia than within any other region in the world (Kathuria 2018). The empirical evidence (chapter 4) indicates that these high trade costs also have a negative impact on investment. Investments in trade facilitation and transportation infrastructure are gradually reducing these high costs and will help not only to increase intraregional trade, but also promote investment within the region. Reduction of trade costs supports investment directly through greater vertical investments along the value chain, as well as indirectly through increases in market learning through the export experience. Some valuable initiatives include progress on electronic data interchange systems at seaports and land borders, development of ports and inland waterways as well as transnational highways, and improvements in air connectivity.

Enhancing digital infrastructure and associated regulatory frameworks is also vital, given that communication costs that are correlated with distance have an impact on FDI entry (Gumpert 2018; Oldenski 2012). The negative impact of distance on investment, conditional on exporting, implies that communication costs may also be an important factor that reduces investment with distance. This issue will be especially important if a post-COVID-19 environment involves less international travel and greater use of digitization in communications and the conduct of business. Security-consistent trade facilitation mechanisms and procedures would ease the flow of goods and services in the region (Kerswell and Kunaka 2015). In the current context of the pandemic, such mechanisms extend to health security and cyber security.

The pandemic can catalyze further trade facilitation, building on some of the positive steps taken by countries, such as accepting electronic copies of trade documentation and India's "faceless assessments" program, which eliminates physical interaction between the taxpayer and the tax authority. Despite progress in electronic management of cross-border trade flows, trade often requires physical submission of paper documents to the various government agencies regulating trade. The development of electronic national single windows and working toward interoperability of such systems would boost global and regional trade. Extending digital acceptance of sanitary and phytosanitary documents (given the high share of vegetables and foodstuffs in intraregional trade) will have positive region-specific effects (De and Kunaka 2019; Nora, Sahu, and Peterson 2020). Overall, many of the trade-facilitation efforts, while valid for global trade, will have a significant impact on intraregional trade.

Regulatory and Promotion Policies for OFDI

Outward investment is becoming the new frontier of investment policy making for developing economies. As more firms from emerging economies invest abroad, governments need to address both regulatory (the extent of liberalization of capital controls) and promotional (the extent of active support given to these firms) aspects of policy. At one time, these policies were considered a macroeconomic issue, bearing on domestic productive capacity and foreign exchange management. However, a value chain approach to competitiveness provides important new microeconomic considerations in favor of relaxation of controls on OFDI for emerging market firms. In the COVID-19 context, the value chain approach offers firms greater agility and flexibility with which to maneuver in crises and build more resilient international partnerships.

Outward investment offers opportunities for firms to access higher-profit segments along a value chain when the associated activities are located across the border, fulfill buyers' higher volume and product scope requirements, secure stable access to inputs, and reduce markups originating from suppliers with market power. OFDI also allows firms to buy technology, brands, or other intellectual property when developing them at home may be capability constrained or take too much time. It provides an opportunity to build stronger relationships with customers and production partners along a value chain.

In this context, it is important to not restrain a country's vibrant firms and to allow them to compete globally with the same options available to firms from other countries. Restrictions on OFDI could imply that firms at home have difficulty competing with foreign firms that use OFDI to gain competitiveness. Such restrictions could, for example, be constraining ferrosilicon exporters from Bhutan that compete with Japanese and Australian investors based in Malaysia that have made strong inroads into Bhutan's traditional market of India. These OFDI restrictions may be viewed as creating inequality of opportunity between home firms and foreign firms. Further, even low-value, trade-supporting investments could be important for Bangladeshi apparel manufacturers to improve direct access to global buyers. The high presence of intermediaries in Bangladesh may account for the low profit margins and lack of spillover benefits (such as staff training, short-term work assignments in buyer headquarters, and more crisis-resilient relationships) that would arise from close relationships with final retailers in the apparel manufacturing sector.

REGULATORY REFORM AND TRANSPARENCY

Gradually relaxing capital controls or being more open to consideration of OFDI proposals is important. Any relaxation must be pursued in the context of sound macroeconomic management within an integrated policy framework, with a range of available instruments (Gopinath 2019). Policies may be designed in a progressive and flexible manner that allows the government space for action under stress. Appropriate reporting by firms will improve the monitoring of policy impacts and help finesse necessary policy adjustments.

For smaller economies, such as Bhutan and Nepal, with very restrictive OFDI arrangements, helping firms open offices abroad could be a first step. Even if policies are in place to technically allow OFDI, governments will need to signal that this behavior is encouraged, making procedures public, transparent, and administratively inexpensive. Bangladesh, despite significant international reserves and a vibrant private sector, has only cautiously approved overseas investments in apparel manufacturing (in Ethiopia, targeting the US market), reconstituted wood products, pharmaceuticals, steel, and engineering, mostly in East Asia. In Afghanistan and Maldives, where the governments state that they have a neutral stance toward OFDI, the relevant policies and procedures need to be readily available and accessible. A lack of publicly available information is more likely to create a situation in which only large or politically connected firms have access to OFDI.

INSTITUTIONAL STRUCTURE

The institutional structure governing OFDI varies across countries and is fragmented compared with IFDI. Currently, most approvals are handled at a department of the central bank, whereas promotional support is divided across various institutions.

PROMOTIONAL SUPPORT FOR OUTWARD INVESTORS

Whereas this report argues for regulatory liberalization of OFDI, it suggests that South Asian countries could at least take a neutral stance on OFDI promotion. This stance is sensitive to the fiscal demands brought on by the pandemic. A more forward-looking approach would encompass certain limited promotional activities, based on a range of criteria, keeping in mind global experience and the marginal cost of provision of support services. Information and networking support could be provided at a low marginal cost by focused trade promotion agencies and inward investment promotion agencies without the need to create new institutions. This method also allows an integrated approach to trade, inward investment, and outward investment.

Some governments have set up formal organizations in foreign countries to support their trade and investments abroad that not only fill information gaps but also facilitate entry support. For example, the Japanese External Trade Organization facilitates Japanese trade and outward investments, and has recently begun to promote IFDI to Japan. The organization has close to 80 offices in 55 countries. It has five offices in India and one each in Bangladesh, Pakistan, and Sri Lanka. Support of this nature may be appropriate for India, given that Indian firms have a large number of investments abroad. Other countries may house effective OFDI support within their embassies abroad.

Potential investors identified legal and management consultancy services and technical assistance for project development and start-up as important sources of support. Given that risk appetite was an important variable in investment entry, an education system that provides entrepreneurship education and encourages links between academia and business could foster more outward investors. Because outward investment is a relatively new concept, cross-border management studies would also be helpful.

Other areas identified by potential investors include access to finance, investment insurance, and financial guarantees (figure 5A.2 in the annex). Financial support for pre-investment activities and start-up costs was the most requested type of OFDI assistance among survey respondents, consistent with the empirical results that investors are often forced to rely on internal funds and intraconglomerate loans for making all types of investments. The demand for investment insurance may reflect the need for trust-compensating mechanisms in the presence of trust deficits, lack of confidence in foreign regulatory institutions, and underdeveloped bilateral relationships. Sensitization of financial institutions to potentially profitable new activities and the development of angel investors and venture capitalists could somewhat address these issues.

Implications for Inward FDI Policy and Promotion

A more symmetric view of IFDI and OFDI may be an innovative and more useful approach to foreign investment policy making. Although this study focuses on OFDI, its approach, including the focus on knowledge connectivity, has important implications for policies to attract inward foreign investment.

RECOGNIZING TRADERS AND NONEQUITY PARTNERS AS POTENTIAL INVESTORS

Given that many firms may follow a gradual approach to investment, governments should be aware that "low-capital" or nonequity modes of engagement may be a first step toward greater commitment. Thus, these initiatives should be supported and given appropriate attention. Focus should not be solely on trying to secure large investments. Governments that require minimum equity capital thresholds for investors to qualify for investment incentives should have a more sophisticated policy design to accommodate this behavior if they seek to attract a critical mass of investors. Some South Asian countries have a disappointing track record for attracting new entrants and often rely on the expansion plans of existing investors.[1]

TARGETING REGIONAL AFFILIATES OF INTERNATIONAL INVESTORS

Smaller South Asian nations may generate more positive results by courting investors that already have regional affiliates in, say, India. The existence of these regional affiliates means extraregional international firms have already incurred the fixed entry costs for South Asia. The entry costs for another South Asian country are likely to be lower relative to those of an international firm with no presence in South Asia, reflecting learning through previous investments in a regional neighbor. This strategy would likely be cheaper and lead to greater success than roadshows to distant advanced economies.

WIDENING THE SCOPE OF INVESTOR TARGETING TO INCLUDE EMERGING MARKET MULTINATIONALS

The growth of globally competitive emerging market multinational enterprises can be seen in the case studies, the survey, and other cited work (for example, Gomez-Mera et al. 2015). These multinationals may have more appropriate technology and, in general, be better suited to navigating emerging market economies. Thus, developing knowledge of high-performing firms in emerging economies, including neighbors, could have significant payoffs. This concept applies equally to the almost-landlocked North Eastern Region of India.

APPROACHING INTERNATIONAL SITE SELECTION AND MANAGEMENT CONSULTANCIES

The exact role and dynamics of international consultancy firms that provide international location selection and management services for large corporations are not well documented (Phelps and Wood 2018).[2] As intermediaries, they are primarily information brokers, but they also add value by getting involved in incentive negotiations and even enforcement. Investment promotion agencies could target such firms to increase national visibility. Besides site selection for corporate clients, some firms have divisions that include investment promotion consulting for national or subnational investment promotion agencies and "lead generation" for organizations seeking to attract inward investment. The potential for conflicts of interest is muted by the importance of reputation for these intermediaries.

TARGETING "HIGH-QUALITY" AND "HIGH-VISIBILITY" FOREIGN CAPITAL

All capital is not of the same caliber (Harding and Javorcik 2013). Governments could target firms that have characteristics such as likely long-term country engagement, higher technology diffusion, greater likelihood of engaging with local firms, and the creation of spillovers from sustainability initiatives. For example, Sri Lankan apparel firms with strong reputations for women's empowerment and environmentally friendly business practices have had positive impacts on local communities, particularly in Andhra Pradesh, India. It may also be useful to target "anchor" investors, that is, firms that are well connected and have high visibility—likely to generate follower firms' interest—and thus could help draw in investment from their suppliers or other global competitors. If these firms are large, they can potentially enhance national comparative advantage, as in the case of Samsung in Vietnam.

OVERCOMING "STICKY" GLOBAL VALUE CHAINS AND STATUS QUO BIAS MAY REQUIRE GREATER-THAN-USUAL EFFORTS

Late-entrant countries into the FDI game may need to signal the country's determination to attract and retain value chain leaders through sustained efforts, including courtship of investors by the highest levels of government.

REDUCING THE FIXED ENTRY COSTS OF INWARD INVESTMENT

Government initiatives in investment facilitation could be viewed through the lens of reducing entry costs, both directly and in accessing information about procedures. Thus, initiatives such as faster and one-stop clearance, simplification of administrative procedures, and greater use of information and communication technology could enhance capital inflows. Beyond entry, there has been increasing recognition of the importance of investment retention and the development of relationships with established investors to foster smooth business conduct and investment expansion. Countries should build on the digitization initiatives relating to investment approvals and facilitation that began during the COVID-19 pandemic.

Emerging Business Practices and Policy Making

Government policy making will benefit from an understanding that economies have a skewed distribution of firms, with a cluster of large, high-performing firms driving cross-border activity and domestic production. The importance of large firms for exporting and job creation has been shown to be true for both advanced and developing economies (Freund 2016). The empirical results in this report confirm the importance of large, high-productivity South Asian firms in making outward investments. While promoting competition, firm entry, job creation, and support to small and medium enterprises, governments at the same time should not constrain the growth of large, high-performing firms. The most positive results emerge when governments and large firms recognize that they are partners in national development.

Policy makers need to be cognizant of the evolving industrial landscape and changes in business dynamics. Policies, capabilities, and incentives should adapt to these changes. The pioneer case studies in the apparel industry, for example, indicate that policy making needs to recognize the importance of more sophisticated logistics infrastructure driven by "fast fashion" and low-inventory stock management strategies (although this may be tempered by the COVID-19 experience). Similarly, in agri-food processing, given the increasing demand for fresh fruits, vegetables, and fish, investments in cold chain infrastructure may be superior to promoting standard value-added activities, such as canning these products.

Some industries are seeing a movement toward asset-light approaches (for example, hotels), which implies that flows of capital may not be of the same order of magnitude as experienced previously. Nevertheless, cross-border relationships that transfer knowledge and skills are still important and need to be facilitated and supported.[3] The dramatic growth in international licensing of intellectual property is depicted in figure 5.1. Government policies, digital infrastructure, and financial architecture should be able to support these welfare-enhancing deals that do not necessarily come with large capital flows.

FIGURE 5.1 Trends in World Trade in Goods versus Intellectual Property Payments, Services Imports, and Foreign Direct Investment Flows, 1990–2017

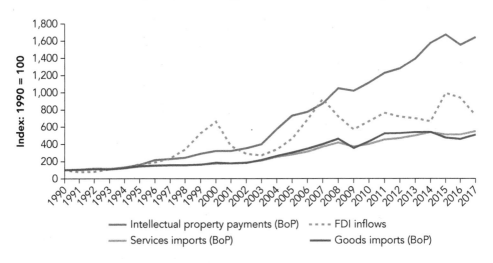

Source: Adapted from UNCTAD 2019.
Note: BoP = balance of payments; FDI = foreign direct investment.

Facilitating services trade payments such as those for intellectual property is crucial in this context. An example of updating policy to the realities of how business operates is the Indian government's extension of automatic approval of manufacturing FDI to contract manufacturers in 2019.[4]

Unilateral National Reforms Can Spur Regional Engagement

In addition to unilateral reform of OFDI discussed earlier, policies that support greater internal integration, an improved investment climate, financial sector reform, entrepreneurship education, trade policy reform, and competition in a country are likely to support regional engagement. For example, the adoption of the unified Goods and Services Tax by the Indian government in 2017 is likely to encourage South Asian exporters and investors. Entrepreneurs outside India viewed the various taxes in different states and additional charges to cross state lines as multiple fixed entry costs. Similarly, differences in state regulations, especially with respect to food safety, also act like multiple entry costs within a country.

Retail FDI in India acts as the link between the apparel communities in India and Bangladesh, providing an example of the interaction between national reforms and networks. India's initial expansion of preferences and elimination of duties for apparel from Bangladesh in 2011 did not elicit much of an increase in exports of ready-made garments from Bangladesh, suggesting the fixed costs of entry were sufficiently high to deter entry. Goods and Services Tax reforms in India in 2017 increased transparency and reduced the number of transactions for exporters. In addition, for Bangladesh, the growing presence of global retailers in India appears to have spurred apparel exports. Reports from India name the retailers Zara and H&M as large importer firms—these firms have retail FDI in India as well as contract manufacturing networks in Bangladesh, and they use these manufacturing networks to import Bangladeshi apparel into India. This is a good example of the entry-cost-reducing nature of networks. In this way, retail FDI is encouraging the formation of a regional value chain in South Asia, similar to how Japanese manufacturing FDI did in East Asia, albeit in a much more limited way.

Implications of the Pandemic for Policy Prioritization and Regional Engagement

The findings of this report are relevant in the post-COVID-19 world because, apart from public health challenges, the pandemic has accelerated the pre-COVID-19 developments in the global economy. These developments include an increase in trade protection measures; the potential restructuring of value chains toward greater regionalization, reshoring, and nearshoring;[5] and diversification pressure induced by, among other factors, the need to make supply chains more resilient and to take into account the trade tensions between the United States and China. Further, just as in the post-global-recession period, foreign investment will be an important building block in the recovery from the pandemic and the recasting of the "next normal." This report provides pointers to innovative approaches to building resilience and gaining from the opportunities arising from the evolving paradigm. The following policy reforms are linked to issues that seem to be growing in importance in the post-COVID-19 world.

OFDI regulatory reform increases the agility and resilience of local firms in times of crisis. OFDI provides another avenue through which national firms can better weather disruptions through more diversified access to information, inputs, and markets as well as cross-border relationship building. Evidence from previous crises has shown that it is the longer and deeper cross-border firm-to-firm relationships that have endured turbulent times. All this remains true even if host country restrictions on foreign investment in strategically important sectors outlast the pandemic.

Timely policies to promote, facilitate, and retain inward investment can help the region benefit from global restructuring opportunities. The pandemic may lead to more opportunities to attract foreign investment to South Asia. It is possible that a greater volume of South Asian OFDI would locate closer to home because of disruptions in traditional markets and rising trade costs. Moreover, as a result of trade tensions between China and the United States, some foreign firms are accelerating their exit from China; more broadly, these firms are seeking more diversification along their value chains. Japan, for example, has for some time pushed a "China plus One" strategy to reduce its dependence on China. To support this initiative, the Japanese government even provides relocation assistance to its multinational firms. This situation implies that timely and effectively targeted investment promotion efforts could yield high payoffs. Many countries have speeded up investment approvals, accelerated the use of online tools and e-platforms, and provided COVID-19-related investment retention services. Given reduced travel and knowledge connectivity, nonequity modes of engagement may become more important than in the past. In such a scenario, local firms may receive access to foreign markets and technology but still require capital financing options.

As trade costs rise, *trade facilitation initiatives and connectivity investments* become more vital. Because health security and other trade costs, such as shipping, have increased during the pandemic, it has become important to accelerate trade facilitation reforms to keep overall trade costs in check. Doing so is important not only for trade flows but also, as shown in this report, for attracting FDI. Digital initiatives to reduce trade costs have been increasingly adopted during the pandemic, and these initiatives should become a permanent feature of the trade facilitation and connectivity agenda.

To ameliorate the disruptions of COVID-19 and anticipated future pandemics and disruptions, the following three factors could receive greater priority.

First, governments and firms will need to accelerate investment in digitization for communications, information flow, and the conduct of business. The COVID-19 pandemic accelerated adoption of digitization, and the post-COVID-19 scenario will involve a sharper reliance on digital capabilities. Opportunities are now available to build on the digitization initiatives in trade and investment facilitation that have occurred during the pandemic. Investment in, and upgrading of, digital capabilities will characterize governments and firms that are better able to navigate the long-term impact of the COVID-19 pandemic.

Second, it will be important for governments to not restrain future growth sectors. Several business sectors—including health care, pharmaceuticals, medical equipment, e-commerce, education (including information technology–enabled education), and information technology–enabled services, to name a few—are likely to increase their weight in national and global economies, and governments should ensure that they do not stifle their growth through undue regulatory barriers, including those related to trade and investment.

Third, government resilience and crisis response capabilities will receive greater weight in investment destination decisions, including both immediate logistical responses to support business continuity and longer-term fiscal responsibility that allows for government action under crisis situations. Although governments may pursue crisis-ameliorating policies in situations of high uncertainty, it is important that these policies not be allowed to continue beyond the crisis. Such policies include restrictive trade, exchange control, and investment-protection measures. In the same way, innovative, security-consistent approaches to opening the economy will have significant payoffs with potential longer-term positive implications through the building of relationships.

Concluding Remarks: Toward a More Engaged South Asia

Despite COVID-19-related setbacks, South Asia is likely to recover its position as one of the fastest-growing regions in the world, and the potential for shared prosperity through greater engagement remains a missed opportunity, with growing costs. This report analyzes issues facing South Asian investors from a global perspective while distilling the key regional implications. The contribution of the analysis to regional engagement comes from focusing on investment and information barriers; highlighting regional opportunities, successful regional pioneers, and the availability of a wide range of engagement options; and spotlighting severe distortions in many outward investment policy arrangements. The report argues for a more integrative approach to global competitiveness that involves trade, IFDI, and OFDI. Similarly, it argues that policy actions regarding connectivity should specifically address knowledge connectivity and digital connectivity in addition to physical connectivity.

In the data collected for this report, 63 percent of the number of first investments were in the region. Thus, the basis for a deeper level of regional engagement exists, fueled by the link between trade, investment, and connectivity. Building on this foundation can help South Asian countries bridge the gap between current and potential opportunities for regional engagement, increase global competitiveness, and diversify the risks that have become embedded in the global environment.

Trade and FDI will continue to be critical for growth and development in the post-COVID-19 world. In South Asia, low levels of intraregional trade and investment indicate the presence of significant unexploited development potential. Moreover, regional value chains and regional trade may possibly become relatively more important in the post-COVID-19 environment, boosting the importance of reforms and investments that would unlock regional trade and investment. Whichever direction the post-COVID-19 world takes, the above-noted messages on trade and investment remain valid, and the associated policy reforms merit consideration.

Annex 5A: Implications for Policy and Operations

FIGURE 5A.1 **Market Opportunities Dominate the Type of Information Support Requested**

What types of information would be most useful to you in supporting intraregional investments?

Source: South Asian Regional Engagement and Value Chains Survey.
Note: OFDI = outward foreign direct investment.

FIGURE 5A.2 **Access to Finance Dominates OFDI Support Requests**

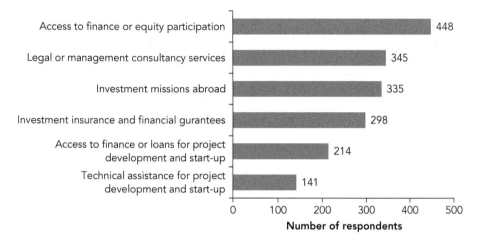

What OFDI promotion and facilitation policies from your home government would be helpful to consider outward foreign direct investment?

Source: South Asian Regional Engagement and Value Chains Survey.
Note: OFDI = outward foreign direct investment.

Notes

1. For example, retained earnings amounted to more than 50 percent of IFDI flows stocks in Bangladesh during 2012–19, except in 2018.

2. However, the formation of a guild of site selectors in 2010 in the United States has been helpful in identifying firms (www.siteselectorsguild.com).

3. In fact, the development of the apparel sector in Bangladesh is attributed to the training offered by the Republic of Korea's firm Daewoo to 130 employees of Bangladesh's Desh Garments, many of whom would later become the entrepreneurial backbone of the industry.

4. Department for Promotion of Industry and Internal Trade, FDI Policy Section, Press Note No. 4 (2019 Series), Section 3, page 2 (https://dipp.gov.in/sites/default/files/pn4_2019.pdf).

5. For updates on trade protection, see Global Trade Alert (https://www.globaltradealert.org/global_dynamics). For a recent discussion of reshoring and nearshoring, see Asian Development Bank (2021).

References

Asian Development Bank. 2021. *Asian Economic Integration Report 2021: Making Digital Platforms Work for Asia and the Pacific.* Manila: Asian Development Bank.

Cai, Jing, and Adam Szeidl. 2018. "Interfirm Relationships and Business." *Quarterly Journal of Economics* 133 (3): 1229–82.

De, Prabir, and Charles Kunaka. 2020. "Connectivity Assessment." In *Playing to Strengths: A Policy Framework for Mainstreaming Northeast India,* edited by Sanjay Kathuria and Priya Mathur, 41–63. Washington, DC: World Bank.

Ecorys. 2014. "Business Networks." Final Report for Director General Enterprise and Industry. Rotterdam.

Freund, Caroline. 2016. *Rich People Poor Countries: The Rise of Emerging-Market Tycoons and Their Mega Firms.* Washington, DC: Peterson Institute for International Economics.

Gomez-Mera, Laura, Thomas Kenyon, Yotam Margalit, Jose Guilherme Reis, and Gonzalo Varela. 2015. *New Voices in Investment: A Survey of Investors from Emerging Countries.* Washington, DC: World Bank.

Gopinath, Gita. 2019. "Making the Case for an Integrated Policy Framework." International Monetary Fund, Washington, DC.

Gumpert, A. 2018. "The Organization of Knowledge in Multinational Firms." *Journal of the European Economic Association* 16 (6): 1929–76.

Harding, Torfinn, and Beata S. Javorcik. 2013. "Investment Promotion and FDI Inflows: Quality Matters." *CESifo Economic Studies* 59 (2): 337–59.

Hovhannisyan, N. 2019. "Business Air Travel and Technology Diffusion." Working Paper 25862, National Bureau of Economic Research, Cambridge, MA.

Howell, Sabrina T., and Ramana Nanda. 2019. "Networking Frictions in Venture Capital, and the Gender Gap in Entrepreneurship." Working Paper 26449, National Bureau of Economic Research, Cambridge, MA.

Kathuria, Sanjay, ed. 2018. *A Glass Half Full: The Promise of Regional Trade in South Asia.* South Asia Development Forum. Washington, DC: World Bank.

Kerswell, Clay, and Charles Kunaka. 2015. "The Security and Trade Facilitation Nexus: Options for South Asian Countries." *SAR Connect* 4, July, World Bank, Washington, DC.

McKenzie, David, and Christopher Woodruff. 2014. "What Are We Learning from Business Training and Entrepreneurship Evaluations around the Developing World?" *World Bank Research Observer* 29 (1): 48–82.

Nora, Erik, Satya Prasad Sahu, and Ivan Peterson. 2020. "COVID-19 Highlights Need for Digitizing and Automating Trade in South Asia." World Bank blog, August 14.

Oldenski, Lindsay. 2012. "Export Versus FDI and the Communication of Complex Information." *Journal of International Economics* 87 (2): 312–22.

Phelps, N. A., and A. M. Wood. 2018. "The Business of Location: Site Selection Consultants and the Mobilisation of Knowledge in the Location Decision." *Journal of Economic Geography* 18 (5): 1023–44.

UNCTAD (United Nations Conference on Trade and Development). 2019. *World Investment Report 2019: Special Economic Zones.* Geneva: UNCTAD.

Consolidated Direct Investment Survey Data Augmentation

The International Monetary Fund's Coordinated Direct Investment Survey reporter and mirror data are augmented in four ways:

- AU1, using reporter data as the base, missing data are augmented with mirror data

- AU2, using mirror data as the base, missing data are augmented by reporter data

- AU3, using the maximum value when two values are available

- AU4, using the minimum value when two values are available

The outcomes of the augmentation for outward foreign direct investment (OFDI) are seen in figure A.1. First, the augmentation dramatically increases the number of bilateral pairs that are covered, from almost 4,400 on a reporter basis to more than 9,200 pairs. Although mirror data provided about 7,000 bilateral pairs, the augmentation program used added 2,200 pairwise data points. Using mirror data and the augmentation dramatically increased data availability for the non-high-income to non-high-income economies. Given that this is the key group the analysis is intended to address, the exercise was very useful. The next big improvements were in high-income to non-high-income economies.

As measured by overall value, the augmented reporter data are higher by US$3 trillion, 12 percent more than the original reporter data, driven mainly by foreign direct investment (FDI) from high-income to non-high-income economies. FDI originating from developing economies rose by just US$600 million. Although small in absolute terms, it represented a 47 percent increase from the reporter data values.

High-income to high-income FDI accounted for the bulk of FDI, 76 percent, whereas high-income to non-high-income FDI amounted to 18 percent. The remaining 6 percent of FDI originating from non-high-income economies was split, with 4.3 percent going to high-income economies and just 1.7 percent going to other non-high-income economies. OFDI from developing economies amounted to US$1.8 trillion in 2015, and US$514 billion of that was South-South investment.

FIGURE A.1 CDIS Data Augmentation Doubles Data Availability and Increases Value by US$3 Trillion

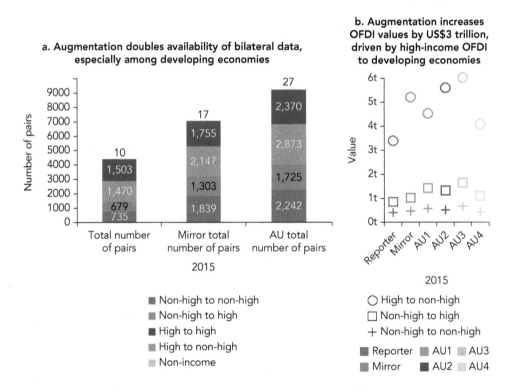

Sources: World Bank calculations using IMF Coordinated Direct Investment Survey data.
Note: The legend refers to income levels, that is, "high to non-high" refers to OFDI from high-income economies to non-high-income (middle- and low-income) economies, according to World Bank income classifications. The IMF data covered several more jurisdictions than the World Bank data, and these were incorporated into the income and regional categories using various sources. For 2015, the unclassified "." pairs represent just 27 bilateral relationships. "Total number of pairs" refers to reporter data. "AU" refers to augmented data. See text for definitions of AU1, AU2, AU3, and AU4. CDIS = Coordinated Direct Investment Survey; IMF = International Monetary Fund; OFDI = outward foreign direct investment.

FIGURE A.2 Top Destinations for Outward FDI Stock from Each South Asian Economy, 2017

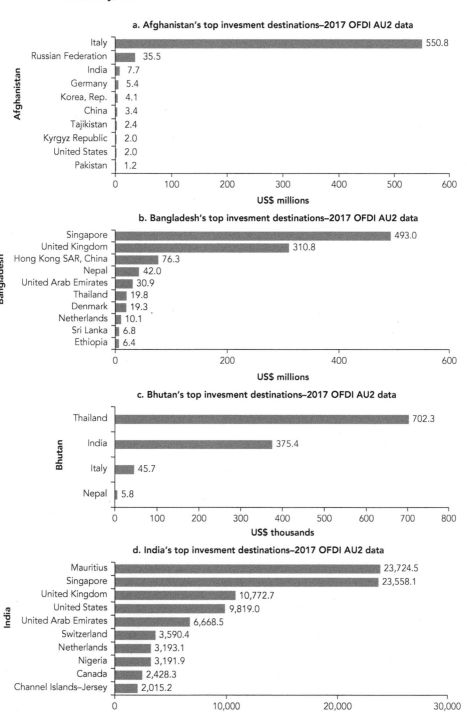

a. Afghanistan's top invesment destinations–2017 OFDI AU2 data

b. Bangladesh's top invesment destinations–2017 OFDI AU2 data

c. Bhutan's top invesment destinations–2017 OFDI AU2 data

d. India's top invesment destinations–2017 OFDI AU2 data

figure continues next page

FIGURE A.2 Top Destinations for Outward FDI Stock from Each South Asian Economy, 2017 *(continued)*

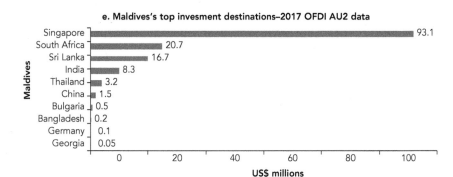

e. Maldives's top invesment destinations–2017 OFDI AU2 data

US$ millions

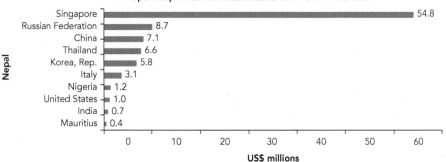

f. Nepal's top invesment destinations–2017 OFDI AU2 data

US$ millions

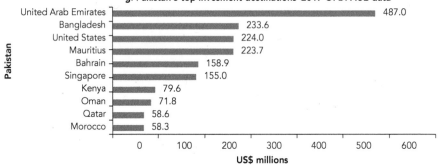

g. Pakistan's top invesment destinations–2017 OFDI AU2 data

US$ millions

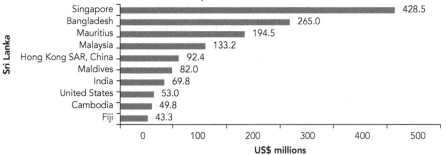

h. Sri Lanka's top invesment destinations–2017 OFDI AU2 data

US$ millions

Source: Augmented International Monetary Fund Coordinated Direct Investment Survey data.
Note: Calculations use AU2 (augmentation 2) data.

FIGURE A.3 **Ease of Investing across Borders: Developing Regions, 2010 (0–100, best)**

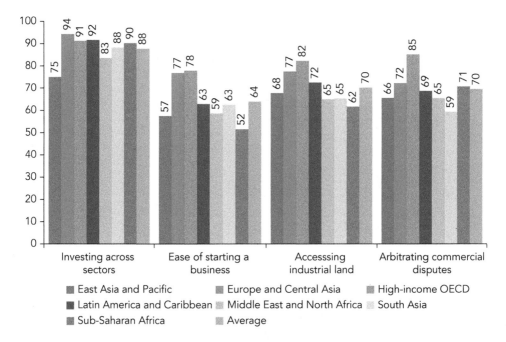

Sources: IFC (International Finance Corporation), MIGA (Multilateral Investment Guarantee Agency), and World Bank, *Investing across Borders 2010: Indicators of Foreign Direct Investment Regulation in 87 Economies* (Washington, DC: World Bank, 2010).
Note: The average is the simple mean across countries and subindexes. OECD = Organisation for Economic Co-operation and Development.

TABLE A.1 Ease of Investing Across Borders: South Asian Economies, 2012

Country	Investing across sectors (0–100)	Average number of procedures required to start a foreign subsidiary	Average number of days required to start a foreign subsidiary	Average length of arbitration proceedings (days)	Average length of recognition and enforcement proceedings (days)	Inflows: Currency conversion and transfer index (0–100)	Outflows: Currency conversion and transfer index (0–100)	Average time to obtain a temporary work permit (weeks)
Afghanistan	87	6	9	No data	No data	100	100	No data
Bangladesh	97	10	45	278	836	57.5	20.00	8
India	81	15	35	569	1,654	50.0	56.25	3
Nepal	80	10	84	No data	No data	32.5	28.75	7
Pakistan	93	13	36	479	5,610	62.5	62.50	6
Sri Lanka	74	7	47	No data	No data	32.5	66.25	5
IAB average	**91**	**9**	**38**	**326**	**557**	**84**	**81**	**8**

Source: Investing across Borders 2012 (http://iad.worldbank.org).
Note: Investing across sectors is the simple mean of the foreign equity cap across the different sectors per country (1–100 best).
The IAB average is the simple mean across 103 countries. IAB = investing across borders.

TABLE A.2 Intraregional Investment Agreements in South Asia

	Afghanistan	Bangladesh	Bhutan	India	Maldives	Nepal	Pakistan	Sri Lanka
Afghanistan								
Bangladesh			DTAA	DTAA, IA		DTAA		DTAA
Bhutan		DTAA		DTAA				
India		DTAA, IA	DTAA			DTAA, IA[a]	DTAA	DTAA, IA[a]
Maldives								
Nepal		DTAA		DTAA			DTAA	DTAA
Pakistan				DTAA		DTAA		IA
Sri Lanka		DTAA		DTAA, IA[a]		DTAA	IA	
Total investment agreements	3	24	0	20[b]	0	4	32	24

Sources: https://investmentpolicy.unctad.org/, accessed June 2019; internet search.
Note: DTAA = Double Taxation Avoidance Agreement; IA = international investment agreement. "Total investment agreements" includes investment agreements with all countries inside and outside South Asia.
a. No longer in force.
b. This was 85 in 2017.

TABLE A.3 North Eastern Region, India: Basic Profile, 2017–18

Name of state	Capital city	Land area (square kilometers)	Population (million, 2011)	GDP (US$, billion)[a]	GDP per capita (US$)[a]
Assam	Dispur	78,438	31.2	44.8	1,151
Manipur	Imphal	22,327	2.9	3.7	1,015
Meghalaya	Shillong	22,429	3.0	4.8	1,258
Mizoram	Aizawl	21,081	1.1	3.0	2,191
Nagaland	Kohima	16,579	2.0	3.8	1,592
Sikkim	Gangtok	7,096	0.6	3.6	4,920
Tripura	Agartala	10,486	3.7	7.2	1,630
North Eastern Region		262,179	45.7	74.3	1,302[b]
India	New Delhi	3,287,265	1,210.9	2,652.2	1,784

Sources: Ministry of Development of North Eastern Region and Ministry of Statistics and Programme Implementation, Government of India.
a. Converted from Indian rupees to US$ using the average exchange rate for fiscal year 2017/18: US$1= 64.4549 Indian rupees. Not official World Bank figures.
b. Weighted by population. Simple average is US$1,967.

FIGURE A.4 Geography of India's North Eastern Region

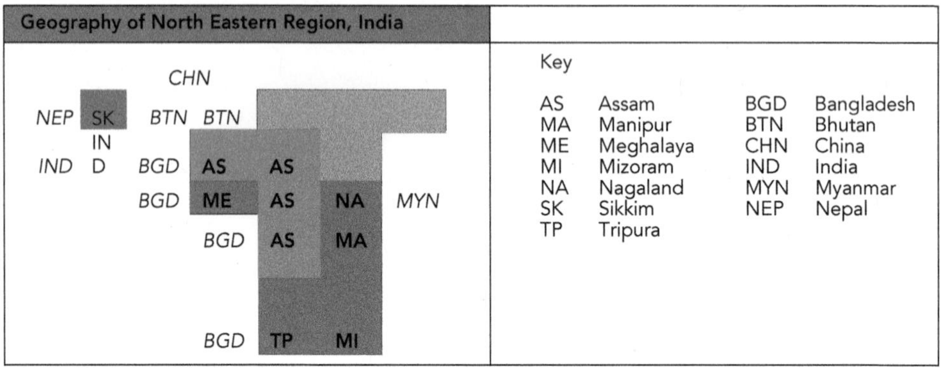

Note: For the scale of land area relative to Bhutan, the NER states are, in alphabetical order, 2.0, 0.6, 0.6, 0.5, 0.4, 0.2, 0.3 times as large. NER: 6.8. See also figure 1A.1 in annex 1A to chapter 1.

TABLE A.4 Investment Destinations, by South Asian Economy

Destination (↓)	Home								
	Afghanistan	Bangladesh	Bhutan	India_General	Maldives	Nepal	Pakistan	Sri Lanka	All
Afghanistan	0 / 0	0 / 0	0 / 0	0 / 0	0 / 0	0 / 0	29 / 34	0 / 0	29 / 34
Bangladesh	0 / 0	0 / 0	2 / 2	39 / 46	2 / 3	0 / 0	13 / 20	9 / 8	65 / 79
Bhutan	0 / 0	0 / 0	0 / 0	6 / 7	0 / 0	0 / 0	1 / 1	1 / 1	8 / 9
India_General	15 / 16	1 / 1	6 / 6	0 / 0	4 / 5	0 / 0	9 / 13	10 / 12	45 / 53
India_North Eastern Region	0 / 0	1 / 1	0 / 0	76 / 94	0 / 0	0 / 0	0 / 0	4 / 4	81 / 99
Maldives	0 / 0	0 / 0	0 / 0	4 / 4	0 / 0	0 / 0	0 / 0	10 / 11	14 / 15
Nepal	1 / 2	1 / 1	0 / 0	22 / 24	0 / 0	0 / 0	1 / 1	1 / 1	26 / 29
Pakistan	21 / 24	0 / 0	0 / 0	3 / 3	0 / 0	0 / 0	0 / 0	4 / 4	28 / 31
Sri Lanka	0 / 0	0 / 0	0 / 0	39 / 52	8 / 11	0 / 0	9 / 9	0 / 0	56 / 72
Total South Asia	37 / 42	3 / 3	8 / 8	189 / 230	14 / 19	0 / 0	62 / 78	39 / 41	352 / 421
Total South Asia, unique firms	33 / 42	2 / 3	6 / 8	149 / 230	14 / 19	0 / 0	46 / 44	22 / 41	272 / 421
Australia and New Zealand	2 / 3	0 / 0	0 / 0	7 / 7	0 / 0	0 / 0	3 / 3	3 / 3	15 / 16
Hong Kong SAR, China; Mauritius; Singapore; United Arab Emirates	11 / 12	2 / 2	0 / 0	33 / 38	0 / 0	0 / 0	18 / 21	7 / 8	71 / 81
Europe and Central Asia	15 / 18	1 / 1	0 / 0	11 / 11	0 / 0	0 / 0	6 / 7	4 / 4	37 / 41
East Asia	17 / 21	1 / 1	0 / 0	24 / 26	0 / 0	0 / 0	25 / 28	5 / 5	72 / 81
Japan	0 / 0	1 / 1	0 / 0	2 / 2	0 / 0	0 / 0	5 / 6	3 / 3	11 / 12
Latin America	0 / 0	0 / 0	0 / 0	2 / 2	0 / 0	0 / 0	0 / 0	1 / 1	3 / 3
Middle East and North Africa	9 / 11	1 / 1	0 / 0	16 / 19	0 / 0	0 / 0	14 / 15	3 / 3	43 / 49
Sub-Saharan Africa	0 / 0	2 / 2	0 / 0	5 / 5	0 / 0	0 / 0	1 / 1	1 / 1	9 / 9
European Union and United Kingdom	8 / 8	2 / 3	0 / 0	28 / 31	0 / 0	0 / 0	24 / 25	9 / 10	71 / 77
United States and Canada	4 / 5	3 / 7	0 / 0	27 / 27	0 / 0	0 / 0	20 / 25	6 / 6	60 / 70
Total non-South Asia	66 / 78	13 / 18	0 / 0	155 / 168	0 / 0	0 / 0	116 / 131	42 / 44	392 / 439
Total non-South Asia unique firms	49 / 78	9 / 18	0 / 0	90 / 168	0 / 0	0 / 0	64 / 131	20 / 44	232 / 439

Source: Compiled from the South Asian Regional Engagement and Value Chains Survey.

Note: India_General refers to India without the North Eastern Region. Investments are measured by firm–investment type–destination combinations. Each bold number is the number of unique firms. Each italicized number is the number of firm–investment type–destination combinations. This table should be read as there are 15 Afghan investors investing in India, making 16 investments. (One firm is making more than one type of investment.) There are 33 unique Afghan investors making a total of 42 investments in South Asia. It is not 37 investors because 4 investors have invested in more than one economy.

Data Description and Empirical Results

Sampling and Summary Statistics

SAMPLING

The survey process was carried out from mid-2017 to early 2019. It was preceded by intensive case studies with entrepreneurs, during which their decision-making processes were discussed at length. The initial search for case study subjects provided the team with a broad sense of high-visibility intraregional investments. It was clear that the apparel sector, hotels, the auto industry, and food-processing firms were important outward investors. The first step was for the regional partners (see table B.1) to come up with a list of outward investor firm names. They were also asked to find names of other firms in the same industry in which they had found an outward investor. The partners were asked to specifically check the four industries, along with logistics companies. They were not to be restricted by these industries and were encouraged to pursue all goods and services industries. The only requirement was that if they did find an outward investor in an industry, they also had to interview other firms in that industry. The initial lists of outward investors were quite small. The team in Washington, DC, contributed to the lists through a mix of different inputs. Trade-supporting investments do not receive much publicity, so they were most often discovered upon interviewing a firm that was not expected to be an investor. An upper limit of 50 percent was set for the share of outward investors in the overall sample. In the final sample, 31 percent were outward investors (see table B.2).

Smaller and fragile economies, which are often neglected because of a lack of data, were included in the data collection. The survey includes family firms, which are

TABLE B.1 **Regional Partners**

Survey country	Partner
Afghanistan	Sustainable Development Policy Institute
Bangladesh	South Asia Network for Economic Modelling
Bhutan	Royal Thimphu College, Professor S. Mehta
India	Federation of Indian Chambers of Commerce and Industry and Bureau of Research on Industry and Economic Fundamentals (BRIEF, India)
Maldives	Institute of Policy Studies of Sri Lanka
Nepal	South Asia Watch on Trade, Economics and Environment
Pakistan	Sustainable Development Policy Institute
Sri Lanka	Breakthrough Business Intelligence

TABLE B.2 **Sample Size, by Country: Full Sample and Investor Firms**

Country	Sample size	Number of outward investors
Afghanistan	203	62
Bangladesh	133	9
Bhutan	74	6
India	300	191
Maldives	99	14
Nepal	103	0
Pakistan	302	86
Sri Lanka	62	31
Total South Asia	1,274	399

Source: South Asian Regional Engagement and Value Chains Survey.

important in several important sectors in South Asian economies, but for which information is not readily available. It also covers large firms that often lead forays into new international markets.

The initial survey design was developed following intensive case studies conducted with pioneering investor firms. Thus, the investor survey attempts to provide a holistic view of the main factors that determine international engagement by firms. The first draft of the survey was shared widely within the World Bank Group, including with staff from the International Finance Corporation, the Multilateral Investment Guarantee Agency, the trade and international integration team in the Development Research Group, and the trade group in the Macroeconomics, Trade, and Investment Global Practice. Members of the potential investor survey team were consulted regularly. The survey was revised based on advice received during a meeting with the above-mentioned groups and experts therein. The revised survey was also shared with regional implementation partners. Again, the survey was modified based on the practical experiences of the partners in the field. The survey was piloted in Bhutan, India, Nepal, Pakistan, and Sri Lanka. The survey was further revised and programmed into Qualtrics, the computer-assisted personal interviewing software that was used to carry out the survey. The survey was carried out with regional partners, mostly think tanks, listed in table B.1.

The Benefits of Own Data Collection through Firm-Level Surveys

The key advantages of data collection through firm-level surveys are

- inclusion of all countries in the region, large and small, in a consistent framework;
- collection of outward investment positions, which are not typically collected;
- capture of known outward investors through a nonrandom part of the sample, which would have most likely been missed in a random sample;
- capture of private and family firms, which do not typically report data, as well as large firms;
- inclusion of the agriculture, manufacturing, and services sectors;
- allows special consideration of India's connectivity-challenged North Eastern Region;
- defines indicators for and collects data on nontypical variables related to social capital and information frictions, which are important in trade and investment analysis for South Asia. These variables include bilateral trust, bilateral knowledge connectivity, and networks.

At the same time, the study did not collect detailed cost, production, and revenue data that may be available in a census of industry, and therefore cannot provide precise estimates of certain factors along the lines of recent econometric analysis of multinational firms based in high-income economies. The goal was to include economically important firms that invest abroad but that typically do not report data (especially for family-owned firms) and to include data from as many firms as possible from all countries (including small economies) in the region. Frontier analysis on outward foreign direct investment (OFDI) focuses on US firms investing abroad because, by law, these firms must fill out statistical surveys for the government. Thus, similar analyses are beyond the scope of what is possible for South Asian firms. For example, in the United States, firms and individuals that own a 10 percent or greater voting interest outside the United States must file a BE-577 report quarterly, a BE-11 report annually, and a BE-10 report once every five years. These reports are administered by the Bureau of Economic Analysis of the US Department of Commerce. Failure to file may lead to civil and criminal penalties. The bureau's website provides the questionnaires (https://www.bea.gov/surveys/diasurv).

Key dependent variable. Foreign investment may be in goods production, services operation, turnkey with own finance, and trade-supporting activities such as a small marketing, sourcing, or representative or liaison office. The data on outward investments are defined according to investor firm, investment type, and destination. Managers were asked to identify the *incidence* of investment by investment type–destination pair (not the number of investments in an investment type–destination pair).

By this definition, 860 investments (defined by firm, investment type, and destination) were identified. However, because a single firm may make more than one type of investment (services, production, and so on), or invest in multiple locations, there are actually 399 unique investor firms. Just under one-third of the sampled firms are investors. Given that one firm may have different types of investments in the same country, there are 744 unique investment destinations by firms (total number of investor-destination pairs). The most common type of investment is trade-supporting investment, with 219 firms making 387 investments around the world. The next most common are services operations investments, with 380, followed more distantly by 118 goods production investments and 25 turnkey investments with some equity finance. For an extensive description of investor data, see the section "Scope of and Strategies for OFDI: Evidence from Firm Surveys and Case Studies," in chapter 3.

TABLE B.3 **Variables and Data Sources**

Variable	Description	Source
Dependent variable		
OFDI_type firm_source_ destination, *(dependent variable)*	Dummy variable that takes the value 1 for firm–investment type–source–destination when the firm has invested in a particular type of investment (incidence measure); 0 otherwise.	REVC Survey
Invest_prod Invest_serv Invest_trade	Three OFDI types: OFDI production; OFDI services operations; OFDI trade-supporting (marketing or sourcing, representative or liaison offices).	
Independent variable		
Productivity	The position of the firm in the home industry's productivity distribution (by percentile, where higher is more productive). Self-reported.	REVC Survey
Turnover	The position of the firm in the home industry's turnover size distribution (by percentile, where higher is larger in size). Self-reported.	REVC Survey
State owned	Dummy variable that takes the value 1 if a firm's state ownership is greater than 50 percent; 0 otherwise.	REVC Survey
Foreign	Dummy variable that takes the value 1 if a firm's status is listed as affiliate or subsidiary of a foreign multinational or has foreign capital ownership; 0 otherwise.	REVC Survey
Family	Dummy variable that takes the value 1 if 32 percent of ownership is controlled by a family; 0 otherwise.	REVC Survey

(Table continues next page)

TABLE B.3 **Variables and Data Sources** (continued)

Variable	Description	Source
Ethnic network	Dummy variable that takes the value 1 if founder or CEO has any ethnic or social ties in destination; 0 otherwise.	REVC Survey
Export history	Dummy variable that takes the value 1 if the first country of export is followed by FDI to the same country ; 0 otherwise.	REVC Survey
Bilateral trust	Average of firm-level bilateral scores based on a question about how much trust a person has in those people in a destination in a range from 1 to 4 (high).	REVC Survey
Informed	Average of firm-level bilateral scores based on a question about "How well-informed are you about opportunities to trade and invest in destination" in a range from 1 to 4 (high).	REVC Survey
Conglomerate or business group	Dummy variable that takes the value 1 if a firm belongs to a conglomerate or business group; 0 otherwise.	REVC Survey
Business community	Dummy variable that takes the value 1 if the CEO or founder of a firm belongs to a business community; 0 otherwise.	REVC Survey
Internal funds	Dummy variable that takes the value 1 if internal funds are a primary or important source of finance; 0 otherwise.	REVC Survey
Intraconglomerate loans	Dummy variable that takes the value 1 if intraconglomerate or intra–business group borrowing is primary or important source of finance; 0 otherwise.	REVC Survey
Home commercial banks	Dummy variable that takes the value 1 if home country commercial banks are primary or important source of finance; 0 otherwise.	REVC Survey
International banks	Dummy variable that takes the value 1 if international banks are primary or important source of finance; 0 otherwise.	REVC Survey
Host commercial banks	Dummy variable that takes the value 1 if host country commercial banks are primary or important source of finance; 0 otherwise.	REVC Survey
Host local investors	Dummy variable that takes the value 1 if host country local investors are primary or important source of finance; 0 otherwise.	REVC Survey
Distance (log)	Natural logarithm of the bilateral population-weighted distance between closest major cities.	CEPII
Contiguity	Dummy variable that takes the value 1 if home country and destination share a common border; 0 otherwise.	CEPII
Common language	Dummy variable that takes the value 1 if source and host country share the same official language; 0 otherwise.	CEPII
Common colonizer	Dummy variable that takes the value 1 for common colonizer post-1945; 0 otherwise.	CEPII

Note: CEO = chief executive officer; CEPII = Centre d'Études Prospectives et d'Informations Internationales; FDI = foreign direct investment; OFDI = outward foreign direct investment; REVC = South Asian Regional Engagement and Value Chains Survey.

TABLE B.4 **Summary Statistics**

Variable	Observations	Mean	Standard deviation	Minimum	Maximum
Dependent variable					
Invest_Prod	24,244	0.005	0.070	0	1
Invest_Serv	24,244	0.014	0.116	0	1
Invest_Trade	24,244	0.016	0.125	0	1
Independent variables					
Prod_Pct	24,244	4.047	2.220	1	8
Trnovr_Pct	24,225	3.861	2.091	1	8
SOE	24,244	0.012	0.108	0	1
Foreign	24,244	0.171	0.376	0	1
Family	24,244	0.516	0.500	0	1
Ethnic_Network	24,244	0.053	0.224	0	1
Export_hist	24,244	0.020	0.139	0	1
Conglom	24,244	0.160	0.366	0	1
Bizcomm	21,983	0.383	0.486	0	1
Informed_Ave	11,559	2.038	1.120	1	4
Trust_Ave	11,484	2.520	0.901	1	4
Internal Funds	24,244	0.219	0.413	0	1
Intra-Conglom	24,244	0.009	0.092	0	1
Home Comm Bank	24,244	0.064	0.245	0	1
Int Bank	24,244	0.015	0.121	0	1
Host Comm Banks	24,244	0.009	0.093	0	1
Host Investor	24,244	0.016	0.127	0	1
Dist (log)	22,835	8.238	0.851	6.0	9.7
Contig	24,244	0.261	0.439	0	1
Comlang	24,244	0.337	0.473	0	1
Comcol	24,244	0.496	0.500	0	1

Source: South Asian Regional Engagement and Value Chains Survey.

TABLE B.5 Correlations

	Invest_Prod	Invest_Serv	Invest_Trade	Prod_Pct	Trnovr_Pct	SOE	Foreign	Family	Ethnic_Netwk	Exporthist	Conglom	Bizcomm	Informed_Ave	Trust_Ave	Internal Funds	Intra-Conglom	Home Comm Bank	Int Bank	Host Comm Banks	Host invest	Dist	Contig	Comlang	Comcol
Invest_Prod	1																							
Invest_Serv	0.1	1																						
Invest_Trade	0.2	0.2	1																					
Prod_Pct	0.0	0.0	0.0	1																				
Trnovr_Pct	0.0	0.0	0.0	0.9	1																			
SOE	0.0	0.0	0.0	0.1	0.1	1																		
Foreign	0.0	0.0	0.0	0.5	0.4	0.0	1																	
Family	0.0	0.0	0.0	0.2	0.2	-0.1	0.1	1																
Ethnic_Netwk	0.0	0.1	0.0	0.2	0.2	0.0	0.3	0.2	1															
Exporthist	0.1	0.1	0.2	0.0	0.0	0.0	0.0	0.0	0.1	1														
Conglom	0.0	0.0	0.0	0.2	0.3	0.0	0.1	0.0	0.0	0.0	1													
Bizcomm	0.0	0.0	0.0	0.2	0.3	0.0	-0.1	0.1	-0.1	0.0	0.2	1												
Informed_Ave	0.1	0.2	0.2	0.2	0.3	0.0	0.1	0.2	0.3	0.2	0.2	0.1	1											
Trust_Ave	0.1	0.1	0.1	0.3	0.2	0.1	0.1	0.2	0.3	0.1	0.1	0.0	0.6	1										
Internal Funds	0.1	0.1	0.2	-0.1	-0.1	0.0	0.0	-0.1	0.0	0.0	0.0	-0.1	0.0	-0.1	1									

(Table continues next page)

TABLE B.5 **Correlations** (continued)

	Invest_Prod	Invest_Serv	Invest_Trade	Prod_Pct	Trnovr_Pct	SOE	Foreign	Family	Ethnic_Netwk	Exporthist	Conglom	Bizcomm	Informed_Ave	Trust_Ave	Internal Funds	Intra-Conglom	Home Comm Bank	Int Bank	Host Comm Banks	Host invest	Dist	Contig	Comlang	Comcol
Intra-Conglom	0.0	0.1	0.0	0.0	0.0	0.0	0.0	0.0	0.0	0.0	0.0	0.1	0.0	0.0	0.2	1								
Home Comm Bank	0.1	0.1	0.1	0.0	0.0	0.0	0.0	0.0	0.0	0.0	0.0	0.0	0.1	0.1	0.2	0.1	1							
Int Bank	0.0	0.1	0.0	0.1	0.1	0.1	0.1	0.1	0.1	0.0	0.0	−0.1	0.1	0.1	0.2	0.0	0.1	1						
Host Comm Banks	0.0	0.0	0.0	0.0	0.0	0.1	0.0	0.0	0.0	0.0	0.0	0.0	0.0	0.0	0.2	0.2	0.0	0.1	1					
Host invest	0.0	0.0	0.1	0.0	0.1	0.0	0.0	−0.1	0.0	0.0	0.0	0.0	0.0	0.0	0.2	0.1	0.0	0.0	0.1	1				
Dist	0.0	0.0	0.1	0.0	0.0	0.0	0.1	−0.1	0.0	−0.1	0.0	−0.1	−0.3	−0.3	0.1	0.0	0.0	0.0	0.0	0.0	1			
Contig	0.1	0.1	0.1	−0.1	−0.1	0.0	−0.2	0.0	0.0	0.1	0.0	0.0	0.3	0.2	0.0	0.0	0.1	0.0	0.0	0.0	−0.4	1		
Comlang	0.0	0.1	0.0	−0.1	−0.1	0.0	−0.1	0.0	−0.1	0.0	0.0	0.0	0.1	0.0	0.0	0.0	0.1	0.0	0.0	0.0	−0.1	0.5	1	
Comcol	0.0	0.1	0.0	0.1	0.1	0.0	0.1	0.0	0.2	0.0	0.0	0.0	0.2	0.2	0.0	0.0	0.1	0.1	0.0	0.0	0.2	0.1	0.4	1

Source: South Asian Regional Engagement and Value Chains Survey.

FIGURE B.1 Comparison of Firm Activities: Full Sample versus Investors

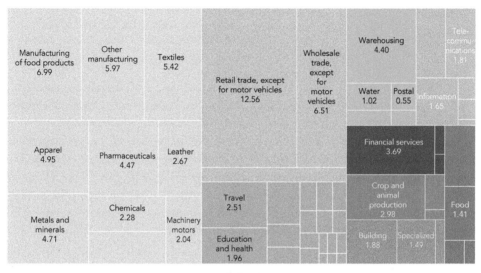

a. All firms

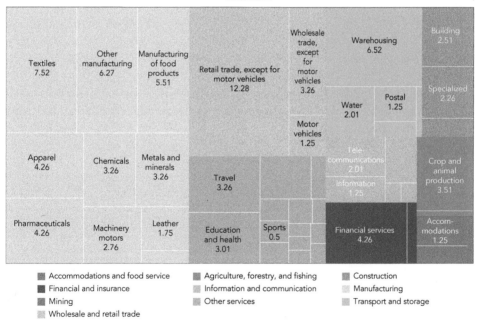

b. Investors

Note: Blank boxes represent sectors with smaller shares of respondent firms.

ESTIMATION STRATEGY

To assess the determinants of firms' decisions to invest abroad, the analysis considers the following empirical specification:

$$Y_{isd} = \alpha + \beta_1 productivity_i + \beta_2 type_i + \beta_3 finance_i + \beta_4 network_{id}$$
$$+ \beta_5 export_{id} + \beta_6 Ent_i + \gamma Z_{sd} + \lambda + \lambda_d + \varepsilon_{isd}. \tag{B.1}$$

In equation B.1, Y_{isd} is an outcome of interest such as the binary decision of firm i from source country s to invest in goods production, services operations, and trade-supporting investments in destination country d; $productivity_i$ is firm productivity; $type_i$ is firm type, including state-owned enterprise, foreign owned, and family owned; $finance_i$ is firm source of financing, including internal funds, business group, home and host commercial banks, and international banks; $network_{id}$ is firm network in country d; $export_{id}$ is firm export experience in country d; Ent_i is a characteristic of the entrepreneur (for example, risk appetite); Z_{sd} is a vector of source–destination country characteristics, such as distance, contiguity, and common language; λ_s and λ_d are vectors of source and destination country dummies to control for all country-specific factors; and ε_{isd} is the error term, which is clustered at the industry level to account for potential correlations in the error term across firms in the same industry.

The identification strategy is based on the fact that a founder's ethnic network is exogenously given and should be orthogonal to other firm-specific factors that could influence the firm investment decision. The ethnic network parameter captures the causal effect of the ethnic network on investment decisions.

Equation B.1 is estimated using linear probability models instead of probit or logit models to avoid potential incidental parameter problems that could arise with fixed effects in unbalanced samples.

RESULTS

TABLE B.6 **Firm Productivity, Distance, and Financing**

Variable	(1) Goods production	(2) Services operations	(3) Trade supporting
Productivity	0.002***	0.004***	0.005***
	(0.000)	(0.001)	(0.001)
State-owned	−0.009**	−0.013*	0.000
	(0.004)	(0.007)	(0.010)
Foreign	0.003	0.006	−0.006
	(0.002)	(0.005)	(0.005)
Family	0.002	−0.005**	0.004
	(0.002)	(0.003)	(0.003)

(Table continues next page)

TABLE B.6 **Firm Productivity, Distance, and Financing** *(continued)*

Variable	(1) Goods production	(2) Services operations	(3) Trade supporting
Internal funds	0.011*** (0.002)	0.028*** (0.005)	0.029*** (0.004)
Intraconglomerate loans	0.029* (0.017)	0.021 (0.015)	0.068* (0.041)
Home commercial banks	0.020*** (0.005)	0.010 (0.007)	0.008 (0.007)
International banks	0.002 (0.006)	−0.007 (0.008)	−0.002 (0.012)
Host commercial banks	−0.005 (0.007)	−0.006 (0.014)	−0.000 (0.027)
Host local investors	0.007 (0.009)	−0.011 (0.013)	0.030* (0.018)
Distance	−0.005*** (0.002)	−0.013*** (0.003)	−0.014*** (0.003)
Contiguity	0.006*** (0.002)	0.011*** (0.003)	0.012*** (0.004)
Common language	−0.003 (0.002)	0.001 (0.003)	−0.001 (0.003)
Common colonizer	0.004** (0.002)	0.011*** (0.003)	−0.005* (0.003)
Constant	0.050*** (0.016)	0.132*** (0.031)	0.146*** (0.028)
Observations	22,799	22,799	22,799
R^2	0.032	0.049	0.040
Destination fixed effects	Yes	Yes	Yes
Source fixed effects	Yes	Yes	Yes

Note: Firm-level clustered standard errors are in parentheses.
*** $p < .01$, ** $p < .05$, * $p < .1$.

TABLE B.7 **Role of Ethnic Networks**

Variable	(1) Goods production	(2) Services operations	(3) Trade supporting
Productivity	0.002*** (0.000)	0.004*** (0.001)	0.005*** (0.001)
State-owned	−0.009** (0.004)	−0.013* (0.008)	0.000 (0.010)
Foreign	0.002 (0.002)	0.006 (0.005)	−0.006 (0.005)
Family	0.002 (0.002)	−0.005** (0.003)	0.004 (0.003)

(Table continues next page)

TABLE B.7 **Role of Ethnic Networks** (continued)

Variable	(1) Goods production	(2) Services operations	(3) Trade supporting
Ethnic network	0.011*	0.050***	0.030***
	(0.006)	(0.012)	(0.009)
Internal funds	0.011***	0.027***	0.029***
	(0.002)	(0.005)	(0.004)
Intraconglomerate loans	0.029*	0.021	0.068*
	(0.017)	(0.015)	(0.041)
Home commercial banks	0.020***	0.011	0.009
	(0.005)	(0.007)	(0.007)
International banks	0.002	−0.007	−0.002
	(0.006)	(0.008)	(0.012)
Host commercial banks	−0.005	−0.007	−0.001
	(0.007)	(0.014)	(0.027)
Host local investors	0.007	−0.011	0.030*
	(0.009)	(0.013)	(0.018)
Distance	−0.005***	−0.011***	−0.013***
	(0.002)	(0.003)	(0.003)
Contiguity	0.006***	0.011***	0.012***
	(0.002)	(0.003)	(0.004)
Common language	−0.003	0.001	−0.001
	(0.002)	(0.003)	(0.003)
Common colonizer	0.004**	0.010***	−0.006*
	(0.002)	(0.003)	(0.003)
Constant	0.047***	0.117***	0.137***
	(0.016)	(0.031)	(0.028)
Observations	22,799	22,799	22,799
R^2	0.032	0.052	0.041
Destination fixed effects	Yes	Yes	Yes
Source fixed effects	Yes	Yes	Yes

Note: Firm-level clustered standard errors are in parentheses.
*** $p < .01$, ** $p < .05$, * $p < .1$.

TABLE B.8 **Role of Past Export Performance**

Variable	(1) Goods production	(2) Services operations	(3) Trade supporting
Productivity	0.002***	0.004***	0.005***
	(0.000)	(0.001)	(0.001)
State-owned	−0.009**	−0.013*	0.001
	(0.004)	(0.008)	(0.010)

(Table continues next page)

TABLE B.8 **Role of Past Export Performance** *(continued)*

Variable	(1) Goods production	(2) Services operations	(3) Trade supporting
Foreign	0.002 (0.002)	0.005 (0.005)	−0.006 (0.005)
Family	0.002 (0.002)	−0.005** (0.003)	0.004 (0.003)
Export history	0.033*** (0.009)	0.078*** (0.014)	0.105*** (0.015)
Ethnic network	0.008 (0.006)	0.043*** (0.012)	0.021** (0.009)
Internal funds	0.011*** (0.002)	0.027*** (0.005)	0.029*** (0.004)
Intraconglomerate loans	0.029* (0.017)	0.021 (0.015)	0.068* (0.041)
Home commercial banks	0.020*** (0.005)	0.011 (0.007)	0.009 (0.007)
International banks	0.002 (0.006)	−0.007 (0.008)	−0.002 (0.012)
Host commercial banks	−0.005 (0.007)	−0.007 (0.014)	−0.001 (0.027)
Host local investors	0.007 (0.009)	−0.011 (0.013)	0.030* (0.018)
Distance	−0.005*** (0.002)	−0.012*** (0.003)	−0.013*** (0.003)
Contiguity	0.005** (0.002)	0.009*** (0.003)	0.009*** (0.004)
Common language	−0.003 (0.002)	0.001 (0.003)	−0.000 (0.003)
Common colonizer	0.004** (0.002)	0.010*** (0.003)	−0.006* (0.003)
Constant	0.046*** (0.016)	0.113*** (0.030)	0.132*** (0.028)
Observations	22,799	22,799	22,799
R^2	0.036	0.060	0.054
Destination fixed effects	Yes	Yes	Yes
Source fixed effects	Yes	Yes	Yes

Note: Firm-level clustered standard errors are in parentheses.
*** $p < .01$, ** $p < .05$, * $p < .1$.

TABLE B.9 **Role of Ethnic Networks and Information Frictions**

Variable	(1) Goods production	(2) Goods production
Productivity	0.002***	0.001***
	(0.001)	(0.001)
State-owned	−0.014**	−0.013*
	(0.006)	(0.007)
Foreign	0.004	0.003
	(0.003)	(0.003)
Family	0.001	0.001
	(0.002)	(0.002)
Export history	0.059***	0.055***
	(0.018)	(0.018)
Ethnic network	0.040***	0.020**
	(0.015)	(0.009)
Bilateral trust	0.010***	
	(0.002)	
Ethnic network × bilateral trust	−0.012**	
	(0.005)	
Internal funds	0.014***	0.015***
	(0.003)	(0.003)
Intraconglomerate loans	0.040	0.041
	(0.035)	(0.034)
Home commercial banks	0.036***	0.035***
	(0.008)	(0.008)
International banks	0.013	0.013
	(0.013)	(0.013)
Host commercial banks	−0.012	−0.012
	(0.012)	(0.012)
Host local investors	0.010	0.010
	(0.016)	(0.016)
Distance	−0.002	−0.003
	(0.002)	(0.002)
Contiguity	0.002	0.002
	(0.003)	(0.003)
Common language	0.006	0.004
	(0.004)	(0.004)
Common colonizer	0.006***	0.004*
	(0.002)	(0.002)
Informed		0.009***
		(0.002)
Ethnic network × informed		−0.006
		(0.004)
Constant	−0.012	0.005
	(0.021)	(0.019)
Observations	10,059	10,059
R^2	0.064	0.065
Destination fixed effects	Yes	Yes
Source fixed effects	Yes	Yes

Note: Firm-level clustered standard errors are in parentheses.
*** $p < .01$, ** $p < .05$, * $p < .1$.

TABLE B.10 **Role of Ethnic Networks and Bilateral Trust across Investment Types**

Variable	(1) Goods production	(2) Services operations	(3) Trade supporting
Productivity	0.002***	0.003***	0.003***
	(0.001)	(0.001)	(0.001)
State-owned	−0.014**	−0.008	0.026
	(0.006)	(0.012)	(0.018)
Foreign	0.004	0.008	−0.003
	(0.003)	(0.006)	(0.006)
Family	0.001	−0.004	−0.001
	(0.002)	(0.004)	(0.003)
Export history	0.059***	0.120***	0.124***
	(0.018)	(0.025)	(0.025)
Ethnic network	0.040***	0.020	0.080***
	(0.015)	(0.036)	(0.028)
Bilateral trust	0.010***	0.013***	0.025***
	(0.002)	(0.003)	(0.004)
Ethnic network × bilateral trust	−0.012**	0.004	−0.023***
	(0.005)	(0.012)	(0.009)
Internal funds	0.014***	0.040***	0.042***
	(0.003)	(0.006)	(0.005)
Intraconglomerate loans	0.040	0.035*	0.036
	(0.035)	(0.019)	(0.026)
Home commercial banks	0.036***	0.025***	0.026***
	(0.008)	(0.010)	(0.008)
International banks	0.013	0.009	−0.014
	(0.013)	(0.015)	(0.015)
Host commercial banks	−0.012	−0.001	−0.015
	(0.012)	(0.028)	(0.017)
Host local investors	0.010	−0.013	0.048**
	(0.016)	(0.017)	(0.019)
Distance	−0.002	−0.012***	−0.007**
	(0.002)	(0.004)	(0.003)
Contiguity	0.002	−0.007	−0.001
	(0.003)	(0.004)	(0.005)
Common language	0.006	0.027***	0.004
	(0.004)	(0.008)	(0.006)
Common colonizer	0.006***	0.016***	0.001
	(0.002)	(0.004)	(0.004)
Constant	−0.012	0.067	−0.032
	(0.021)	(0.043)	(0.036)
Observations	10,059	10,059	10,059
R^2	0.064	0.107	0.092
Destination fixed effects	Yes	Yes	Yes
Source fixed effects	Yes	Yes	Yes

Note: Robust standard errors are in parentheses.
*** $p < .01$, ** $p < .05$, * $p < .1$.

TABLE B.11 **Role of Ethnic Networks and Information Frictions across Investment Types**

Variable	(1) Goods production	(2) Services operations	(3) Trade supporting
Productivity	0.001*** (0.001)	0.002** (0.001)	0.002** (0.001)
State-owned	−0.013* (0.007)	−0.006 (0.013)	0.028 (0.018)
Foreign	0.003 (0.003)	0.006 (0.006)	−0.006 (0.006)
Family	0.001 (0.002)	−0.005 (0.004)	−0.002 (0.003)
Export history	0.055*** (0.018)	0.111*** (0.025)	0.115*** (0.025)
Ethnic network	0.020** (0.009)	0.025 (0.018)	0.040*** (0.015)
Informed	0.009*** (0.002)	0.016*** (0.003)	0.022*** (0.003)
Ethnic network × informed	−0.006 (0.004)	0.001 (0.007)	−0.013** (0.007)
Internal funds	0.015*** (0.003)	0.041*** (0.006)	0.044*** (0.005)
Intraconglomerate loans	0.041 (0.034)	0.036* (0.018)	0.038 (0.027)
Home commercial banks	0.035*** (0.008)	0.023** (0.009)	0.023*** (0.008)
International banks	0.013 (0.013)	0.010 (0.015)	−0.013 (0.016)
Host commercial banks	−0.012 (0.012)	−0.000 (0.028)	−0.013 (0.017)
Host local investors	0.010 (0.016)	−0.015 (0.017)	0.046** (0.020)
Distance	−0.003 (0.002)	−0.011*** (0.004)	−0.008*** (0.003)
Contiguity	0.002 (0.003)	−0.010** (0.004)	−0.003 (0.005)
Common language	0.004 (0.004)	0.027*** (0.007)	0.000 (0.006)
Common colonizer	0.004* (0.002)	0.012*** (0.004)	−0.004 (0.004)
Constant	0.005 (0.019)	0.067* (0.036)	0.010 (0.030)
Observations	10,059	10,059	10,059
R^2	0.065	0.112	0.097
Destination fixed effects	Yes	Yes	Yes
Source fixed effects	Yes	Yes	Yes

Note: Firm-level clustered standard errors are in parentheses.
*** $p < .01$, ** $p < .05$, * $p < .1$.

TABLE B.12 **Role of Conglomerates**

Variable	(1) Goods production	(2) Services operations	(3) Trade supporting
Productivity	0.002*** (0.000)	0.003*** (0.001)	0.005*** (0.001)
State-owned	−0.009** (0.004)	−0.013* (0.008)	0.001 (0.010)
Foreign	0.002 (0.002)	0.005 (0.005)	−0.006 (0.005)
Family	0.002 (0.002)	−0.005* (0.003)	0.004 (0.003)
Conglomerate or business group	0.005** (0.002)	0.011** (0.004)	0.001 (0.003)
Export history	0.033*** (0.009)	0.078*** (0.014)	0.105*** (0.015)
Ethnic network	0.008 (0.006)	0.043*** (0.012)	0.021** (0.009)
Internal funds	0.011*** (0.002)	0.027*** (0.005)	0.029*** (0.004)
Intraconglomerate loans	0.028* (0.017)	0.019 (0.015)	0.068* (0.041)
Home commercial banks	0.020*** (0.005)	0.011 (0.007)	0.009 (0.007)
International banks	0.002 (0.006)	−0.007 (0.008)	−0.002 (0.012)
Host commercial banks	−0.004 (0.007)	−0.005 (0.014)	−0.001 (0.027)
Host local investors	0.007 (0.009)	−0.011 (0.013)	0.030* (0.018)
Distance	−0.005*** (0.002)	−0.012*** (0.003)	−0.013*** (0.003)
Contiguity	0.005** (0.002)	0.009*** (0.003)	0.009*** (0.004)
Common language	−0.003 (0.002)	0.001 (0.003)	−0.000 (0.003)
Common colonizer	0.004** (0.002)	0.010*** (0.003)	−0.006* (0.003)
Constant	0.044*** (0.016)	0.110*** (0.031)	0.131*** (0.028)
Observations	22,799	22,799	22,799
R^2	0.037	0.061	0.054
Destination fixed effects	Yes	Yes	Yes
Source fixed effects	Yes	Yes	Yes

Note: Firm-level clustered standard errors are in parentheses.
*** $p < .01$, ** $p < .05$, * $p < .1$.

TABLE B.13 **Role of Risk Appetite**

Variable	(1) Goods production	(2) Services operations	(3) Trade supporting
Productivity	0.002*** (0.000)	0.003*** (0.001)	0.004*** (0.001)
State-owned	−0.006 (0.004)	−0.018** (0.007)	0.017* (0.010)
Foreign	0.003 (0.002)	0.004 (0.005)	−0.004 (0.006)
Family	0.001 (0.001)	−0.005** (0.002)	0.003 (0.003)
Export history	0.033*** (0.010)	0.068*** (0.013)	0.101*** (0.016)
Risk appetite	0.003*** (0.001)	0.001 (0.003)	0.009*** (0.003)
Ethnic network	0.004 (0.005)	0.044*** (0.012)	0.022** (0.009)
Internal funds	0.010*** (0.002)	0.024*** (0.005)	0.032*** (0.005)
Intraconglomerate loans	0.035* (0.018)	0.019 (0.015)	0.069 (0.045)
Home commercial banks	0.025*** (0.006)	0.008 (0.006)	0.006 (0.007)
International banks	−0.001 (0.006)	−0.002 (0.008)	−0.010 (0.010)
Host commercial banks	−0.005 (0.007)	−0.003 (0.015)	−0.004 (0.027)
Host local investors	0.006 (0.010)	−0.011 (0.014)	0.028 (0.019)
Distance	−0.004*** (0.002)	−0.009*** (0.003)	−0.014*** (0.003)
Contiguity	0.006*** (0.002)	0.009*** (0.003)	0.009** (0.004)
Common language	−0.002 (0.002)	0.002 (0.003)	0.001 (0.004)
Common colonizer	0.005*** (0.002)	0.011*** (0.002)	−0.007** (0.003)
Constant	0.041** (0.017)	0.095*** (0.030)	0.140*** (0.029)
Observations	20,658	20,658	20,658
R^2	0.037	0.060	0.057
Destination fixed effects	Yes	Yes	Yes
Source fixed effects	Yes	Yes	Yes

Note: Robust standard errors are in parentheses.

*** $p < .01$, ** $p < .05$, * $p < .1$.

TABLE B.14 **Robustness 1: Excluding Non–South Asia Region Destination Investors**

Variable	(1) Goods production	(2) Services operations	(3) Trade supporting
Productivity	0.002***	0.003***	0.002***
	(0.000)	(0.001)	(0.001)
State-owned	−0.006	−0.015**	0.020**
	(0.005)	(0.007)	(0.009)
Foreign	0.002	0.006	−0.000
	(0.003)	(0.005)	(0.006)
Family	0.001	−0.002	−0.001
	(0.001)	(0.003)	(0.003)
Export history	0.034***	0.061***	0.073***
	(0.010)	(0.014)	(0.014)
Risk appetite	0.004***	−0.002	0.009***
	(0.001)	(0.003)	(0.003)
Ethnic network	0.003	0.042***	0.018**
	(0.005)	(0.012)	(0.009)
Internal funds	0.010***	0.028***	0.040***
	(0.002)	(0.005)	(0.005)
Intraconglomerate loans	0.036*	0.015	0.079*
	(0.019)	(0.015)	(0.044)
Home commercial banks	0.025***	0.008	0.012*
	(0.006)	(0.007)	(0.007)
International banks	−0.001	−0.005	−0.016
	(0.006)	(0.008)	(0.010)
Host commercial banks	−0.004	−0.001	−0.006
	(0.007)	(0.014)	(0.026)
Host local investors	0.007	−0.008	0.032*
	(0.010)	(0.014)	(0.019)
Distance	−0.004**	−0.009***	−0.015***
	(0.002)	(0.003)	(0.003)
Contiguity	0.007***	0.009***	0.010**
	(0.002)	(0.004)	(0.004)
Common language	−0.003	−0.002	−0.009***
	(0.002)	(0.003)	(0.003)
Common colonizer	0.005***	0.012***	−0.001
	(0.001)	(0.002)	(0.003)
Constant	0.036**	0.097***	0.127***
	(0.018)	(0.032)	(0.031)
Observations	18,685	18,685	18,685
R^2	0.044	0.072	0.067
Destination fixed effects	Yes	Yes	Yes
Source fixed effects	Yes	Yes	Yes

Note: Robust standard errors are in parentheses.
*** $p < .01$, ** $p < .05$, * $p < .1$.

TABLE B.15 **Robustness 2: Excluding the North Eastern Region of India as Destination**

Variable	(1) Goods production	(2) Services operations	(3) Trade supporting
Productivity	0.002*** (0.000)	0.003*** (0.001)	0.004*** (0.001)
State-owned	−0.006 (0.004)	−0.018** (0.007)	0.017* (0.010)
Foreign	0.003 (0.002)	0.004 (0.005)	−0.004 (0.006)
Family	0.001 (0.001)	−0.005** (0.002)	0.003 (0.003)
Export history	0.033*** (0.010)	0.068*** (0.013)	0.101*** (0.016)
Risk appetite	0.003*** (0.001)	0.001 (0.003)	0.009*** (0.003)
Ethnic network	0.004 (0.005)	0.044*** (0.012)	0.022** (0.009)
Internal funds	0.010*** (0.002)	0.024*** (0.005)	0.032*** (0.005)
Intraconglomerate loans	0.035* (0.018)	0.019 (0.015)	0.069 (0.045)
Home commercial banks	0.025*** (0.006)	0.008 (0.006)	0.006 (0.007)
International banks	−0.001 (0.006)	−0.002 (0.008)	−0.010 (0.010)
Host commercial banks	−0.005 (0.007)	−0.003 (0.015)	−0.004 (0.027)
Host local investors	0.006 (0.010)	−0.011 (0.014)	0.028 (0.019)
Distance	−0.004*** (0.002)	−0.009*** (0.003)	−0.014*** (0.003)
Contiguity	0.006*** (0.002)	0.009*** (0.003)	0.009** (0.004)
Common language	−0.002 (0.002)	0.002 (0.003)	0.001 (0.004)
Common colonizer	0.005*** (0.002)	0.011*** (0.002)	−0.007** (0.003)
Constant	0.041** (0.017)	0.095*** (0.030)	0.140*** (0.029)
Observations	20,658	20,658	20,658
R^2	0.037	0.060	0.057
Destination fixed effects	Yes	Yes	Yes
Source fixed effects	Yes	Yes	Yes

Note: Robust standard errors are in parentheses.

*** $p < .01$, ** $p < .05$, * $p < .1$.

TABLE B.16 **Robustness 3: Logit Estimation**

Variable	(1) Goods production	(2) Services operations	(3) Trade supporting
Productivity	0.462*** (0.077)	0.355*** (0.067)	0.323*** (0.050)
State-owned	—	—	—
Foreign	−0.018 (0.398)	0.482* (0.268)	−0.565 (0.398)
Family	0.398 (0.262)	−0.637*** (0.188)	0.337* (0.183)
Export history	1.570*** (0.332)	1.643*** (0.224)	2.004*** (0.196)
Ethnic network	0.818 (0.643)	1.555*** (0.360)	1.199*** (0.398)
Internal funds	1.475*** (0.306)	1.267*** (0.189)	1.156*** (0.183)
Intraconglomerate loans	0.844 (0.626)	0.044 (0.467)	1.252* (0.641)
Home commercial banks	1.224*** (0.363)	0.442** (0.218)	0.293 (0.249)
International banks	0.926 (0.626)	0.254 (0.458)	0.637 (0.587)
Host commercial banks	−0.313 (0.623)	−0.046 (0.580)	−0.302 (1.018)
Host local investors	0.099 (0.415)	−0.808 (0.527)	0.335 (0.313)
Distance	−2.656*** (0.628)	−2.299*** (0.329)	−1.547*** (0.232)
Contiguity	0.174 (0.439)	0.241 (0.211)	0.344* (0.198)
Common language	0.125 (0.472)	−0.249 (0.307)	−0.523* (0.292)
Common colonizer	0.664 (0.904)	−1.631 (1.009)	−1.258** (0.513)
Constant	17.184*** (5.613)	15.865*** (2.984)	9.473*** (2.061)
Observations	18,364	18,550	20,981
Destination fixed effects	Yes	Yes	Yes
Source fixed effects	Yes	Yes	Yes

Note: Firm-level clustered standard errors are in parentheses. Coefficients are not marginal effects.
— = not available.

*** $p < .01$, ** $p < .05$, * $p < .1$.

Glossary

Affiliate: The company receiving the investment abroad.

Asset-light business model: A strategy that reduces the traditional amount of capital needed to start a business, and instead offers a share of revenue to capital owners, such as hotels run using management contracts and shared economy–type businesses.

Brownfield investment: The lease or purchase of a preexisting facility in a foreign country.

Export platform foreign direct investment: Investing in a foreign location with the primary purpose of serving a third market.

Foreign direct investment enterprise: An incorporated enterprise in which a foreign investor has at least 10 percent of the shares or voting power.

Fixed entry costs: Costs incurred in the process of market entry that do not vary with the quantity of output.

Goods production investment: Investment in agriculture and manufacturing.

Greenfield investment: The process of a company building its own facilities abroad from the ground up.

Horizontal foreign direct investment: Duplication of production abroad for sales in the destination to avoid trade costs.

Investment hubs: Jurisdictions offering investor services that facilitate international investment. Larger than tax havens, these jurisdictions have substantial real economic activity and attract multinational enterprises through their favorable investment conditions.

Parent: The company making the investment abroad.

Relational contracting: Relationships in which contracting parties behave in an expected manner to sustain the relationship in the long term, although such behavior is not explicitly stipulated in a transactional contract.

Roundtripping: The channeling abroad by direct investors of local funds and the subsequent return of these funds to the local economy in the form of foreign direct investment.

Services operations investment: Investment in facilities such as hotels, hospitals, schools, warehouses, retail, banks, logistics firms, headquarters, call centers, research and development centers, or offices in general.

Sticky global value chains: A propensity for a global value chain relationship to exist beyond its optimal period because of relation-specific investments already incurred within a value chain; it represents a status quo bias.

Sticky knowledge: Imperfect information flows between parties resulting from motivational factors and information barriers.

Sunk entry costs: Unrecoverable fixed costs that must be incurred to make the entry decision into a market, regardless of whether the market is eventually entered.

Switching costs: Additional costs incurred to switch suppliers or distributors or engage in new relationships; higher expected profits could be necessary to switch partners.

Tax havens: Jurisdictions whose economies are mostly dedicated to the provision of offshore financial services.

Trade-supporting services investment: Investment in small sourcing, marketing, or representative offices, with five or fewer employees.

Transfer pricing: Firms and their subsidiaries or related firms overinvoice or underinvoice for goods and services to shift profits to a low-taxation territory.

Turnkey operations or concession contracts with some own financing (a minimum threshold of 10 percent) as a contractor: Engineering, procurement, and construction projects and other similar forms of contracting that are common in the construction industry, public utilities provision, and some public asset management.

Vertical foreign direct investment: Foreign direct investment driven by factor price differences to produce a product or value chain activity abroad. A firm chooses to minimize costs by fragmenting the production process, setting up different stages of production in different countries according to comparative advantage.